Outdoors
with **Kids**

· ·

Boston

100 FUN PLACES TO EXPLORE IN AND AROUND THE CITY

KIM FOLEY MACKINNON

Appalachian Mountain Club Books
Boston, Massachusetts

AMC is a nonprofit organization, and sales of AMC Books fund our mission of protecting the Northeast outdoors. If you appreciate our efforts and would like to become a member or make a donation to AMC, visit outdoors.org, call 800-372-1758, or contact us at Appalachian Mountain Club, 5 Joy Street, Boston, MA 02108.

outdoors.org/publications/books

Distributed by The Globe Pequot Press, Guilford, Connecticut.
Front cover photograph © Carmen Martínez Banús / iStockphoto
All interior photographs by Kim Foley MacKinnon © Appalachian Mountain Club, except for images on pages 1, 25, 34, 102, 147, 203, 207, 219, 223, and 227 © Jerry and Marcy Monkman; 20 © Kimberly Duncan-Mooney; 23 © Sharon Beesley / nyctaughtme.blogspot.com; 36 courtesy of Franklin Park Coalition; 53 © Jaren Wicklund / iStockphoto; © xril / iStockphoto; © Athena Lakri; 72 by Megan Begley © Appalachian Mountain Club; 78 and 129 by Pat Bagley © Appalachian Mountain Club; 85 © mommyniri.com; 108 courtesy of Westford Cub Scout Pack 102; 148 Wikimedia Creative Commons; courtesy of South Shore Natural Science Center; 171 Wikimedia Creative Commons; 181 by K. McMahon courtesy of The Trustees of Reservations.
Maps by Ken Dumas © Appalachian Mountain Club
Cover design by Matt Simmons
Interior design by Joyce Weston

Library of Congress Cataloging-in-Publication Data
MacKinnon, Kim Foley.
  Outdoors with kids Boston : 100 fun places to explore in and around the city / Kim Foley MacKinnon.
    p. cm. – (AMC outdoors with kids)
  Includes index.
  ISBN 978-1-934028-60-5 (pbk.)
  1. Boston (Mass.)–Guidebooks. 2. Family recreation–Massachusetts–Boston–Guidebooks. 3. Outdoor recreation–Massachusetts–Boston–Guidebooks. I. Title.
  F73.18.M255 2012
  917.44'61044–dc23
                        2011042988

The paper used in this publication meets the minimum requirements of the American National Standard for Information Sciences-Permanence of Paper for Printed Library Materials, ANSI Z39.48-1984. ∞

Outdoor recreation activities by their very nature are potentially hazardous. This book is not a substitute for good personal judgment and training in outdoor skills. Due to changes in conditions, use of the information in this book is at the sole risk of the user. The author and the Appalachian Mountain Club assume no liability for accidents happening to, or injuries sustained by, readers who engage in the activities described in this book.

Interior pages contain 30% post-consumer recycled fiber.
Cover contains 10% post-consumer recycled fiber.
Printed in the United States of America,
using vegetable-based inks.

10 9 8 7 6 5 4 3 2 1   12 13 14 15 16

Dedicated to Rob and Sadie with love.

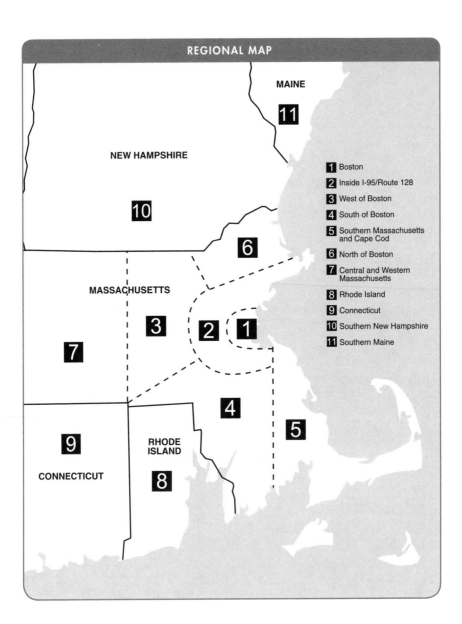

REGIONAL MAP

MAINE

11

NEW HAMPSHIRE

10

1 Boston
2 Inside I-95/Route 128
3 West of Boston
4 South of Boston
5 Southern Massachusetts and Cape Cod
6 North of Boston
7 Central and Western Massachusetts
8 Rhode Island
9 Connecticut
10 Southern New Hampshire
11 Southern Maine

MASSACHUSETTS

6

3   2   1

7

4

5

9   RHODE ISLAND

CONNECTICUT   8

CONTENTS

THE "10 BEST" LISTS

AT-A-GLANCE TRIP PLANNER

# Trip	Page	Best for Ages	Fee	Public Transit	Dog Friendly	Stroller Friendly
BOSTON						
1. Boston Harbor Islands: Georges Island	16	All	$	🚌		
2. Boston Harbor Islands: Spectacle Island	18	All	$	🚌		🚼
3. Boston Common	20	All		🚌	🐕	🚼
4. Charles River Reservation: Esplanade	22	All		🚌	🐕	🚼
5. Belle Isle Marsh Reservation	24	All		🚌		🚼
6. Castle Island and Pleasure Bay	26	All		🚌	🐕	🚼
7. Arnold Arboretum	28	0–4		🚌	🐕	🚼
8. Allandale Woods	31	0–4		🚌	🐕	
9. Bussey Brook Meadow	33	0–4		🚌	🐕	🚼
10. Franklin Park	35	All		🚌	🐕	🚼
11. Forest Hills Cemetery	38	All		🚌	🐕	🚼
12. Jamaica Pond	40	0–4		🚌	🐕	🚼
13. Millennium Park	42	0–4		🚌	🐕	🚼
14. Boston Nature Center and Wildlife Sanctuary	44	0–4		🚌		🚼
15. Stony Brook Reservation	46	All		🚌	🐕	🚼
16. Neponset River Reservation	48	All		🚌		🚼
INSIDE I-95/ROUTE 128						
17. Fresh Pond Reservation	52	0–4		🚌	🐕	🚼
18. Danehy Park	54	0–4		🚌	🐕	🚼
19. Mount Auburn Cemetery	56	All		🚌		🚼
20. Chestnut Hill Reservation	58	5–8		🚌	🐕	🚼
21. Larz Anderson Park	60	All		🚌		🚼
22. Hall's Pond Sanctuary and Amory Woods	63	All		🚌		🚼
23. Hammond Pond Reservation	65	5–8		🚌	🐕	

Hike Walk	Bike	Swim Paddle	Playground	Camp	Trip Highlights
Walk					Old fort to explore, Boston views
Walk		Swim			Beach, fun to collect sea glass
Walk			Playground		Beautiful gardens, frog pond
Walk	Bike	Swim	Playground		Riverside path, playgrounds, biking
Walk		Paddle			Salt marsh, observation tower
Walk	Bike	Swim	Playground		Fort Independence, beaches, views
Walk	Bike				Nation's oldest arboretum, bonsais, paved paths
Walk					Urban wild, pond, easy hiking
Walk					Forest, wetlands, meadows
Walk	Bike		Playground		Zoo, woods, fields
Walk					Victorian landscape, lake, fountain, sculptures
Walk		Paddle			1.5-mile pond loop, sailing, paddling
Walk	Bike	Paddle	Playground		Urban park, nature trail
Walk					Look for wildlife, exhibits
Walk	Bike	Swim	Playground		Biking trails, pond
Walk	Bike	Paddle	Playground		Salt marsh, bike paths, playgrounds
Walk	Bike		Playground		Butterfly meadow, woods, bike path
Walk	Bike		Playground		Spray park, grassy hills, and sports fields
Walk					Country's oldest landscaped cemetery, bird area
Walk	Bike				Paved walking path, waterworks museum
Walk	Bike		Playground		Lagoon, gazebo, views
Walk					Boardwalk around pond, great bird-watching
Walk					Rock climbing, pond

Hike Walk	Bike	Swim Paddle	Playground	Camp	Trip Highlights
🚶					Historic house, small farm, animals
🚶					Ponds, wetland, meadows, vernal pools
🚶					635-foot summit hike, views, observation tower
🚶		Paddle		△	Boardwalk hike, pond, bog
🚶		Swim	Playground		Swimming, easy trails
🚶					Rocky ledges, marsh, views
🚶	Bike	Swim/Paddle	Playground		Ponds, paddling, playgrounds
🚶		Paddle			Miles of trails, hills, ponds
🚶	Bike				Tree-lined bike path
🚶	Bike	Swim	Playground		Swimming, small summit to Eagle Rock
🚶					Dungeon Rock, tunnels
🚶		Swim/Paddle	Playground		Waterfront promenade, beach
🚶					Farm animals, hills, tractor ride
🚶					Outdoor art, museum, pond
🚶		Paddle			Superb place to see wildlife
🚶		Swim/Paddle			Swimming, views, historic site
🚶	Bike				Revolutionary War sites
🚶	Bike	Paddle			Working dairy farm, meadows, fields
🚶	Bike				11 miles of easy, paved trail
🚶		Paddle			Beaver dams, along Nashua River, boardwalk
🚶					Charming botanical garden
🚶					Boardwalk, marshes, waterfall, mill site
🚶					Great for young hikers, woods
🚶					Pond loop walk, meadow
🚶	Bike	Paddle			Whimsical children's garden, paddling

Hike Walk	Bike	Swim Paddle	Playground	Camp	Trip Highlights
Walk			Playground		Former mill site, ponds, waterfall
Walk					Working farm, fields, meadows
Walk					Former mill site, wetlands, hay field
Walk			Playground		Ponds, wetlands
Walk		Paddle			Scenic river walk
Walk	Bike		Playground		Stone bridges, ponds, urban park
Walk					Vernal pools, boardwalk, swamp, summit
Walk					Meadows, pastures, woods, views
Walk					Cave, rock-climbing
Walk					Boardwalks, marshland, ponds
Walk	Bike	Paddle			Ponds, historic mansion, disc golf
Walk		Swim, Paddle	Playground		Beach, lookout tower, marshes
Walk					Rock climbing, historic site
Walk					Views, carriage paths, marshes
Walk					Working farm, animals, river
Walk	Bike	Paddle		Camp	12 miles of bike paths, freshwater spring
Walk		Swim, Paddle	Playground		Beach, promenade, carousel
Walk					Interpretive center, pond, animals
Walk		Swim			Barrier beach
Walk	Bike	Swim, Paddle		Camp	Miles of bike trails, ponds, camping
Walk	Bike	Swim		Camp	Sandy beach, jetty, fishing
Walk				Camp	Salt marsh, beach, pine woods, pond
Walk	Bike	Swim, Paddle			22-mile bike trail, beaches, lighthouses
Walk		Swim, Paddle	Playground		Paddling, playground, fishing
Walk	Bike	Paddle			Historical sites, canals
Walk	Bike	Paddle		Camp	Forest, ponds, trails, fishing, old quarry

Hike Walk	Bike	Swim Paddle	Play-ground	Camp	Trip Highlights
🏃		🛶		⛺	Rock tunnels, pond, boardwalk
🏃		🏊			White sand beach, views, dunes
🏃					Working farm, bridle paths
🏃					Tidal pools, rock scrambling, ocean views
🏃		🛶			Exhibits, butterfly garden, interpretive displays
🏃		🏊🛶			Wildlife haven bird sanctuary, beaches
🏃		🛶			Meadows, woods, beaver ponds, otters
🏃					Challenging hike to mountain peak
🏃			🛝		Rock climbing, caves
🏃					Boardwalk, frog pond, great nature center
🏃		🏊🛶	🛝	⛺	Paddling, camping, waterfalls
🏃	🚲	🛶			Observation tower, bike paths, fishing
🏃					Wetlands, woods, wildflower field
🏃					Fossilized dinosaur footprints
🏃					Woods, wetlands, pond, brook
🏃	🚲		🛝		Former railway, parks, views
🏃		🏊			Oceanside promenade, views
🏃					Grasslands, beaver ponds, meadows
🏃		🏊		⛺	Caves, pond, camping
🏃	🚲				Pond, paved trail, mountain biking
🏃				⛺	Great first summit for kids, views
🏃					Largest rhododendron area in New England
🏃					Bird refuge, vernal pools, harbor views

Hike Walk	Bike	Swim Paddle	Play-ground	Camp	Trip Highlights
🚶	🚴		🔗		Lighthouse, ocean views
🚶	🚴		🔗	⛺	Climbing, mountain biking, views
🚶	🚴	🏊	🔗	⛺	Water sports galore

PREFACE

I have been writing about families and activities in New England for more than a decade, for a number of different publications. I have written other guidebooks about New England in which certainly I covered outdoor activities, but not at all as in-depth as I have done for this book.

Most people who know me would describe me as a city girl, which I certainly am. However, I grew up in the country, I am an explorer at heart, and I love the outdoors, especially if camping is involved. Combining that with the joy of discovering new places and sharing them with others, especially my daughter, made me thrilled to write this book.

This guide covers everything from urban wilds to the stunning Cape Cod National Seashore to birding at the Joppa Flats in Newburyport. With the enormous number of great places to explore the outdoors with kids in Massachusetts, the scope of the book easily could have been limited to eastern Massachusetts, but I did include a few not-to-miss spots in Western Massachusetts, Maine, New Hampshire, Rhode Island, and Connecticut. Keeping the book to 100 destinations was difficult!

Each place in the guide is truly kid-tested and approved. Besides my then-12-year-old daughter, I enlisted her friends as well as my friends with kids of all ages to tag along with us. I let the kids take me where they wanted to go, rather than telling them what particular trail to choose or activity to engage in. This policy led us to places I might not have gone, on paths that I might not have chosen, but that's what exploring is all about. Being allowed some freedom, within reason, is a gift we can give to kids, one I think they will appreciate both now and later in life.

A connection to the outdoors is vital for families. My daughter can navigate a trail map as easily as she can a subway guide. We have a patch of grass in our backyard, but it's no substitute for spending a day or a night on a mountain, catching a glimpse of a creature in the wild, or following a trail just because you think something neat might be around the bend. I hope your family enjoys these adventures as much as we did.

ACKNOWLEDGMENTS

Nobody ever really creates a book alone, especially not one like this. As I did my field research, my constant companion was my daughter, Sadie, who now knows more about the New England outdoors than she ever thought she would. She has a list of favorite places she can't wait to return to. Thanks for hanging in there, Sadie. I never would have written this book without you.

In addition to my daughter, a core group of her friends accompanied us on trips; eventually our outings came to be called Kim Kamp, with me as head counselor. My very special thanks to Hazel Law, Griffin Li, and Ione and Felix Madsen Hardy, who made our research so much fun on dozens of trips. Thanks to Alejandro Abellas-Seitz, Cecelia Galligan, Lenny Esser, Jackie Kam, Becky Paul, Theo Shapiro, and Maddy Ward for joining us when they could.

Some adults deserve my deep appreciation as well. Sarah Madsen Hardy, Hilary Law, Elizabeth Seitz, and Bob Curley helped me tremendously with field work and friendship.

My co-camp counselor—my husband, Rob—was wonderful as always, offering support and love, especially when I broke my foot on one hike and despaired of ever getting back on track.

Thanks to Appalachian Mountain Club Books Editor Kimberly Duncan-Mooney, who was patient and kind, and offered invaluable advice. Other AMC staff I'd like to thank are Publisher Heather Stephenson, Production Manager Athena Lakri, Editorial Intern Ellen Duffer, Vice President for Communications and Marketing Kevin Breunig, Director of Education Programs Pam Hess, *AMC Outdoors* Senior Editor Marc Chalufour, Director of Conservation and Recreation Policy Heather Clish, and the Boston Youth Opportunities Program team. Thank you to copyeditor Janet Renard, proofreader Ken Krause, and mapmaker Ken Dumas. My gratitude goes to Heather and Steve DePaola, AMC trip leaders who reviewed the manuscript, and to AMC's Great Kids, Great Outdoors blogger Kristen Laine.

INTRODUCTION

Endless distractions abound to keep us and our kids inside: television, computers, video games, social media sites, even just cell phones. The draw of the overwhelming amount of media at our fingertips can be hard to resist, especially for kids.

To get you started, this book offers 100 outdoor adventures, as well as a number of other ideas for enjoying the great outdoors with children. It's not enough for us as parents to send our kids outside to play. We can't count on physical education at school either. It's up to us to teach our kids about the environment and what wonders it can hold. Just as we provide healthy, balanced meals for our children, we need to make sure kids get outside. There's no better way to do that than by being a good example ourselves.

When our children see that we parents enjoy the outdoors and when they realize that we are spending time with them, sharing something we love with them, they will come to cherish the experience as well. The simple joy of discovering a new trail, spying an animal in its natural habitat, or accomplishing a difficult climb as a family can't be overstated.

Some of the suggested activities in this book can be done in a couple of hours, some are likely to take all day, and some can easily form the basis of a weekend trip. I've included a broad range of activities, from hiking up mountains (Trips 82, 95, 99) to exploring caves (Trips 33, 57, 83) to biking on trails that used to be railroad tracks (Trips 32, 42, 90). As Boston-area dwellers, we are lucky to be able to get to beaches, forests, mountains, lakes, ponds, and even islands in quite a short time.

New England is full of special places, sometimes hidden in urban or suburban neighborhoods and sometimes entirely worth a long drive. In doing research for this book, I was frankly astounded by the many fantastic places I had never heard of and the discoveries I made of places I know my family and I will return to.

In choosing adventures to be included here, I have tried to offer a wide range of habitats and settings so that everyone can find something appealing. For the most part, no special gear or athletic ability is needed, just a little curiosity. In addition, many activities described here are free or can be enjoyed at a very low cost. More than one-third are accessible by public transit.

As the parent of an only child, I've learned that sometimes more is better. Having more than two people can change the whole dynamic of an outing. While my daughter might not be entirely thrilled about a long hike with only me for company, when she has a couple of pals to walk with, her attitude can completely change.

One of my personal heroes is nineteenth-century landscape architect Frederick Law Olmsted, who played an enormous role in designing many of the urban green spaces Americans enjoy today. Olmsted thought it vital to the mental health and well-being of city dwellers to have green spaces to escape to.

To me, this 1870 quote by Olmsted is as relevant as ever: "We want a ground to which people may easily go when the day's work is done, and where they may stroll for an hour, seeing, hearing, and feeling nothing of the bustle and jar of the streets where they shall, in effect, find the city put far away from them."

In this book, you'll find his imprint at Arnold Arboretum (Trip 7), Franklin Park (Trip 10), Jamaica Pond (Trip 12), Lynn Woods Reservation (Trip 34), and World's End (Trip 62). His designs, however, are quite far-reaching: he planned New York's Central Park, for example, and his work can be seen as far away as Washington State.

As you make your own plans to put the city behind you, try not to get too hung up on making your kids go on a certain trail or path. Exploring a new place and trying new things can be half the fun.

And remember, while it's good to unplug ourselves and our kids from distracting technology on a regular basis, that doesn't mean technology can't enhance a trip on occasion. For example, for geocaches (see page 150), you'll need a device with GPS. For kids who love tech toys, this is perfect. Put them in charge of finding coordinates as you hike and researching geocaches online before you go out. In the end, all that matters is that you and your family are enjoying the outdoors together.

HOW TO USE THIS BOOK

With 100 destinations to choose from, you may wonder how to decide where to go. The regional map at the front of this book and the locator maps at the beginning of each section will help you narrow down the trips by location, and the At-a-Glance Trip Planner that follows the table of contents will provide more information to guide you toward a decision. The four "10 Best" lists might also influence your selection.

You can involve even young children in the planning process. Is he crazy about animals? Does she love to splash in the water? Are they always the first ones on top of the monkey bars? When kids have some input, they are more invested in the excursion and in having a good time.

Don't let a child's current interests limit you, however. In researching this guide, I discovered that we may have a future rock climber in the family when I took my daughter to places where she could climb and scramble on rocks. Our trips used to revolve around swimming; now we have another option for outdoor adventure, simply because we explored something new.

Once you settle on a destination and turn to a trip in this guide, you'll find a series of icons that indicate whether the destination is accessible via public transit; is stroller-friendly; offers hiking, bicycling, swimming, or paddling; has a playground or camping facilities; or charges fees. (*Note:* A fee icon is used only when payment is mandatory. No fee icon is used for the instances where donations are requested or certain areas of a destination require a fee. In those cases, more information is provided in the text.) An icon also indicates what ages are best suited for activities there.

The trip overview (in italic type) summarizes the main activities or points of interest that children will enjoy at the destination. Information on the basics follows: address, hours, fees, contact information, bathrooms, water/snacks, and available maps. The recommendations are based on my perception.

The directions explain how to reach the destination by car and, for some trips, by public transit (note: if a walk of more than 1 mile is necessary, instructions are not included here. Check the destination's website if you are interested in taking public transportation that requires longer walks). Information about parking and global positioning system (GPS) coordinates for parking lots are also included. When you enter the coordinates into your GPS device, it will provide driving directions. Whether or not you own a GPS device, it is wise to consult an atlas.

We've included maps for some of the trips. You'll also find URLs and information on where you can find maps for those outings. Hours, fees, and other details are all subject to change, so be sure to check websites or call the locations before heading out.

The Remember section provides been-there insights to help you sidestep potential glitches or alerts you to sights or experiences that are worth the extra effort to pursue. The Where to Eat Nearby section provides details about restaurants, cafés, and so on for before or after your trip.

Every trip includes a Plan B section, which gives ideas for nearby activities in case the original plan does not work out. Plan B should never be seen as a failure. Sometimes the weather doesn't cooperate. Sometimes a long hike isn't in the cards for a cranky child. Keep in mind that you're trying to share and foster a love of the outdoors with your kids, not make them go on a march. You can always come back on another, better day.

All of the destinations in this book have some sort of "payoff," from beaver lodges to boardwalks to fire towers to vernal pools. Talk to children about these special aspects of places you visit. They may be motivated by reaching a fire tower or by looking for salamanders in a vernal pool.

There are other payoffs to taking children outdoors, of course: payoffs in family time, in children's growing confidence and skills, in their increased comfort in the outdoors and connection to the natural world. Those are part of every destination.

STEWARDSHIP AND CONSERVATION

Frequent, unstructured outdoor play can increase children's health, school performance, self-esteem, and feelings of connection to nature. Kids who feel connected to nature today are likely to be tomorrow's conservation leaders. The Appalachian Mountain Club (AMC) is committed to helping kids build strong connections to the outdoor world, including its protection. When you bring young people outdoors, you should teach them to take care of the natural resources around them.

The first step in raising a conservation-conscious child takes place when that child falls in love with a special place. Foster a sense of fun at the outdoor destinations you visit, and then go one step further: Teach your children the Leave No Trace guidelines (see below). Join volunteer groups and participate in park cleanups or sign up for a naturalist-led walk to explore the plants, animals, rocks, trees, and waterways.

AMC's regional chapters are a great resource. Join AMC for access to the chapters' family committees, which offer programs to get kids outdoors and teach conservation strategies. Suitable for adults and children of all ages, these programs can be close to home or farther afield, and they include hiking, paddling, apple picking, winter weekends, exploring conservation areas and parks, and more.

LEAVE NO TRACE

The Appalachian Mountain Club is a national educational partner of Leave No Trace, a nonprofit organization dedicated to promoting and inspiring responsible outdoor recreation through education, research, and partnerships. The Leave No Trace program seeks to develop wildland ethics—ways in which people think and act in the outdoors to minimize their impact on the areas they visit and to protect our natural resources for future enjoyment. Leave No Trace unites four federal land management agencies—the U.S. Forest Service, the National Park Service, the Bureau of Land Management, and the U.S. Fish and Wildlife Service—with manufacturers, outdoor retailers, user groups, educators, organizations such as AMC, and individuals.

The Leave No Trace ethic is guided by these seven principles:

1. **Plan Ahead and Prepare.** Know the terrain and any regulations applicable to the area you're planning to visit, and be prepared for extreme weather or other emergencies. This will enhance your enjoyment and ensure that you've chosen an appropriate destination. Small groups have less impact on resources and on the experiences of other backcountry visitors.

2. **Travel and Camp on Durable Surfaces.** Travel and camp on established trails and campsites, rock, gravel, dry grasses, or snow. Good campsites are found, not made. Camp at least 200 feet from lakes and streams, and focus activities on areas where vegetation is absent. In pristine areas, disperse use to prevent the creation of campsites and trails.

3. **Dispose of Waste Properly.** Pack it in, pack it out. Inspect your camp for trash or food scraps. Deposit solid human waste in catholes dug 6 to 8 inches deep, at least 200 feet from water, camps, and trails. Pack out toilet paper and hygiene products. To wash yourself or your dishes, carry water 200 feet from streams or lakes and use small amounts of biodegradable soap. Scatter strained dishwater.

4. **Leave What You Find.** Cultural or historical artifacts, as well as natural objects such as plants and rocks, should be left as found.

5. **Minimize Campfire Impacts.** Cook on a stove. Use established fire rings, fire pans, or mound fires. If you build a campfire, keep it small and use dead sticks found on the ground.

6. **Respect Wildlife.** Observe wildlife from a distance. Feeding animals alters their natural behavior. Protect wildlife from your food by storing rations and trash securely.

7. **Be Considerate of Other Visitors.** Be courteous, respect the quality of other visitors' backcountry experience, and let nature's sounds prevail.

AMC is a national provider of the Leave No Trace Master Educator course. AMC offers this 5-day course, designed especially for outdoor professionals and land managers, as well as the shorter 2-day Leave No Trace Trainer course at locations throughout the Northeast.

For Leave No Trace information and materials, contact the Leave No Trace Center for Outdoor Ethics, P.O. Box 997, Boulder, CO 80306. Phone: 800-332-4100 or 302-442-8222; fax: 303-442-8217; web: lnt.org. For a schedule of AMC Leave No Trace courses, see outdoors.org/education/lnt.

GETTING STARTED

Creating a lifetime connection to the outdoors starts with sharing fun experiences. Getting your kids outside doesn't need to be difficult—focus on enjoyment and exploration, one hike, day at the beach, bike ride, or winter walk at a time.

GETTING OUTSIDE NEAR HOME

A great way to get started is to get outdoors in your backyard or neighborhood. Whether it's walking to a local park or climbing trees in your yard, make time to play in nature and reap the benefits. Here are some ideas for projects and activities you can do close to home and in all types of weather.

In Your Neighborhood
- Build Fairy Houses: Construct tiny "homes" from sticks, twigs, leaves, rocks, and other natural materials. (Don't use living plants.)
- Feed the Birds: Set up a bird feeder (you can make a simple one by spreading peanut butter on a pinecone). See which types of birds come; have the kids keep a log of their visits.
- Plant Something: Start small with a flowerpot or window box. Or plant a vegetable garden, a flower garden, a butterfly garden, an herb garden, or a tree.
- Follow a Map: Devise a local treasure hunt, or try orienteering or geocaching (see page 150).
- Take the Inside Outside: Bring out your kids' traditionally indoor toys and set up a play space outside. Getting out of a routine can be entertaining.
- Embrace the Dark: Go on a night walk and gaze at the moon and stars. The world will feel different and bigger.

In a Park
- Have a Picnic: Have your kids help you plan a picnic and enjoy eating together at your favorite park. After eating, they can play.
- Celebrate Outdoors: Plan birthday parties, family visits, or holiday traditions that involve getting outside.
- Volunteer: Many parks have volunteer organizations that plant flowers, donate toys for the sandbox, and hold events. If your local park doesn't have such an organization, consider starting your own.

Through the Seasons
- During spring, look for signs of life in streams, ponds, puddles, or vernal pools. Local nature centers often make note of the seasonal vernal pools and organize events around salamander crossings.

- When it's raining, head out with umbrellas or put kids in bathing suits and let them run around and splash in puddles.
- During fall, try leafy crafts: Have kids collect leaves they like and iron them between sheets of wax paper to make a bookmark or window decoration. Or make a leaf sailboat from fallen pinecones, sticks, or pieces of bark. A leaf can be the sail, a stick the mast, and a pinecone or piece of bark the boat body.
- In winter, go sledding, look for animal tracks, build a snow fort, or make snow sculptures.

GROWING UP IN THE OUTDOORS

As parents or caregivers, we learn quickly that children have different needs at different ages. That's true of children in the outdoors as well. Remember, your enthusiasm is contagious. If you show excitement for the outdoors, your children will become excited too.

Babies, Toddlers, and Preschoolers (up to age 4)

With very small children, your primary goal is to create a positive association with being outdoors.
- It's surprisingly easy to bring babies on many outdoor excursions. Babies are easily carried and their needs are relatively simple: Keep them fed, warm, and dry. Nursing moms shouldn't hesitate about getting outside with their babies. No need to pack food for a baby who's nursing!
- Once children begin walking, you may cover less distance than with babies. Small children love repetition and engage with nature on a micro level. Young explorers may count every wildflower or try to jump over every rock on a trail, or want to turn around after half a mile or half an hour. Children at this age respond well to simple games, songs, and storytelling.
- Small children have a limited understanding of time, distance, and danger, and require constant supervision, especially near water and on steep terrain.

Young Children (ages 5 to 8)

Young children want to do everything you do and they'll try hard to keep up. This makes them great company outdoors.
- Children these ages are eager to learn new skills and information. Simple lessons work well.
- Young children are easily distracted or discouraged, but are also readily engaged and are easily motivated by clear goals and imaginative games. Offer encouragement and support for their efforts.

- Children at this stage still need you to set boundaries and safety guidelines. They're old enough, though, that you can share your reasoning with them. You can also start asking children to carry their own backpack.
- Inviting a friend along on an outdoor adventure lets children share the experience with someone their own age—and often makes your job easier.
- Young children may be able to join in child-focused group activities in the outdoors, but may not have long enough attention spans to join mixed-age groups.

Older Children (9 to 12)

Older children can take on more trip responsibilities and may enjoy testing their limits in outdoor activities. They may also focus more on peer relationships.

- Being outdoors offers parents the chance to engage their children with lessons about nature, history, weather, or any number of topics.
- Enlist older children in trip planning and decision-making; reading maps and assisting in navigation; and carrying personal gear.
- Leave electronic devices behind or turn them off. Talking on a phone, texting, or playing an electronic game is distracting and noisy.
- Children at this age often want to bring friends along on outings, but may be more reluctant to try something new in front of their peers or to follow safety guidelines.
- Some preteens will be ready to join organized mixed-age groups and educational activities.

TRIP PLANNING

When you're heading farther than the local park, you will want to map out your day and activity ahead of time. Just be prepared for changes.

Choose Your Goals

For most outdoor adventures, shorter is better with young children. Consider your child's pace and stamina when selecting destinations and routes.

- Think about payoffs: Hike to a waterfall or bicycle to a beach with public swimming.
- For cycling, plan trips that are not as hilly as adult trips and that minimize traffic and maximize children's safety. Bike paths are often fun for families, but can be busy; when kids are just learning to ride, you may be better off heading to a park or reservation with bike trails.

Before You Go

- Check the weather forecast. Be prepared for changes in the weather conditions.

- Leave a trip plan with someone you trust before you head out.
- Check directions, available parking, and facility hours.

Once You're There

- Go over your route with children. Give them trail names when hiking and talk about stopping points and turnaround times. Tell children to always stop at a trail junction. Remind them that the group must stay together.
- Make a contingency plan for if you get separated, and make sure children understand it.
- Find the bathroom. Each trip description in this book gives information on where bathrooms are located.

Schedules and Routines

- Keep children's schedules and routines in mind. If your daughter eats lunch every day at 11:30 A.M. but you're holding out for the picnic tables at the end of the trail, no one is going to have fun.
- Flexibility is important, too. If kids are having a blast climbing on rocks, there's no need to make them stop just because it's lunchtime.

Sharing the Outdoors with Others

- Inviting other children can make a big difference in fun and motivation.
- Having other adults along on a trip can give you extra sets of eyes—and arms. But be careful that socializing does not take your attention away from children. This is especially important with small children.
- Grandparents and older adults also can be great additions to outings.

Fees, Deals, and Discounts

Many of the destinations in this guide are free or have a minimal cost. Some ask for voluntary donations. The following tips can help you save money while getting outdoors.

- Becoming a member of the Appalachian Mountain Club links you to a local chapter that organizes outings and offers discounts on everything from guidebooks and maps to Family Adventure Camps. Visit outdoors.org for more information about deals, discounts, and events.
- Consider joining Mass Audubon and The Trustees of Reservations. These memberships grant you free or discounted access to parks, nature centers, beaches, and historical properties, plus offer discounts on seasonal camps and special events.
- If you're a Boston resident, visit your local library to pick up parking passes for Massachusetts Department of Conservation and Recreation (DCR)

sites that charge a day-use fee. Parking fees are currently $2 at day-use areas, $5 at inland water areas, and $7 or $9 at ocean beaches.

- Consider an annual pass to DCR sites, currently $35 for Massachusetts residents.
- Many towns and cities offer free programs at public parks, and park rangers lead a number of free programs at state parks. During summer months, the nonprofit Highland Street Foundation runs "Free Fun Fridays" at cultural institutions around the state; these have included the Boston Harbor Islands, Garden in the Woods, the Arnold Arboretum, and other outdoor destinations.

CLOTHING AND GEAR

Good-fitting, well-functioning clothes and equipment—from rain jackets and backpacks to hiking boots—can mean the difference between a good time and a miserable one. But you don't need to spend a lot of money; you can often find well-made snowsuits, synthetic long underwear, and life jackets for children at thrift stores or gear swaps. You also don't need all of the items listed below for every type of outing. For a day in the park, a fleece jacket, sturdy shoes, and long pants may do the trick.

Outdoor Clothing Basics
- Put kids in long-sleeved shirts and long pants for increased sun protection or to keep bugs away from tender skin.
- Lightweight and easily packed, hats offer quick warmth, shade children from sun, and protect from wind and cold.
- Teach kids to wear clothes that are quick-drying and retain warmth even when wet. That means steering clear of jeans, sweats, and cotton shirts; instead, choose wicking synthetics, fleeces, wools, and quick-drying nylons.
- Dress children in layers. Light wicking layers go under heavier layers, which are under warm outer layers and wind protection. Adding or removing layers keeps kids from being soaked with sweat or rain, and from becoming too hot or too cold.

Footwear
- Choose appropriate footwear. For hiking, wear closed-toe shoes with good ankle support. For biking, wear closed-toe shoes, not sandals or flip-flops. For paddling, pick closed-toe shoes that can get wet repeatedly and dry quickly. For snowshoeing, choose thick snow boots or hiking boots that hold their shape under snowshoe straps or buckles.

- Synthetic liner socks under wool socks offer the most warmth and blister protection when hiking, skiing, or snowshoeing. If you need smaller sizes that outdoor manufacturers don't make, kids' nylon dress socks work decently as liners.

Helmets
- Helmets are a must for bicycling, including riding in trailers and in bike seats. Fit is important for safety; the helmet should sit level on a child's head and fit securely with the strap fastened.
- Babies may not have the neck strength to wear a helmet until after age 1.
- Although it may be tempting to buy a used helmet at a yard sale, you may have trouble assessing its condition and whether it meets current safety standards. New helmets are relatively inexpensive and worth the investment.

Dressing for Summer
- Sun hats protect children from intense sun. Look for lightweight hats with wide brims or visors long enough to shade a child's entire face. "Safari" hats with removable neck protection also work well, as do bandannas.
- Protect children's eyes with sunglasses, especially if you're traveling on water or over open landscapes. Expect to lose a few pairs along the way.

Dressing for Winter
- Don't overdress your children for winter. When active, people generate heat quickly. Dress in layers and remove a layer as necessary.
- One-piece snowsuits work best for younger children. Older children should practice the same layering system as adults.
- Balaclavas are great winter hats for kids because they cover both head and neck, leaving just an opening for the face.
- Keep toes warm—invest in a pair of wool or fleece socks.
- Mittens keep small hands warmer than gloves, so unless children need to use their fingers, mittens are best in winter. Wool socks can double as mittens.
- Remember sunglasses when out on the snow.
- Attach plastic bags over hands or mittens and socks or shoes to protect against rain or to add warmth in cold conditions.

Snowshoes and Skis
- Select snowshoes by weight, and look for ones that are easy for children to put on and take off.
- Waxless skis are the best choice for children who are learning the basics of cross-country skiing.

- Many Nordic centers and downhill ski resorts rent snowshoes and cross-country ski equipment for children.

Dressing for Wind or Rain
- Getting wet is often a safety risk, so be sure children have rain gear that is waterproof, not just water resistant. For extended trips, rain pants are a good addition to a rain jacket. Ponchos aren't recommended because they don't cover enough of the body and are useless in wind. If you plan to be out and active in rain for any length of time, breathable rain gear works best.
- Wearing a visored hat under a raincoat helps keep the hood of the raincoat out of a child's eyes.
- Wind protection is especially important when hiking or snowshoeing in the mountains or in exposed areas, paddling on the ocean or open water, bicycling, or cross-country skiing.

Dressing Babies for the Outdoors
- In hot weather, try thin, cotton one-pieces without feet to keep babies from overheating.
- In cooler weather, babies may need a hat or mittens before you do because they're not moving their bodies.
- In winter, babies stay warmer in snowsacks, rather than snowsuits with legs. If you ski or snowshoe with a child in a back carrier or open sled, remember that the child is not exercising and warming up as you are. Dress a baby in warm layers, minimize exposed skin, and check often to be sure the baby's nose, face, neck, and limbs are warm.
- Choose brimmed hats with a strap under the chin so they stay on.
- Pack twice as many diapers, covers, and clothing changes as you think you'll need. Bring several sturdy plastic bags to carry out soiled diapers and clothing.

PACKING

No single packing list can cover every activity in this book. The basic list below should work well for most day hikes. I've also provided specific tips for children's packs and for carriers, trailers, and sleds.

Basic Pack
You'll want to have the following items in your bag or backpack on outings in every season.
- ❏ Cell phone: Be sure to have emergency phone numbers on hand, though service is unreliable in rural and remote areas.

- ❑ Water: Bring enough for yourself, plus more to share. Two quarts per person is usually adequate, depending on the weather and the length of the trip.
- ❑ Food: Crankiness is increased by hunger. Pack high-energy snacks such as nuts, dried fruit, or granola bars. Pack a lunch for longer trips. Include children in this task as much as possible.
- ❑ Outerwear: wind protection, rain protection, warm jackets. Pack for the range of weather you're likely to encounter.
- ❑ Extra clothing: Extra socks, mittens, hats, and sunglasses come in handy and don't take up much room. Bringing extra warm clothes in all but the hottest weather is a good idea. If your activity takes you to a lake, river, stream, or ocean, a change of clothing may be required for everyone.
- ❑ Wet wipes
- ❑ Plastic bags
- ❑ Sunscreen
- ❑ First-aid kit: adhesive bandages, athletic or hospital tape, gauze, blister protection, small scissors, children's antihistamines, nonprescription painkillers, and tweezers for removing splinters
- ❑ Toilet paper or a pack of tissues
- ❑ Map and compass
- ❑ Whistle
- ❑ Flashlight or headlamp
- ❑ Insect repellent
- ❑ Extra clothes to leave in the car for the trip home

Optional Items

- ❑ Binoculars
- ❑ Camera
- ❑ Books: guidebooks, nature guides, picture books for young children
- ❑ Journal or loose paper, plus pens, pencils, or crayons
- ❑ Bandannas
- ❑ Fishing poles
- ❑ Trekking poles

Carriers, Trailers, and Pulks

At very young ages, for trips that don't involve a stroller, children are usually carried in a front pack or backpack, in a bike trailer, or on a sled behind skis. As children get older, bike seats and bike extensions may help you enjoy the outdoors together.

- Front packs are a good idea for babies up to about 6 months of age. They get the benefit of your body warmth, and you have a close-up view of them.
- You can move older babies to a child backpack when they're able to hold up their heads unaided.
- Children can ride in bike trailers as soon as they're able to hold their heads up independently. Be careful on bumpy terrain, however, and remember bike helmets, as with any cycling activity.
- Attached bike seats are appropriate when children can hold their heads upright while wearing a helmet and can comfortably sit upright on their own.
- For a period of a few years in between riding in a bicycle trailer and riding longer distances on a separate bicycle, your child may enjoy riding on a one-wheel child bike extension, complete with pedals, that attaches to the back of your bicycle. This may extend the distance you are able to enjoy riding together, but requires training and good communication.
- When cross-country skiing, it's easier and safer to use a sled built specifically for pulling children, called a pulk, than it is to ski with a baby in a backpack or front child carrier. You may start using a pulk with a child between 6 and 12 months old. The sled has two poles that are secured to the adult with a padded waist belt. Many cross-country ski areas have pulks available for rent.

Paddling Gear
- When paddling, store gear in specialized dry bags or in double-bagged, heavy-duty plastic bags.
- If you do a lot of paddling, you may want to invest in sized-down paddles so children can participate.
- Children should always wear personal flotation devices (PFDs). Parents should set an example by wearing PFDs as well.

Children's Packs
For many reasons—including safety, increasing skills and responsibility, and engaging them in the outdoors experience—children should carry some of their gear as early as possible.
- Food: Carrying their own snacks or lunches lets children replenish their energy on the go and also minimizes arguments among siblings over who has more of a favored food.
- Water: Carrying their own water encourages children to drink on the trail.
- Clothing: When kids have their own jackets, rain gear, or wind protection, they're more likely to put them on and take them off when needed.
- Whistle: Teach children how to use a whistle for safety.

- Map and compass: Older children can help with route-finding (and learn a valuable skill while they're at it).
- Address and phone number: Put this important information in a water-proof bag and in a place (such as a pack or pocket) where your child knows to find it.
- Fun stuff: sketch pad, magnifying glass, binoculars, ball, coloring books, harmonica. Young children may want to bring a favorite toy or stuffed animal.

SAFETY

Being prepared and taking a few precautions can reduce problems on your outings.

Sun and Heat

Children's sweat glands don't fully develop until adolescence, so they have a harder time managing extreme heat than adults.
- Apply sunscreen thoroughly before setting out for activities.
- During very hot weather, seek out shade or water to play in.
- Make sure children drink plenty of liquid to prevent heat exhaustion or heat stroke. Be alert for symptoms, including nausea, headache, dizziness, pale skin, and shallow breathing.
- If a child becomes overheated, move to a cool, shady spot. Apply wet cloths, loosen clothing, and have the child sip water.

Hypothermia

Hypothermia is a life-threatening condition that occurs when the body's core temperature drops. Hypothermia can happen in any season, even summer. Wet, windy conditions can be as dangerous as severe cold.
- The best treatment for hypothermia is prevention. Cool to cold temperatures combined with moisture and wind cause hypothermia, so stay dry and choose clothing that keeps you warm even when wet, such as wool and fleece. Remember your rain coats. Keep well hydrated and nourished.
- Know the signs: loss of judgment, shivering, stumbling, trouble speaking, and difficulty with motor skills such as unzipping a coat.
- A child who has become chilled should immediately be removed from the windy and cold conditions and changed into dry, warm clothes. Give the child warm, sweet liquids to drink and food with protein and sugar, if possible.
- To check a baby, feel the neck, torso, and limbs. If limbs feel cool to touch, a baby may be at risk for hypothermia.

Dehydration
- Make sure children drink plenty of water when active outdoors.
- Bring your own water. Never drink untreated water from outdoor sources.

Insects
- In the Northeast, some mosquitoes are infected with the eastern equine encephalitis virus, a rare but potentially fatal disease that can be transmitted to humans. The threat is generally greatest in the evening hours, when mosquitoes are most active.
- Ticks carry Lyme disease. Have children wear long sleeves, and long pants tucked into socks. After every outdoor adventure, don't forget to check for ticks (visit cdc.gov/ticks for tips).
- If any child on your trip is allergic to bee or wasp stings, he or she (or a designated adult) should carry an Epi kit.
- Insect repellent containing DEET is not recommended for children. Teach older children to wash their hands after applying repellent, if possible, and to avoid getting it in their eyes or mouths.

Plants and Animals
- Poison ivy is ubiquitous in the Northeast. Teach children to identify its clusters of three leaves that shine in the sun but are dull in the shade. If a child comes into contact with poison ivy, wash the affected area with soap as soon as possible.
- Train young children not to eat berries or plants.
- Teach children to observe, but not feed, wild animals. Explain that they shouldn't get between a mother and her young, such as a mother bear and cubs or a moose cow and calves.

Lightning
- If you're caught in a lightning storm, seek shelter, preferably in a building or car. If neither is nearby, seek shelter among trees that are of equal height. Avoid peaks, towers, and single trees in open areas. Remove packs or anything containing metal. Squat down, if possible on a foam pad, with your heels touching, knees apart, and hands off the ground.
- If you're on water and see a storm approaching, immediately head for shore.
- Count the number of seconds between lightning and thunder to estimate how far you are from the storm. Estimate one mile for every five seconds. If the number of seconds is decreasing, the storm is headed your way.

Water Safety

Children should always be supervised while around water. Remember these swimming safety tips, adapted from the American Red Cross:

- Never leave a young child unattended near water and do not trust a child's life to another child; teach children to always ask permission to go near water.
- Have young children and inexperienced swimmers wear U.S. Coast Guard–approved life jackets around water and in boats, but do not rely on life jackets alone. Be sure a jacket fits the user. Check buckles and straps.
- The Coast Guard does not recommend taking infants on board recreational boats and cautions that Infant Type II personal flotation devices up to 18 pounds may not always perform as expected.
- Establish rules for your family and enforce them without fail. For example, no swimming unless you can touch bottom.
- Know how to safely operate the type of watercraft you will use. Plan what you will do if a boat capsizes. Enroll in a boating safety class.

Getting Lost

- When hiking, sign in and out at trail registers to leave a record in case of emergency.
- Adults in the group should be able to use a map and guidebook. Keep the group together, with everyone within eye sight. Try a game, such as everyone counting off, to keep track.
- Teach children to stay together, keep to the trail, and wait at trail junctions if the group gets spread out. Point out landmarks as you go along to help build images of the trail in children's minds.
- Teach children to stay in one place, preferably in the open, if they get lost and to blow their whistles (three short blasts). The best thing adults can do in this situation is to stay calm and to keep the rest of the group together.
- Consider enrolling in a program like AMC's Lost and Alone workshops, which teach children how to stay with a group in the outdoors and also what to do if they become separated from the group.

Section 1

Boston

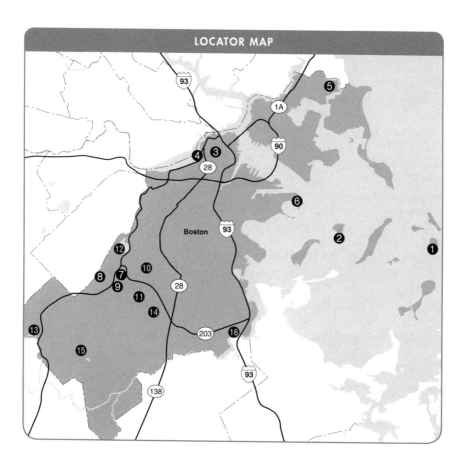

Trip 1

Boston Harbor Islands: Georges Island

Georges Island is a short ferry ride away and offers a fort to explore, complete with a drawbridge, dungeons, spooky tunnels, and plenty of space to run around.

Address: 66 Long Wharf, Boston, MA (for the ferry)

Hours: Ferry: 10 A.M. to 5 P.M., May through mid-October; island: 9 A.M. to sunset daily

Fee: Ferry: adults, $14; children ages 4–11, $8; island: free

Contact: bostonharborislands.org; 617-223-8666; nps.gov/boha

Bathrooms: At the visitor center

Water/Snacks: Water fountain inside the visitor center; concessions outside

Map: USGS Boston North

Directions by Car: Take I-93 South to Exit 24A (Government Center). Take the right fork, then stay left. At the traffic light, turn onto Atlantic Avenue. *GPS coordinates (ferry ticket booth): 42° 21.636' N, 71° 2.990' W.*

Directions by Public Transit: Take the Blue Line to Aquarium. Take a right out of the station, then another right at Christopher Columbus Park and look for the ferry ticket booth. The walk takes less than five minutes.

Thirty-nine-acre Georges Island is home to Fort Warren and serves as the hub for visiting most of the Boston Harbor Islands, which comprise a 34-island national park less than 10 miles from Boston's shores. After a pleasant 25-minute ferry ride, you'll arrive at the dock, where you can watch a brief movie about the island's history at the excellent visitor center. The fort, now a National Historic Landmark, was built in 1833 and served by turns as a training ground, a patrol point, and a Civil War prison.

Older kids will love exploring the warren of dark passageways, rooms, and towers. For intrepid explorers, a flashlight is a must to avoid stumbling. Spiral staircases leading to dead ends, cannon placements, rooftop vistas, and observation points on the ramparts are irresistible to children, but remind them to be cautious. Don't forget to bring a camera; Boston views from the island can't be beat.

Free park-ranger-led tours of the fort give visitors an in-depth history of the island. Special events, such as fishing clinics, musical performances and other live shows, and even vintage 1860s baseball games played by costumed teams

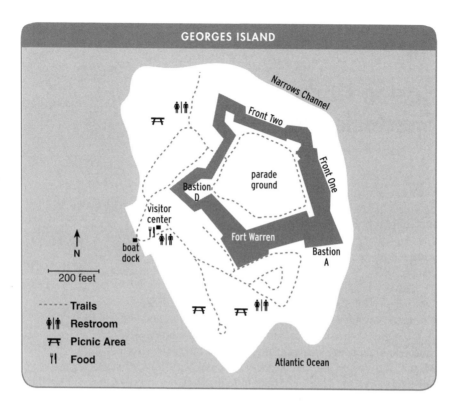

GEORGES ISLAND

Narrows Channel

Front Two

Front One

parade ground

Bastion D

visitor center

boat dock

Fort Warren

Bastion A

N

200 feet

Trails

Restroom

Picnic Area

Food

Atlantic Ocean

are offered in summer. You can't swim at this island, but you can wander along the gravel beach. While you can bring a stroller on the ferry, much of the fort and island are not stroller-friendly. You'll want to bring a baby carrier for infants.

Remember: Four islands in the park allow camping: Grape, Bumpkin, Lovells, and Peddocks. Visit the park website for more information.

PLAN B: The New England Aquarium, one dock over, and the Boston Children's Museum, a few blocks away, are great alternatives.

WHERE TO EAT NEARBY: Plan ahead and bring supplies to cook out at one of several cooking grills.

Trip 2

All Ages

Boston Harbor Islands: Spectacle Island

Spectacle Island offers swimming, an enormous variety of family-friendly programs, and a fascinating history.

Address: 66 Long Wharf, Boston, MA (for the ferry)
Hours: Ferry: 10 A.M. to 5 P.M., May through mid-October; island: dawn to dusk daily
Fee: Ferry: adults, $14; children ages 4–11, $8; island: free
Contact: bostonharborislands.org; 617-223-8666; nps.gov/boha
Bathrooms: At the visitor center
Water/Snacks: Water fountain and snack bar inside the visitor center
Map: USGS Boston North; nps.gov/boha/parkmgmt/upload/spectacle.pdf
Directions by Car: Take I-93 South to Exit 24A (Government Center). Take the right fork, then stay left. At the traffic light, turn onto Atlantic Avenue. *GPS coordinates (ferry ticket booth): 42° 21.636′ N, 71° 2.990′ W.*
Directions by Public Transit: Take the Blue Line to Aquarium. Take a right out of the station, then another right at Christopher Columbus Park and look for the ferry ticket booth. The walk takes less than five minutes.

Spectacle Island, part of the 34-island national park known as the Boston Harbor Islands, has a storied past. It served as fishing and hunting grounds for native peoples; grazing lands for livestock of colonial settlers; a quarantine station in the 1700s; a popular recreation spot in the 1800s; then, less glamorously, a horse-rendering factory site and garbage dump in the early 1900s. Happily, the island was rehabilitated into a recreation area once again when clay and sediment from Boston's Big Dig construction project was used to seal over the landfill in more recent years.

One of the main activities here is combing the rocky beaches for sea glass, pottery, and other debris. You are not supposed to keep anything you find, but that doesn't take away from the pleasure of the hunt. All sorts of ranger-run programs teach about the island's past and make a game of it for kids. The visitor center offers self-guided treasure hunts that vary according to age and difficulty—children can return with their finds to get a sticker or stamp. On one of our visits, a ranger led kids in looking for sea glass and then making a

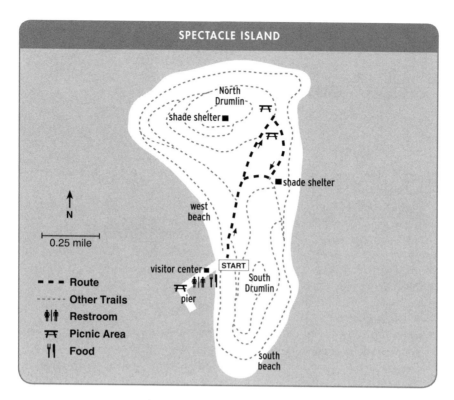

SPECTACLE ISLAND

North Drumlin

shade shelter ■

shade shelter ■

west beach

↑ N

0.25 mile

- - - Route
------ Other Trails
Restroom
Picnic Area
Food

visitor center ■

START

South Drumlin

pier

south beach

temporary mosaic. A rich variety of programs is offered in summer: jazz bands on the porch of the visitor center, clambakes, fishing clinics, kite-flying workshops, and much more. Kids will love the Hula-Hoops available for anyone to play with, found next to the visitor center.

The island is one of the few that allows swimming, and lifeguards supervise the beach area. If the kids agree to leave the beach, you can explore about 2.5 miles of trails. Spectacle Island offers the highest viewing point of any of the islands, at 155 feet, with stunning views of Boston. Take the trail to the North Drumlin to see the city from afar.

Remember: If you plan on swimming, water shoes are essential! The beach is rocky and painful for bare feet. Spectacle has a strict pack-in, pack-out policy, so you won't find any trash cans.

PLAN B: If it proves to be a rainy day or another reason keeps you on shore, the New England Aquarium, one dock over, and the Boston Children's Museum, a few blocks away, are great alternatives.

WHERE TO EAT NEARBY: A snack bar is on the island. Plenty of shops on the mainland sell picnic supplies.

Trip 3

Boston Common

America's oldest park is a place of community and a green oasis in the heart of busy downtown.

Address: 148 Tremont Street, Boston, MA (visitor center)
Hours: All hours daily
Fee: Free
Contact: cityofboston.gov/freedomtrail/bostoncommon.asp; 617-426-3115
Bathrooms: At the Frog Pond
Water/Snacks: Vendors throughout the park
Map: USGS Boston
Directions by Car: Public parking is very limited; driving is discouraged. If you decide to drive, an underground parking lot is on Charles Street between Beacon and Boylston streets. *GPS coordinates (parking garage)*: 42° 21.260′ N, 71° 4.096′ W.
Directions by Public Transit: Take the Red or Green Line to Park Street, or the Green Line to Boylston Street. Both stations open onto Boston Common.

The Boston Common offers plenty of green space for picnicking.

Boston Common, almost 50 acres, is the United States' oldest park, established in 1634. Once used for grazing livestock, it now offers a respite from the city sidewalks. The Frog Pond (a spray pool in summer and an ice-skating rink in winter) and the adjacent Tadpole Playground are great for kids, but wandering through the city's backyard, smelling the flowers, and admiring the view are also enticing.

Boston Common is the anchor for the Emerald Necklace, a system of connected parks that wend through many of Boston's neighborhoods. The Common has long been a place of public assembly, hosting everything from bonfires and fireworks celebrating the repeal of the Stamp Act and the end of the Revolutionary War to civil rights rallies, including one led by Martin Luther King Jr. Today, in summer you can see a Shakespeare play, watch an informal softball game, or enjoy concerts at the bandstand. In winter, you can skate on the Frog Pond, sled down the park's central hill, or simply admire the holiday lights that adorn the park's trees.

Remember: You can learn more about the park's history and pick up maps at the Visitor Information Center at 148 Tremont Street.

PLAN B: The equally historic Public Garden is just next door, across Charles Street. In summer, take a ride on the Swan Boats at the pond. Don't forget to look for the Make Way for Ducklings statue, a kid favorite.

WHERE TO EAT NEARBY: All around the Common, you'll find a number of restaurants for any budget.

Trip 4

All Ages

Charles River Reservation: Esplanade

The Charles River, one of Boston's defining natural features, offers recreational activities for everyone.

Address: Along the Charles River, Boston, MA
Hours: Dawn to dusk daily
Fee: Free
Contact: mass.gov/dcr; 617-626-1250
Bathrooms: Portable toilets near the Hatch Shell
Water/Snacks: Water fountains along the river
Map: USGS Boston; mass.gov/dcr/parks/charlesRiver/brochures.htm
Directions by Car: Public parking is very limited; driving is discouraged. *GPS coordinates:* 42° 21.434′ N, 71° 4.395′ W.
Directions by Public Transit: Take the Red Line to Charles Street/MGH. Take the footbridge over Storrow Drive and head west. The Hatch Shell is a short walk from here.

The Charles River Reservation runs 20 miles from downtown Boston to Riverdale Park in West Roxbury and offers myriad recreational activities, from strolling on its banks or biking and inline skating on paved paths, to sailing lessons and rentals. If you live in Boston, it's easy to take the river for granted, but that's a mistake. It's one of our best—and free—outdoor spaces.

The Esplanade, officially known as the James J. Storrow Memorial Embankment, is probably the most famous area of the park. *Esplanade* translates from the French as "promenade along a shore," the perfect description for this 3-mile stretch along the Boston shore of the Charles River, from the Museum of Science to the Boston University Bridge. The site of the Hatch Memorial Shell, well known as the stage for the Boston Pops Fourth of July concert, is here. In summer, free family movies are often shown on Friday nights.

Overall this section of the reservation contains miles of paths and riverbank to enjoy, plus a wading pool, a number of sports fields, and two playgrounds—the Esplanade Playground at the Longfellow Bridge and Stoneman Playground farther west near the Fairfield Street footbridge. You couldn't ask for a more scenic spot to spend time with your family. In addition to all the activities you can enjoy on your own, the nonprofit Esplanade Association

The grassy paths along the Charles River are perfect for impromptu foot races.

runs a number of special events throughout the year, including concerts, a dog parade, and exercise classes. Visit esplanadeassociation.org for a calendar.

Remember: Except for special events, you can't park near the Esplanade; it's really better to take public transit if you can. Keep your dog on a leash and clean up after it.

PLAN B: The Museum of Science, near the north end of the Esplanade, is a great alternative option, with exhibits that appeal to kids.

WHERE TO EAT NEARBY: Cross over the footbridge to the Back Bay for any kind of dining you could want. Charles Street offers a wide range of quick food options, including pizza and sandwiches.

Trip 5

All Ages

Belle Isle Marsh Reservation

Belle Isle Marsh offers an easy walk through Boston's last remaining salt marsh and a two-story observation tower to climb.

Address: Bennington Street, East Boston, MA
Hours: 9 A.M. to dusk daily
Fee: Free
Contact: mass.gov/dcr/parks/metroboston/belleisle.htm; 617-727-5350
Bathrooms: None
Water/Snacks: None
Map: USGS Boston Marblehead South
Directions by Car: From Boston, take MA 1A north. Take a right onto Boardman Street. At the traffic circle, take the second exit onto Saratoga Street, then take a slight left onto Bennington Street. The entrance and parking lot will be ahead on the right. *GPS coordinates:* 42° 23.518′ N, 70° 59.626′ W.
Directions by Public Transit: Take the Blue Line to Suffolk Downs and exit onto Bennington Street, then turn left. The entrance is 500 yards ahead on the right.

The 152-acre Belle Isle Marsh Reservation offers easy walks that take you through Boston's last remaining salt marsh. The reservation is a critical habitat for many salt-marsh plants and wildlife now rare to the region. Salt marshes used to be common along the shore of Massachusetts, but development destroyed most of them, so the area is a living time capsule and needs to be protected.

The Massachusetts Department of Recreation and Conservation (DCR) maintains 28 acres of landscaped park, perfect for families. Paved pathways are stroller-friendly and benches are available for resting. Paddlers will enjoy launching their canoe or kayak in the marsh. Kids will enjoy climbing the observation tower.

Boardwalks built over the marsh allow you to catch glimpses of fish in the water below. Birds and butterflies flock here, so it is a great place to spot herons, egrets, and other winged creatures. The Friends of Belle Isle Marsh group (friendsofbelleislemarsh.org) offers a current bird sighting list on its website, which details the hundreds of different birds that visit and where they were

Children love spotting the birds and butterflies that flock to Belle Isle.

spotted. It's worth downloading the list and checking it out with your child before you go so that on your visit you can make a game of spotting some of the same birds.

On occasion, the DCR offers guided walks that cover the natural and cultural history of Belle Isle. Check the website for details. The Friends of Belle Isle Marsh group offers fun family programs, such as canoeing on Father's Day.

Remember: Restrooms are not available at Belle Isle. You can find some public restrooms at Revere Beach. You can rent kayaks at the Belle Isle Boat Yard and the Winthrop Town Landing.

PLAN B: Revere Beach, America's oldest public beach, is a short drive away. Walk along miles of beach or visit the playground.

WHERE TO EAT NEARBY: Several places to eat are along Chelsea Street, which is a ten-minute drive from Belle Isle.

Trip 6

All Ages

Castle Island and Pleasure Bay

There's no castle and it's not an island, but Castle Island is a Boston treasure, with stunning views, beaches, playgrounds, and historic Fort Independence.

Address: William J. Day Boulevard, South Boston, MA
Hours: Dawn to dusk daily
Fee: Free
Contact: mass.gov/dcr; 617-727-5290
Bathrooms: By the entrance to the park; at the fort
Water/Snacks: Water fountains near the bathrooms; concessions by the parking lot
Map: USGS Boston South; mass.gov/dcr/parks/trails/CastleIs.gif
Directions by Car: From Boston, take I-93 South to Exit 15 (Columbia Road/ JFK). Turn left onto Columbia Road. At the traffic circle, take the third exit for William J. Day Boulevard and drive to the end. Plenty of parking is available in a large lot. *GPS coordinates:* 42° 20.326′ N, 71° 0.806′ W.
Directions by Public Transit: Take the Red Line to Broadway and take City Point bus #9 to East Broadway at Farragut Road. Walk through Marine Park and along the causeway to Castle Island. The walk takes about ten minutes.

Castle Island is a 22-acre urban park connected to the mainland by causeways. It is home to Fort Independence, a pentagon-shaped granite fort built between 1834 and 1851. The fort is actually the eighth one to be built here. The first fort on Castle Island was built in 1634.

The park is popular with families, who bring kids here to learn how to ride bikes, skateboard, roller-skate, climb on the play structures, splash in the water, and picnic. Since Castle Island is across the water from Logan International Airport, it's a fantastic place to watch planes taking off and landing, and no matter what age your children are, they will be impressed by how close to the ground the planes seem to be.

The two paved walking paths—Pleasure Bay Loop, which is 1.84 miles long, and Castle Island Loop, which is less than 1 mile long and goes around the fort—offer views that can't be beat.

Pleasure Bay, the M Street Beach, and Carson Beach, also part of the park system, stretch along 3 miles of parkland and beach on the South Boston

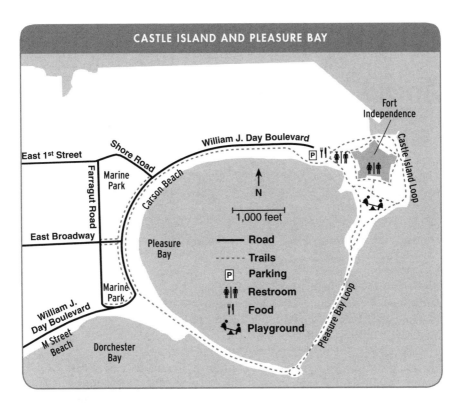

CASTLE ISLAND AND PLEASURE BAY

shoreline of Dorchester Bay. From Carson Beach, a walkway leads from Castle Island to the Kennedy Library.

Remember: The Castle Island Association conducts guided tours of the fort from Memorial Day through Columbus Day; call ahead for hours, which vary. Keep your dog on a leash and clean up after it.

PLAN B: If you want to visit a real island (by boat), the nearby Boston Harbor Islands (Trips 1 and 2) make great day trips.

WHERE TO EAT NEARBY: The popular snack bar serves hot dogs, chicken fingers, fries, ice cream, and other foods.

Trip 7

Arnold Arboretum

The arboretum is a haven for families who bring their kids in strollers, teach them to ride bikes, or just amble along and enjoy great views.

Address: 125 Arborway, Boston, MA
Hours: Park: dawn to dusk daily; visitor center: 9 A.M.. to 4 P.M. weekdays, 10 A.M. to 4 P.M. weekends
Fee: Donations accepted
Contact: arboretum.harvard.edu; 617-524-1718
Bathrooms: At the Hunnewell Building visitor center
Water/Snacks: Water fountain at the visitor center.
Map: USGS Boston South; arboretum.harvard.edu/wp-content/uploads/Web_ Map.pdf
Directions by Car: From Boston, take Storrow Drive to the Fenway/Park Drive exit. Follow signs to Riverway/Boylston Street and drive down Boylston Street through three lights, where Boylston Street flows into Brookline Avenue. Take Brookline Avenue to the Riverway and make a left. The Riverway becomes the Jamaicaway, then the Arborway. Stay on the Arborway/MA 203 East. On-street parking is available at most entrance gates along the Arborway and along Bussey Street. *GPS coordinates:* 42° 18.461' N, 71° 07.203' W.
Directions by Public Transit: Take the Orange Line to Forest Hills; exit through the Arnold Arboretum door. The arboretum is across the street.

One of the oldest parks in the United States, the Arnold Arboretum has been enjoyed since 1872. It is the second-largest park in Boston's Emerald Necklace, designed by landscape architect Frederick Law Olmsted, and its paved paths invite people out for a stroll, kids on bikes, and people exercising their dogs. In winter, cross-country skiers cut paths through the snow and sledders enjoy the snowy hills.

Amateur botanists will like that many of the trees and plants are labeled for easy identification. A small bonsai tree collection is always popular with kids. The arboretum's excellent website also offers downloadable podcast guides, a tree-of-the-month fact sheet, and bird checklists. A letterbox puzzle (see page 150) is also a fun way to explore the arboretum. This is found on the same downloadable sheet as the tree-of-the-month information. If the visitor center is open, stop in for maps and check out exhibits and artwork.

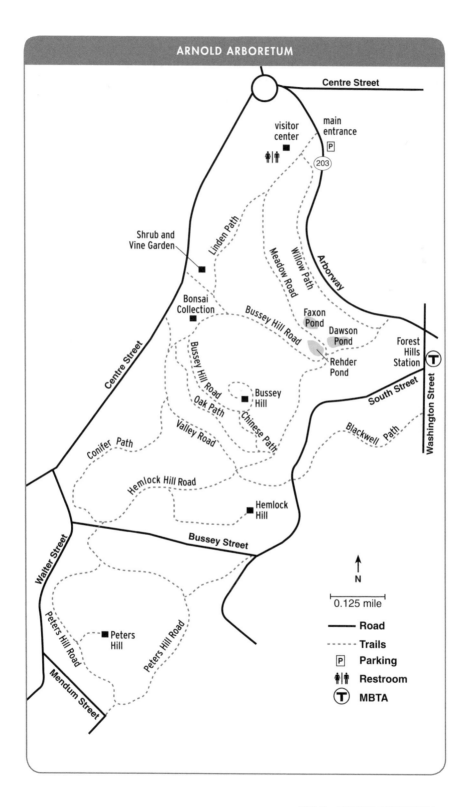

From April through October, the arboretum offers free monthly Family Drop-In Activities. The events range from crafts to scavenger hunts. On weekends in May, June, September, and October, arboretum interpreters are at the ready with hands-on fun and stories about the grounds. The second Sunday in May is celebrated as Lilac Sunday, a festival that has become a Mother's Day tradition for many families.

Remember: Except on Lilac Sunday, picnicking is not allowed on the arboretum's grounds, so plan to eat elsewhere. Tree climbing, plant picking, and walking on plant beds and mulched areas are prohibited. Keep your dog on a leash and clean up after it.

PLAN B: Jamaica Pond (see Trip 12), a short distance north of the Arnold Arboretum, offers fishing and sailing.

WHERE TO EAT NEARBY: Restaurants and shops are on Centre Street, South Street, and Hyde Park Avenue, and in nearby Roslindale Square. A detailed map of restaurants is available at the visitor center.

Trip 8

Ages 0–4

Allandale Woods

Easy trails, meandering streams, and a small pond in this 90-acre Urban Wilds Initiative property offer plenty of diversions for kids.

Address: 7 VFW Parkway, West Roxbury, MA
Hours: Dawn to dusk daily
Fee: Free
Contact: cityofboston.gov/parks; 617-635-4505
Bathrooms: None
Water/Snacks: None
Map: USGS Boston South; cityofboston.gov/parks/urbanwilds/AllandaleWoods.asp
Directions by Car: From I-95, take Exit 20 and follow MA 9 east. After 2.9 miles, bear right at Florence Street. Turn right onto Hammond Pond Parkway and continue to the traffic circle, then take the third exit onto Newton Street. Take a slight right onto West Roxbury Parkway, then take the third exit at the traffic circle onto Grove Street. Turn right onto Allandale Road. After 1.1 miles, turn right onto Centre Street. Take a slight right onto Veterans of Foreign Wars Parkway and take a right into the lot of the Annunciation Church. Parking spaces are set aside specially for hikers. *GPS coordinates:* 42° 17.844′ N, 71° 8.029′ W.
Directions by Public Transit: Take the Orange Line to Forest Hills and switch to the #38 bus. Get off the bus on Centre Street at the VFW Parkway stop.

Sandwiched between the busy VFW Parkway and Allandale Road is a 90-acre section of woods that is completely unexpected. Allandale Woods, a second-growth forest, is classified by the City of Boston as an "urban wild," meaning it is part of the original ecosystem of the area. It stretches from the Fens and the Charles River Basin, along the Boston–Brookline boundary, and through the Sawmill Marshes to the Charles River in West Roxbury. Along the way, it abuts private homes and streets.

Several trails lead into the woods, but the most convenient one is behind the church, where you can leave your car. The dirt trails, maintained by volunteers, take you to Rock Pond, where you can go fishing, to a very long stone boundary wall built in the 1930s. The wall is irresistible to kids, most of whom will instantly feel the need to walk on it as far as they can. You'll also find gentle hills, a cattail marsh, and intertwining streams to splash in.

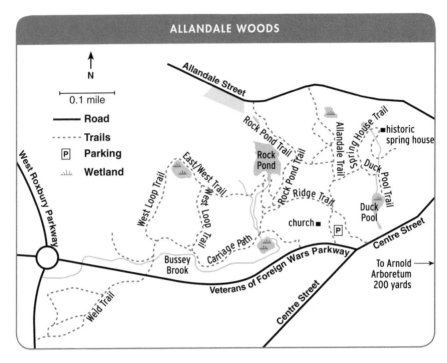

ALLANDALE WOODS

N

0.1 mile

—— Road
----- Trails
P Parking
Wetland

West Roxbury Parkway

Allandale Street

Rock Pond Trail

Rock Pond

Allandale Trail

Springhouse Trail

historic spring house

Duck Pool Trail

West Loop Trail

East/West Trail

West Loop Trail

Rock Pond Trail

Ridge Trail

Duck Pool

church ■

P

Centre Street

Carriage Path

Bussey Brook

Veterans of Foreign Wars Parkway

Centre Street

To Arnold Arboretum 200 yards

Weld Trail

Remains of a historic springhouse and abandoned rusty farming implements are scattered about in a section near the main trail—make sure to keep children clear of these. Joggers and people walking their dogs are frequent visitors, and you'll definitely hear traffic if you are close to the roads, but once you venture in farther, you'd never know you were in Boston. When the woods are cloaked in snow, strap on your snowshoes and explore the quiet trails and frozen streams.

Remember: Some of the trails will take you almost into people's backyards; try to be a good neighbor and keep rambunctious kids to the more interior paths. Keep your dog on a leash and clean up after it.

PLAN B: Millennium Park (see Trip 13) is a short distance west from Allandale Woods, with lots of climbing structures.

WHERE TO EAT NEARBY: Restaurants and shops can be found on the VFW Parkway, as well as in nearby Roslindale Village.

Trip 9

Ages 0–4

Bussey Brook Meadow

This 20-acre Urban Wilds Initiative property, almost hidden away, is just steps from a busy subway station and the Arnold Arboretum.

Address: Washington and South streets, Jamaica Plain, MA
Hours: Dawn to dusk daily
Fee: Free
Contact: arboretumparkconservancy.org; 617-556-4110
Bathrooms: None
Water/Snacks: None
Map: USGS Boston South; arboretumparkconservancy.org/Blackwell%20Map. html
Directions by Car: From Boston, take Storrow Drive to the Fenway/Park Drive exit. Follow signs to Riverway/Boylston Street and drive down Boylston Street through three lights, where Boylston Street flows into Brookline Avenue. Take Brookline Avenue to the Riverway and make a left. The Riverway becomes the Jamaicaway, then the Arborway. Stay on the Arborway/MA 203 East. On-street parking is available at most entrance gates along the Arborway and along Bussey Street. *GPS coordinates:* 42° 17.982′ N, 71° 6.913′ W.
Directions by Public Transit: Take the Orange Line to Forest Hills and exit through the Arnold Arboretum door. The entrance gate for the park is on Washington Street, across the street from the station.

Bussey Brook Meadow is a sweet little green space. This urban wild was named after Benjamin Bussey, the man who in 1842 bequeathed the lands that would become the Arnold Arboretum. This particular section adjacent to the arboretum was underdeveloped for years. In 2002, however, the Arboretum Park Conservancy, along with the arboretum and the City of Boston, worked to add this land to the arboretum's holdings. However, while Bussey Brook Meadow is groomed, it is nothing like the well-manicured lawns of the larger property.

The stroller-friendly Blackwell Path meanders through forest, wetlands, and a meadow that is full of wildflowers. Visitors can enter through gates across the street from the Forest Hills T station or on South Street. Along the path are interpretive signs, one of which states that the nonprofit hopes that the path encourages commuters to visit the arboretum. Kids especially will love to see the many butterflies that visit, and in winter, they'll enjoy spotting

The tall grasses of this urban wild invite exploration.

animal tracks in snow. Tracks made by red foxes, white-tailed deer, muskrats, and even coyotes have been spotted here.

Remember: Bring bug spray in summer, as the mosquitoes are quite active. Keep your dog on a leash and clean up after it.

PLAN B: You can head into the Arnold Arboretum (Trip 7) for more paths and to visit the interpretive center.

WHERE TO EAT NEARBY: On the other side of the Forest Hills T station, a few restaurants are on Washington Street. Nearby Roslindale Village offers lots of dining options.

Trip 10

Franklin Park

Franklin Park is home to more than just a zoo. Here you can also explore a forest, enjoy concerts, visit playgrounds, run around fields, and go sledding.

Address: 1 Circuit Drive, Boston, MA
Hours: Dawn to dusk daily
Fee: Free
Contact: franklinparkcoalition.org; 617-635-7275
Bathrooms: At the clubhouse (open to all park users, not just golfers)
Water/Snacks: None
Map: USGS Boston South; emeraldnecklace.org/static/filelib/Franklin_Park_Map.pdf
Directions by Car: From Boston, take Storrow Drive to the Fenway/Park Drive exit. Follow signs to Riverway/Boylston Street and drive down Boylston Street through three lights, where Boylston Street flows into Brookline Avenue. Take Brookline Avenue to the Riverway and make a left. The Riverway becomes the Jamaicaway, then the Arborway. Stay on the Arborway/MA 203 East. Just past the Arboretum, take the left lane to stay on the overpass. At the traffic circle, take the second exit to the entrance of the park and turn right onto Circuit Drive. *GPS coordinatates (golf course clubhouse parking lot):* 42° 18.105′ N, 71° 5.327′ W.
Directions by Public Transit: Take the Orange Line to Green Street. Out of the station, take a right on Green Street. Eventually Green Street becomes Glen Road. Follow Glen Road to the park (a ten-minute walk).

When people hear "Franklin Park," they often think "zoo," but the approximately 500-acre park is much more than that. This is the largest park and crowning jewel of Frederick Law Olmsted's Emerald Necklace. Created in the 1880s, it was named for none other than Benjamin Franklin.

In addition to the zoo, a 200-acre forest, tennis courts, baseball fields, a cross-country course, and an 18-hole public golf course—where you can hike, cross-country ski, and sled in winter—are on the property. A stroller-friendly, 2.5-mile loop path winds through woods, over old stone bridges, and past a pond. The Playstead, an area for recreation and sports, is a popular spot. Playgrounds, basketball courts, a baseball field, tennis courts, and a cricket pitch make the park a fantastic place for sports lovers.

Franklin Park offers miles of paved paths, enjoyed by bikers of many ages.

Cars do drive along the 6 miles of roads that pass through the park, so be aware, but you can stroll or bike along 15 miles of pedestrian and bridle paths. The Franklin Park Coalition sponsors a number of events in the park throughout the year. Visit franklinparkcoalition.org for details and a calendar.

Remember: Keep your dog on a leash and clean up after it.

PLAN B: You can easily find enough to keep you busy at the park, but no doubt your kids will beg to go to the zoo. If you are a Boston resident with a library card, you can get discounted tickets from your local library.

WHERE TO EAT NEARBY: A restaurant and concessions are available at the zoo, and Jamaica Plain has a variety of restaurants for every taste and budget.

Throughout this book you'll find wonderful refuges where you can see creatures in their natural environments and learn about ecosystems. You can even visit injured wildlife recuperating at Great Blue Hill (Trip 26) or Drumlin Farm (Trip 36).

While spotting a local creature in the wild can't be beat, sometimes children want to see something exotic, such as an elephant or a giraffe. When a guaranteed visit with animals is called for, zoos are the perfect choice.

Buttonwood Zoo

Buttonwood has a focus on local animals and its Berkshires to the Sea exhibit describes 200 miles of wildlife habitat from the Berkshire Mountains to Buzzards Bay. In addition, kids can visit two Asian elephants. *In New Bedford; bpzoo.org.*

Capron Park Zoo

This small zoo has a lot to see, from a rainforest exhibit to African lions to lemurs. A splash fountain is fun for kids on hot days, so bring a bathing suit and a towel. *In Attleboro; capronparkzoo.com. Near Borderland State Park (Trip 59).*

Ecotarium

The Ecotarium has a 40-foot-high treetop canopy walkway that is an exciting adventure for children and adults alike. Inside the center, visit three floors of exhibits and see a variety of rescued animals that couldn't live on their own. Nature trails and a working, one-third scale passenger train are also on the property. *In Worcester; ecotarium.org. Near Purgatory Chasm State Reservation (Trip 83).*

Franklin Park Zoo

Besides the lions, tigers, and giraffes that are kid favorites, the Franklin Farm exhibit is always a big hit. Children can pet cows and goats, and check out baby chicks. *In Boston; zoonewengland.org. Within Franklin Park (Trip 10).*

Roger Williams Park Zoo

This zoo has more than 100 species of animals from around the globe including dromedaries, moon bears, red pandas, and snow leopards. *In Providence, Rhode Island; rogerwilliamsparkzoo.org. Near East Bay Bike Path (Trip 90).*

Southwick's Zoo

This is the largest zoo in New England, with 175 acres of land and huge number of animals. The 35-acre deer forest is a kid favorite. *In Mendon; southwickszoo.com.*

Stone Zoo

The barnyard here is inviting with sheep, goats, and a pygmy zebu (a miniature humped-cattle species). Other favorites include black bears, flamingos, and jaguars. *In Stoneham; zoonewengland.org. Near the Middlesex Fells (Trip 31).*

Trip 11

All Ages

Forest Hills Cemetery

A cemetery may seem an unlikely place for a walk with kids, but the Forest Hills Cemetery has beautiful paths and art to enjoy in a peaceful city setting.

Address: 95 Forest Hills Avenue, Jamaica Plain, MA
Hours: Dawn to dusk daily
Fee: Free
Contact: foresthillscemetery.com; 617-524-0128
Bathrooms: None
Water/Snacks: None
Map: USGS Boston South; foresthillscemetery.com/wp-content/uploads/2011/06/Forest_Hills_Map_2011_03.pdf
Directions by Car: From Boston, take Storrow Drive to the Fenway/Park Drive exit. Follow signs to Riverway/Boylston Street and drive down Boylston Street through three lights, where Boylston Street flows into Brookline Avenue. Take Brookline Avenue to the Riverway and make a left. The Riverway becomes the Jamaicaway, then the Arborway. Stay on the Arborway/MA 203 East. Take a right at Forest Hills Avenue (the cemetery driveway), and look for parking along this roadway. *GPS coordinates: 42° 17.891' N, 71° 6.466' W.*
Directions by Public Transit: Take the Orange Line to Forest Hills and exit through the Hyde Park Avenue door. Cross the avenue and take a left on Tower Street. Walk to the end and enter Forest Hills' pedestrian gate. (To get to the main gate, follow the path to the left.)

Some people may think it odd to include a cemetery in a book about exploring the outdoors with kids, but they will understand once they have been to Forest Hills Cemetery, which is so much more than a burial site. The 275-acre green space was named to the National Register of Historic Places in 2004.

Founded in 1848, the cemetery features Victorian landscape design with shady paths, a lake, a fountain, a waterfall, and scenic vistas. You can find works by important sculptors throughout the cemetery, and you can pick up a fantastic visitors guide and map at the main entrance. It's interesting to note that in its early days, the cemetery was actually a place where the public went for art openings—the Museum of Fine Arts wasn't founded until 1870.

In that spirit, the Forest Hills Educational Trust—which offers walking tours, exhibitions, special events, concerts, and poetry readings throughout

Modern sculptures dot the landscape at the Forest Hills Cemetery.

the year—began the Contemporary Art Sculpture Path in 2001 with year-long exhibits. The artworks are listed in the guide and are found throughout the cemetery. Many famous people are buried here, including abolitionist William Lloyd Garrison, suffragist Lucy Stone, poet E. E. Cummings, and playwright Eugene O'Neill.

For a nice loop walk, use the map from the visitors guide to find your way to the center of the cemetery, where you'll find lovely Lake Hibiscus. Circle the lake, and then wander along lanes and avenues on your way back to the main entrance. If you need a theme for your walk, have kids look for all the memorials and monuments that feature animals, a popular motif during Victorian times. The most famous one is the 1854 Barnard Monument, which features a life-size sculpture of a dog.

Remember: Forest Hills is still an active burial ground, so remind kids to be respectful of people who may be there to mourn loved ones. Keep your dog on a leash and clean up after it.

PLAN B: The Mass Audubon's Boston Nature Center and Wildlife Sanctuary (Trip 14) is a short walk south and has exhibits inside as well as trails to explore.

WHERE TO EAT NEARBY: Jamaica Plain and nearby Roslindale Village have restaurants galore, ranging from gourmet to casual.

Trip 12

Jamaica Pond

A charming and easy 1.5-mile loop around the pond offers plenty of chances for viewing waterfowl, fishing, walking dogs, and renting boats.

Address: Jamaicaway and Perkins Street, Jamaica Plain, MA
Hours: All hours daily
Fee: Free
Contact: cityofboston.gov; 617-357-8300
Bathrooms: None
Water/Snacks: Water fountain by the bandstand
Map: USGS Boston South
Directions by Car: Take the Jamaicaway to Kelly Circle, then bear north on Parkman Drive at the traffic circle. Turn right onto Perkins Street; look for parking spots on the right. Limited parking is on the Perkins Street side of the pond. *GPS coordinates:* 42° 19.252′ N, 71° 07.339′ W.
Directions by Public Transit: Take the Orange Line to Stony Brook. Walk down Boylston Street, which turns into Moraine Street, then cross the Jamaicaway. (Walk is about 1 mile total.)

Jamaica Pond is a beautiful oasis in a busy urban neighborhood. The 68-acre pond is a kettle hole that was formed by glaciers melting more than 10,000 years ago. It is part of Boston's Emerald Necklace, the chain of parks designed by Frederick Law Olmsted. For nearby residents and visitors alike, the pond serves as a gathering place, a fishing hole, a jogging path, and a center of calm.

Families bring their children to stroll along the mostly smooth, flat, paved path that circles the pond or just to watch the ducks and turtles on its shores. From spring through fall, the nonprofit organization Courageous Sailing offers sailing classes on the pond in cooperation with the Boston Department of Parks & Recreation. (Call 617-522-5061 for information or visit courageoussailing.org.) Sailboats, rowboats, and kayaks are also available to rent. In snowy months, bring your snowshoes and traipse along the easy path. The "Bowl," next to the pond, is a safe and fun place to sled.

Since the state stocks the pond with fish every year, many people come to try their hand at catching trout, pickerel, bass, and catfish. Children 15 and under don't need a fishing permit, so feel free to have your child bring along a pole and some bait for an afternoon of fun.

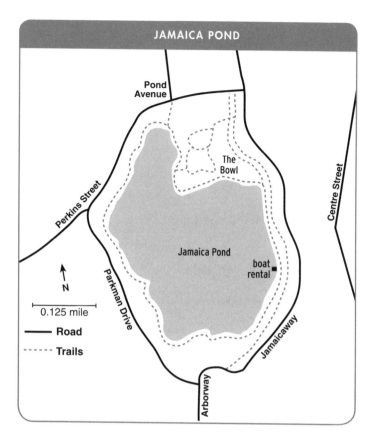

The annual Jamaica Pond Lantern Parade, coordinated by Spontaneous Celebrations, is a fall staple for many families. The October festival draws thousands of people walking around the pond with candle lanterns in a parade of lights. Since it's so close to Halloween, many kids come in costumes.

Remember: As tempting as it may be, don't feed the ducks or any other wildlife you encounter. No private crafts are allowed on the pond, and neither is swimming, as the pond is a backup water reserve. Keep your dog on a leash and clean up after it.

PLAN B: If you want to stretch your legs further or find a little more green space with fewer people, the Arnold Arboretum (Trip 7) is a short walk south.

WHERE TO EAT NEARBY: You can find a variety of restaurants (from pizza joints to sub shops to sit-down restaurants) on Centre Street.

Trip 13

Millennium Park

Two playgrounds, beautiful, grassy hills, a canoe and kayak launch, and multiple athletic fields await visitors to Millennium Park.

Address: Gardner Street, West Roxbury, MA
Hours: Dawn to dusk daily
Fee: Free
Contact: newtonconservators.org/34millennium.htm; cityofboston.gov/parks; 617-635-4505
Bathrooms: Portable toilets by the playground
Water/Snacks: Water fountain by the playground
Map: USGS Boston South; newtonconservators.org/map34millennium.htm
Directions by Car: From Boston, take MA 9 West. Take a left onto Hammond Street. At the first traffic circle, take the third exit onto LaGrange Street. In about 1.5 miles, take a right onto VFW Parkway. After you pass the Home Depot, make a right onto Gardner Street and follow it until you see a sign for the park. The upper parking lot is closer to the playgrounds; the lower lot is closer to the trails. *GPS coordinates: 42° 16.891′ N, 71° 10.838′ W.*
Directions by Public Transit: Take the Orange Line to Forest Hills and switch to the #36 bus toward Rivermoor. Get off at Charles Park Road and walk 0.2 mile on Gardner Street.

Millennium Park, built in 2000 on top of a former landfill and capped with dirt from the Big Dig, is a magnet for families, who bring their kids to fly kites, roll or sled down hills, enjoy the two playgrounds, or play soccer on one of the many athletic fields.

Because of its elevation, the park commands great views and can get quite windy, which makes it a popular kite-flying spot. If you have your own canoe or kayak, you can use the boat launch for the Charles River at the southern end of the park.

The 6 miles of walking trails include a short, paved nature trail that leads around the fields and is a popular stroller cruise. You can also take trails leading to Nahanton Park in Newton. A bridge across Sawmill Brook connects the park with the Oak Hill Trails that run through Brook Farm and connects to Helen Heyn Riverway. The trails—simply called Short, Medium, and Long—

Grassy hills and lush trees help to make visitors feel far away from the city.

range from 0.5 mile to 1.4 miles long. The longest trail takes you by Sawmill Brook and the river, so I recommend that for the best scenery.

Remember: The park can get crowded with children's sports leagues in spring and fall, so if you are looking for a secluded walk, head elsewhere. Keep your dog on a leash and clean up after it.

PLAN B: Allandale Woods (Trip 8), just down the road on VFW Parkway, is peaceful and not usually crowded. The Jim Roche Community Ice Arena is about two minutes away, also on VFW Parkway.

WHERE TO EAT NEARBY: Restaurants are along VFW Parkway as well as on nearby Providence Highway.

Trip 14

Boston Nature Center and Wildlife Sanctuary

Visitors will enjoy easy walking trails and a surprising amount of wildlife in such an urban setting.

Address: 500 Walk Hill Street, Mattapan, MA
Hours: Trails: dawn to dusk daily; nature center: 9 A.M. to 5 P.M. Monday through Friday, 10 A.M. to 4 P.M. weekends and Monday holidays
Fee: Free for Mass Audubon members; $2 suggested donation for nonmembers
Contact: massaudubon.org; 617-983-8500
Bathrooms: At the nature center
Water/Snacks: Water fountain in the nature center
Map: USGS Boston South; massaudubon.org/Nature_Connection/Sanctuaries/ images/maps/boston_trails.pdf
Directions by Car: From Boston, take Storrow Drive to the Fenway/Park Drive exit. Follow signs to the Riverway. The Riverway becomes the Jamaicaway, then the Arborway. Stay on the Arborway/Route 203 East (Morton Street). Turn right onto Harvard Street, then take the first right onto West Main Street. Follow the road to the left, and turn right at the sign for Boston Nature Center and the parking lot. *GPS coordinates:* 42° 17.252′ N, 71° 6.111′ W.
Directions by Public Transit: Take the Orange Line to Forest Hills. Leave the station on the Hyde Park Avenue side, cross the street, and turn right. Take a left onto Walk Hill Street. Proceed up Walk Hill Street to the intersection of American Legion Highway. Cross the highway and follow Walk Hill Street until you see the Mass Audubon/Boston Nature Center sign on the left. (Total distance is about 1.25 miles.)

You never know what might turn up when you take a walk at this 67-acre urban sanctuary. On one hot summer afternoon, after dodging a multitude of day campers playing on the lawn, my group went out the back door of the nature center, followed the easy 0.5-mile Snail Trail to Fox Trail, where in just a couple of minutes, all noise fell away. Rabbits hopped down the trail in front of us. A few minutes after that, a large turkey and three small chicks made their way across our path. This is a perfect hike for toddlers.

The 2 miles of trails here are easy to navigate and range from grassy meadows to boardwalks through wetlands. Download the winter quest (see page 150

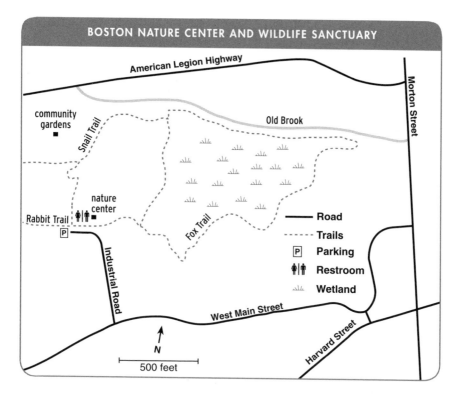

BOSTON NATURE CENTER AND WILDLIFE SANCTUARY

for more on questing) on the center's website and follow the guide to thirteen stations. The naturalist's notes and clues will teach kids all about winter wildlife and flora and fauna.

This is a popular and busy Mass Audubon property, offering environmental education programs to Boston elementary schools weekly. The sanctuary's George Robert White Environmental Conservation Center was built green to teach about environmentally sustainable design. Inside, you'll find displays about the building and about the animals and birds in the area.

Remember: The nature center has birding kits that you can borrow for 1.5 hours. Each kit includes binoculars, bird guide books, and a list of common birds found at the center. Call ahead to reserve one if you have a budding birder in the family.

PLAN B: Forest Hills Cemetery (Trip 11) is just next door.

WHERE TO EAT NEARBY: Numerous places to grab a quick bite are on American Legion Highway.

Trip 15

All Ages

Stony Brook Reservation

Ice skate, fish, hike, swim, or enjoy a variety of other activities at this 475-acre reservation, whose many boulders and outcroppings tell the story of its glacial past.

Address: Enneking Parkway and Turtle Pond Parkway, Hyde Park, MA
Hours: Dawn to dusk daily
Fee: Free
Contact: mass.gov/dcr; 617-333-7404
Bathrooms: At the ice rink and at the pool
Water/Snacks: Water fountains and snack machines at the ice rink and at the pool
Map: USGS Boston South; mass.gov/dcr/parks/trails/stonybrook.pdf
Directions by Car: From Boston, take I-93 South to Exit 15. Turn right onto Columbia Road, then left onto Blue Hill Avenue. Turn right onto River Street, then right onto Gordon Avenue. Take the second left onto Enneking Parkway. Follow it to the small parking lot ahead on the left (room for four cars). *GPS coordinates: 42° 15.512′ N, 71° 8.149′ W.*
Directions by Public Transit: Take the Orange Line to Forest Hills and switch to the #40 bus toward Georgetowne. Get off at the intersection of Turtle Pond Parkway and Dedham Parkway within the park.

Stony Brook Reservation, founded in the late 1800s, appeals to lots of different outdoor enthusiasts. Some like to ice-skate at the rink on the property. Others enjoy the 12 miles of trails, some of which are paved, that run through West Roxbury and Hyde Park. Still others enjoy fishing at Turtle Pond.

The terrain here comprises hills, valleys, forests, rocky outcroppings, and wetlands. Facilities include ball fields, tennis courts, picnic areas, a pool, and playgrounds. The 5 miles of paved biking trails are perfect for kids learning to ride a bike and offer a safer—and leafier—alternative to the road for commuter bicyclists. Some sections feature boulders perfect for kids who might like to climb. In winter, kids can enjoy cross-country skiing or snowshoeing, or simply lace up their snow boots and search for animal tracks along the reservation's quiet trails.

Remember: Cars can pull over in a number of sanctioned parking places along Turtle Pond Parkway, which intersects Enneking. When crossing the

Kids who like to climb and scramble will enjoy exploring the boulders at Stony Brook Reservation.

street, make sure to watch out for cars that speed along the parkway. Keep your dog on a leash and clean up after it.

PLAN B: The Boston Nature Center and Wildlife Sanctuary (Trip 14) is minutes away and offers exhibits and easy trails.

WHERE TO EAT NEARBY: On the northwest border of the reservation, you can drive or bike to Washington Street into Roslindale for restaurants. Just a few blocks east of the reservation, Hyde Park Avenue leads to dining options.

Neponset River Reservation

Biking or walking through the Neponset River Reservation offers urban dwellers a respite from the city.

Address: Hallett Street, Dorchester, MA
Hours: Dawn to dusk daily
Fee: Free
Contact: mass.gov/dcr; 617-727-5290
Bathrooms: Portable toilets along the trail
Water/Snacks: Water fountain near the playground
Map: USGS Boston South; mass.gov/dcr/parks/metroboston/neponset.htm
Directions by Car: From Boston, take I-93 South to Exit 11B and merge onto Granite Avenue. In about 0.5 mile, turn right onto Hill Top Street, then make your first right onto Hallett Street and the parking lot at Pope John Paul II Park. *GPS coordinates: 42° 17.092′ N, 71° 2.644′ W.*
Directions by Public Transit: Take the Red Line to North Quincy and switch to the #210 bus toward Fields Corner. Get off at Neponset Circle at Walnut Street, and walk south 0.2 mile to the park.

The Neponset River Reservation covers a lot of ground. Along the 3-mile Neponset River Greenway Trail following the river, you'll find picnic tables, soccer fields, playgrounds, paths for walking and biking, and a restored salt marsh.

The Pope John Paul II Park, where this trip originates, is a 65-acre park with walkways, fields, and a playground. It's on the site of a former landfill, which makes the spot even more special since the Department of Conservation and Recreation was able to restore this formerly contaminated site. This urban green space is actually a bit underutilized, so don't be surprised to have areas all to yourself.

Biking through the salt marsh is enjoyable, because it's so different from its urban setting. The marsh offers a diverse habitat for plants and animals, including a number of threatened and endangered species. If you're lucky, you might spot a snowy egret or a great blue heron. The marsh has the distinction of being the first salt marsh in the commonwealth to be publicly owned.

Remember: You can paddle your own canoe or kayak on the river if you have one.

Neponset River is a peaceful oasis where you can paddle alongside water birds.

PLAN B: Head to Quincy Quarries Reservation (Trip 61) for rock climbing and to see where stone for the Bunker Hill Monument came from.

WHERE TO EAT NEARBY: Along Gallivan Boulevard and Granite Avenue in Dorchester, you'll see several spots to dine.

Section 2

Inside I-95/Route 128

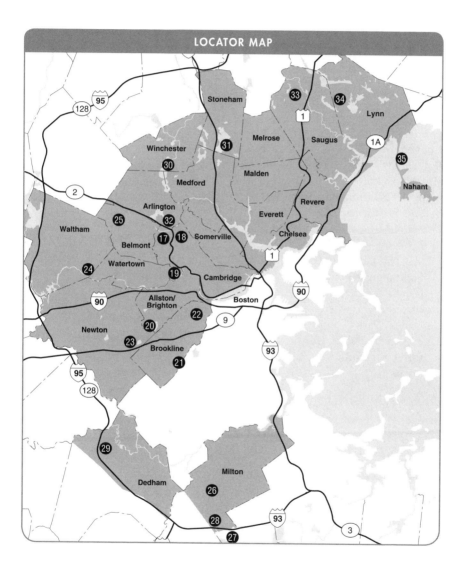

LOCATOR MAP

Trip 17

Fresh Pond Reservation

Fresh Pond Reservation is a hub of activity, popular with families, joggers, bicyclists, and nature lovers.

Address: 250 Fresh Pond Parkway, Cambridge, MA
Hours: Dawn to dusk daily
Fee: Free
Contact: cambridgema.gov; 617-349-4762
Bathrooms: At the water department facility next to the parking lot
Water/Snacks: None
Map: USGS Lexington; cambridgema.gov/CityOfCambridge_Content/
  documents/map.pdf
Directions by Car: From Boston, take Storrow Drive West to Soldiers Field
  Road. Cross Eliot Bridge and follow signs for Fresh Pond Parkway (MA 2).
  Stay to the right on Gerrys Landing Road and continue onto Fresh Pond
  Parkway. The pond will be on the left. The lot has limited parking for
  Cambridge residents and cars with handicap plates only. Exceptions include
  special events when nonresidents can get a permit. Public lots are at nearby
  Danehy Park (Trip 18). *GPS coordinates:* 42° 22.984′ N, 71° 8.581′ W.
Directions by Public Transit: Take the Red Line to Alewife. Exit the station and
  turn right on Alewife Brook Parkway/MA 2 and walk about 0.5 mile to the
  pond.

Fresh Pond Reservation is part of the reservoir system for the City of Cambridge. While the 155-acre kettle-hole pond is surrounded by a chain-link fence to protect the water, the 162 acres surrounding it offers plenty of space for activities. A 2.25-mile paved loop around the pond is open to runners, walkers, bikers, inline skaters, and parents pushing strollers.

In the 1800s, the pond was privately owned and was the site of an ice business, which shipped ice as far away as Europe, China, and India. The pond became the city's drinking-water supply in 1852. Around the perimeter of the pond, you'll find a tot lot, a butterfly meadow, woods, community gardens, and a golf course.

The volunteer group Friends of Fresh Pond runs a variety of educational nature events for families. Activities include bird-watching, leaf-pile jumping,

Paved paths near the reservoir are great for beginner cyclists.

digging in mulch, leaf rubbing, and book readings. Check the group's website (friendsoffreshpond.org) for a calendar.

Remember: Dogs are not allowed in the lawn areas. On Fridays, April through November, a Kids' Walk is held at 9 A.M. to discover plants and animals.

PLAN B: Walk over to Danehy Park (Trip 18) for playgrounds, playing fields, and picnic tables.

WHERE TO EAT NEARBY: A grocery store with a café and prepared foods is in the Fresh Pond Mall, and restaurants are along Fresh Pond Parkway.

Trip 18

Danehy Park

This urban park is a haven for bicyclists, dog walkers, joggers, and families.

Address: 99 Sherman Street, Cambridge, MA
Hours: Dawn to dusk daily
Fee: Free
Contact: cambridgema.gov; 617-349-4301
Bathrooms: At the comfort station near the tot lot by Sherman Street
Water/Snacks: In the comfort station
Map: USGS Lexington; cambridgema.gov/CityOfCambridge_Content/
documents/danehy.pdf
Directions by Car: From Boston, take Massachusetts Avenue/MA 2A across
the bridge into Cambridge. Follow Mass Ave for 3 miles, then turn left onto
Rindge Avenue. Turn left onto Sherman Street; you'll see the parking lot
ahead on the right. *GPS coordinates: 42° 23.335′ N, 71° 07.972′ W.*
Directions by Public Transit: Take the Red Line to Alewife. Walk down Rindge
Avenue, and take a right onto Sherman Street. The walk takes about 15 minutes.

The open fields at Danehy Park call out for kite flyers.

Danehy Park is a 50-acre recreational facility built on the site of the former city landfill, yet one more of the reclaimed spaces that are so valuable in the urban landscape. The park offers wide-open spaces, paved paths, sports fields, playgrounds, a spray park, a dog park, picnic tables and grills, and a 2-acre wetlands area.

The separate bike path is great for bicyclists and walkers. The park is the perfect place to teach kids how to ride a bike or, if the fields are empty, to let a toddler roam free. The gentle hills are popular for sled rides in winter. The spray park lets kids cool down in summer while parents sit on nearby shaded benches. The comfort station, equipped with a water fountain and bathrooms, is a nice perk.

Remember: In summer, special family programs include arts events and movie nights. Call 617-349-6200 for details.

PLAN B: The Fresh Pond Reservation (Trip 17) is minutes away by foot and has a 2.25-mile loop trail easy to navigate on foot or with a stroller.

WHERE TO EAT NEARBY: At the Fresh Pond Shopping Mall, just behind the park, you can find a grocery store with a café. Several dining options are across the street from the mall.

Trip 19

Mount Auburn Cemetery

America's first large-scale designed-landscape cemetery is rich in art, architecture, and nature.

Address: 580 Mount Auburn Street, Cambridge, MA
Hours: 8 A.M. to 5 P.M. daily, October through April, 8 A.M. to 7 P.M. daily, May through August
Fee: Free
Contact: mountauburn.org; 617-547-7105
Bathrooms: Outside Story Chapel
Water/Snacks: Water fountain outside Story Chapel
Map: USGS Lexington; ground map available at Story Chapel
Directions by Car: From Boston, take Storrow Drive West to the Arlington/Fresh Pond Parkway exit. Bear right over the Charles River on Eliot Bridge and follow signs for Arlington/Fresh Pond Parkway. Get in the left lane at the traffic lights in front of Mount Auburn Hospital and follow signs for MA 16 West/Watertown. At the next traffic light, bear left onto Mount Auburn Street. Ample parking is available in the lot. *GPS coordinates: 42° 22.516′ N, 71° 8.713′ W.*
Directions by Public Transit: Take the Red Line to Harvard Square, where you can take either the Watertown Square or Waverley Square bus (#71 or #73) to Mount Auburn Street at Aberdeen Avenue, just outside the cemetery.

Mount Auburn Cemetery, founded in 1831, was the first large-scale designed-landscape cemetery open to the public in the United States and is now a National Historic Landmark. As with the Forest Hills Cemetery (Trip 11), Mount Auburn is so much more than a burial site. The 175-acre property has ponds, meadows, woods, gardens, fountains, sculptures, monuments, and chapels. It's considered a wildlife sanctuary for birds; the Mass Audubon Society designated it an Important Bird Area.

Start your visit at Story Chapel (to the right of the cemetery office), which is home to the visitor center. You can watch a video about the cemetery's history and pick up maps as well as special materials for kids. Mount Auburn is committed to educating children and offers a letterbox challenge (see page 150), a scavenger hunt, and a family guide to the Washington Tower, an observation tower you can climb for views of Boston.

From the 62-foot Washington Tower at Mount Auburn Cemetery, visitors enjoy a panoramic view, including Harvard Stadium and the buildings of Boston.

The Friends of Mount Auburn Cemetery offers guided walking tours and special events throughout the year. Check the cemetery's website for a calendar.

Remember: Let your kids know that the cemetery is a place of contemplation for many and is therefore not the place for rambunctiousness. Bicycles, picnics, and pets are not allowed.

PLAN B: Fresh Pond Reservation and Danehy Park (Trips 17 and 18), where the kids can run and play to their hearts' content, are five minutes away by car.

WHERE TO EAT NEARBY: Plenty of food choices are available in either direction on Mount Auburn Street.

Trip 20

Ages 5–8

Chestnut Hill Reservation

The reservation offers an easy 1.5-mile loop walk around its reservoir and views of a serene setting in the city.

Address: Beacon Street and Chestnut Hill Avenue, Allston/Brighton, MA
Hours: Dawn to dusk daily
Fee: Free
Contact: mass.gov/dcr; 617-333-7404
Bathrooms: None (unless you visit the rink and pool)
Water/Snacks: None (unless you visit the rink and pool)
Map: USGS Lexington
Directions by Car: From Boston, take Beacon Street west to Cleveland Circle. Cross Chestnut Hill Avenue. The reservation is on the right. Look for on-street parking on Beacon Street or Chestnut Hill Avenue. *GPS coordinates:* 42° 20.134′ N, 71° 9.047′ W.
Directions by Public Transit: Take the Green Line C train to Cleveland Circle. Cross Chestnut Hill Avenue at the light. The reservation is on the right.

Chestnut Hill Reservoir and pumping station pumped millions of gallons of drinking water to Boston, Brookline, and numerous other communities during its prime in the late 1800s and well into the next century. The reservoir was constructed at a time when civic pride was at a high pitch, which is why the pumping station, across Beacon Street, looks somewhat like a castle.

The station, now a museum (see Plan B below), operated until the 1970s, when Boston began getting its water from the Quabbin Reservoir. If need arises, though, Chestnut Hill is able to serve as an emergency backup source. Today, the reservation is listed on the National Register of Historic Places and is a City of Boston Landmark.

You can take your kids for a pleasant stroll on the 1.5-mile path around the reservoir. This is also a good place for kids to bike or roller-skate. In colder months, take a wintry walk and look for signs of wildlife.

Remember: You can't swim or ice-skate on the reservoir; head to Reilly Rink and Pool (335 Chestnut Hill Avenue), part of the reservation's property, to enjoy those activities. Keep your dog on a leash and clean up after it.

The 1.5-mile loop around the reservoir is an enjoyable walk with kids.

PLAN B: The Waterworks Museum, housed in the former pumping station, was built by architect Henry Hobson Richardson, who also built Boston's Trinity Church. Inside, all the machinery is pretty fascinating to look at for adults and kids alike. A movie and exhibit stations detail the history of the building and the era. The museum is open Wednesdays through Sundays. Visit waterworksmuseum.org for information.

WHERE TO EAT NEARBY: Numerous restaurants are on Beacon Street in either direction from the reservation.

Trip 21

Larz Anderson Park

Larz Anderson is a charming spot to picnic, visit a lagoon, fly a kite, and take in fantastic views of Boston.

Address: Goddard Avenue, Brookline, MA
Hours: Dawn to dusk daily
Fee: Free
Contact: brooklinema.gov; 617-730-2069
Bathrooms: Next to the playground; at the ice-skating rink in winter
Water/Snacks: None
Map: USGS Boston South; brooklinema.gov/images/stories/Recreation/
LarzAndersonPark.pdf
Directions by Car: From I-95, take Exit 20 and follow MA 9 east and bear right at Florence Street. Take a right onto Lee Street and follow to the end, then take a left onto Newton Street. Follow Newton Street for approximately a quarter-mile. The road will fork; go to the left on Goddard Avenue. The park and the main lot are a quarter-mile ahead on the right. You can also park at the Larz Anderson Auto Museum or at the top of the main ridge. *GPS coordinates (parking lot):* 42° 18.764′ N, 71° 8.319′ W.
Directions by Public Transit: Take the Orange Line to Forest Hills and switch to the #41 bus toward Cleveland Circle. Get off at Clyde Street at Whitney Street and walk 0.2 mile to the corner of Newton and Goddard streets.

This 64-acre former private estate turned public property was bequeathed to the Town of Brookline in the 1950s; it is now the town's largest park, with easy walking paths, sports fields, a playground, an ice-skating rink, a lagoon, plenty of places to picnic, and an auto museum. The Temple of Love gazebo is a wonderful place to gaze out at the peaceful scenery. Head up to the highest point on the main ridge for fantastic views of Boston.

The main ridge is a popular spot to watch Boston's Fourth of July fireworks or to fly kites, because there's always a wind. In winter, the many hills call to sledders when snow is on the ground. Overall, Larz Anderson Park offers a lovely outdoor respite from the city and is an extremely popular gathering place for groups.

From May through October, the Auto Museum holds a series of lawn events on the weekends, showcasing different kinds of vehicles, from Cor-

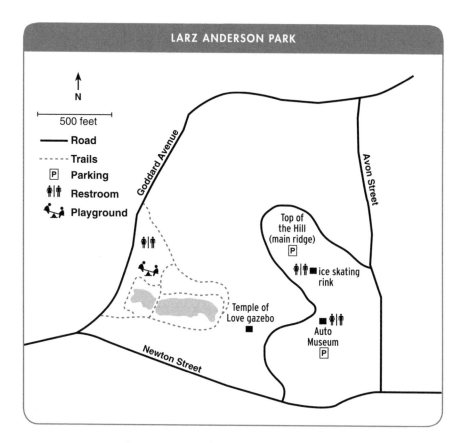

Map legend:
- Road
- Trails
- P Parking
- Restroom
- Playground

500 feet

N

Goddard Avenue

Avon Street

Top of the Hill (main ridge) P

ice skating rink

Temple of Love gazebo

Auto Museum P

Newton Street

vettes to motorcycles to Minis. The events are always lots of fun, for both adults and kids.

Remember: The grills, picnic areas, Temple of Love gazebo, and other areas are often rented out to groups by the Town of Brookline. Call ahead to reserve a space if you want to cook out.

PLAN B: If it is a rainy day, head to the Larz Anderson Auto Museum. Not only is there a stunning collection of classic cars, but there is also a dedicated kids' playroom, filled with toys that have—you guessed it—wheels.

WHERE TO EAT NEARBY: Centre Street in Jamaica Plain offers plenty of family-friendly dining options.

Are any two words sweeter than "snow day" to kids? When winter sets in, snow days offer the chance to sled down hills, ice-skate at a local rink, or build snow forts in the backyard. The Boston area also has more places than you might think to skate outdoors, a special treat when snow is falling or it's dark out.

Outdoor Rinks

Charles Hotel

This cute little winter rink is set up on what is normally the patio area in front of the hotel. It's perfect for younger kids, and the hotel even provides crates for beginners to use as leverage. A small concession stand sells hot chocolate when you need to warm up. In Cambridge; charleshotel.com.

Frog Pond

The Frog Pond is one of the most beautiful places anywhere to skate outdoors, especially at night, when the city lights are your backdrop. It can get busy, but it's magical. On Boston Common (Trip 3); bostoncommonfrogpond.org.

Kendall Square

Managed by Charles River Recreation, this rink in an outdoor courtyard is right outside of the MIT campus. A café sells snacks and hot chocolate. In Cambridge; paddleboston.com/skating2/skating.php

Larz Anderson

This outdoor rink in the heart of the Larz Anderson Park (Trip 21) is a fun spot for some ice time. In addition, fantastic hills call out for sledding. In Brookline; townofbrooklinemass.com.

Kelly Rink

This popular rink is the only outdoor rink run by the Department of Conservation and Recreation. In Jamaica Plain (near Trips 11 and 12); mass.gov/dcr.

Indoor Rinks

The Department of Conservation and Recreation manages a number of ice rinks in Boston and Cambridge. Public skating hours vary at each one. Most of them rent ice skates. Make sure to call ahead to check hours in case classes, sporting events, or private events are being held. Visit mass.gov/dcr for location, information, and phone numbers.

Sledding

For excellent sledding, try Boston Common (Trip 3), Arnold Arboretum (Trip 7), Jamaica Pond (Trip 12), Danehy Park (Trip 18), Larz Anderson Park (Trip 21), Blue Hills Reservation (Trip 26), Elm Bank Reservation (Trip 48), and Borderland State Park (Trip 59).

Trip 22

All Ages

Hall's Pond Sanctuary and Amory Woods

This is a great place to spot a variety of birds and enjoy a quiet walk on a boardwalk that takes you around the pond and through the woods.

Address: 1120 Beacon Street, Brookline, MA
Hours: Dawn to dusk daily
Fee: Free
Contact: brooklinema.gov/parks; 617-730-2088
Bathrooms: Portable toilets near the ball field (seasonal)
Water/Snacks: None
Map: USGS Boston South
Directions by Car: From I-93 South, take Exit 26 (MA 3N) and follow signs to Storrow Drive West. Take the left ramp off Storrow to Fenway and merge onto Charlesgate. Continue onto Boylston Street. Take a slight right onto Park Drive and a left onto Beacon Street. Go about 0.5 mile and take a right onto Amory Street; the sanctuary is on the right. The parking lot is adjacent to the sanctuary, and plenty of metered on-street parking is available nearby. *GPS coordinates (parking lot): 42° 20.809′ N, 71° 6.792′ W.*
Directions by Public Transit: Take the Green Line C train to Kent Street. When you get off the train, cross Beacon Street to the sanctuary.

Hall's Pond Sanctuary and Amory Woods make up a 5-acre gem of protected space in busy Brookline. What many people might not know is that the pond used to be called Swallow Pond and was owned in 1850 by the family of Minna Hall. Hall and her cousin Harriet Hemenway were founders of the Mass Audubon Society.

Today, the town-owned property is just one of two natural ponds remaining in Brookline and the sanctuary is a bird and animal paradise. Great blue herons, black-crowned night herons, kingfishers, and red-winged blackbirds are just a few of the species that visit. Children who love to see glimpses of wildlife will no doubt be rewarded with sightings of any number of birds and maybe some painted turtles too.

A boardwalk takes visitors about halfway around the pond and over the wetlands. There's also a formal garden area, and a short trail with overlooks

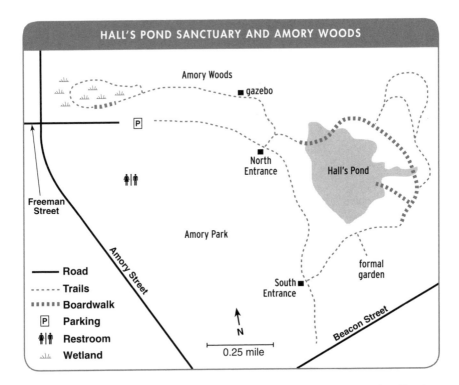

Amory Woods

■ gazebo

P

North
Entrance

Hall's Pond

Freeman
Street

Amory Park

Amory Street

formal
garden

South ■
Entrance

——— Road
- - - - - Trails
▪▪▪▪▪▪ Boardwalk
P Parking
Restroom
Wetland

N

0.25 mile

Beacon Street

and a gazebo. The garden, which you enter underneath an arched trellis, has been the project of the Friends of Hall's Pond for 25 years. The Friends help with upkeep of the sanctuary and hold events periodically.

Remember: Stay on the paths! A lot of poison ivy grows around the pond.

PLAN B: A playground is adjacent to the sanctuary on Amory Street.

WHERE TO EAT NEARBY: Coolidge Corner, which offers many places to eat, is just a few blocks away on Beacon and Harvard streets.

Trip 23

Hammond Pond Reservation

Behind a mall, you will discover an unlikely and surprisingly peaceful hike.

Address: Hammond Pond Parkway and MA 9, Newton, MA
Hours: Dawn to dusk daily
Fee: Free
Contact: mass.gov/dcr; 617-333-7404
Bathrooms: None
Water/Snacks: None
Map: USGS Newton
Directions by Car: From Boston, take MA 9 West to the Hammond Pond Parkway exit. Enter the Chestnut Hill Shopping Center and park in the lot on the left. *GPS coordinates:* 42° 19.332′ N, 71° 10.354′ W.
Directions by Public Transit: Take the Green Line D train to the Chestnut Hill stop. Walk down Hammond Street, then through the shopping center to Hammond Pond Parkway. The walk takes about 15 minutes.

This is one of those surreal city places that transports you instantly from the modern urban world to a nice slice of nature. Access to the Hammond Pond Reservation is from a parking lot next to the Chestnut Hill Shopping Center, but once you're in the reservation you'll feel far away from the shoppers.

The pond, while quite large, is not much deeper than 4 feet at its deepest point. The trail around the pond is a magnet for families and dog walkers. The outcroppings of Roxbury Puddingstone are irresistible to rock climbers and are just feet away from the parking lot. Serious climbers bring all the requisite gear, but kids will find plenty of places to climb around. Puddingstone, used in many nineteenth- and early-twentieth-century buildings in Boston, happens to be the official rock of Massachusetts.

Remember: Keep your dog on a leash and clean up after it.

PLAN B: For families pushing strollers or looking for less shade and more sun, the Chestnut Hill Reservation (Trip 20) is minutes away.

WHERE TO EAT NEARBY: Restaurants are along MA 9, as well as in the mall.

Trip 24

All Ages

Gore Place

At this historic property you can rent an activity backpack that will have kids racing around to explore the grounds and farmyard.

Address: 52 Gore Street, Waltham, MA
Hours: Grounds, dawn to dusk daily
Fee: Grounds: free; mansion tour: adults, $12; children ages 5–12, $5; children under age 5, free
Contact: goreplace.org; 781-894-2798
Bathrooms: None (unless you pay to rent a backpack or take a tour)
Water/Snacks: None
Map: USGS Newton
Directions by Car: From Boston, take the Mass Pike (I-90 West) to Exit 17 for Watertown Square. Continue on Centre Street, which turns into Galen Street. Turn left onto Main Street. Drive 1.25 miles to Gore Street. Park in the lot and walk up to the house; the barnyard is beyond the house to the left. *GPS coordinates:* 42° 22.418′ N, 71° 12.713′ W.
Directions by Public Transit: Take the Red Line to Central Square and walk to the corner of Green Street and Magazine Street. Take the #70 bus to Main Street at Warren Street in Waltham. Walk 0.2 mile to Gore Street.

Gore Place, a Federal period house built in 1806, was the estate of Massachusetts governor Christopher Gore. Rescued from demolition in the 1930s and restored by the nonprofit Gore Place Society, the 48-acre property consists of the mansion, manicured grounds, gardens, and a barnyard that tots will adore.

You can go right into the fenced-in barnyard to say hello to the animals—sheep, goats, chickens, and seemingly dozens of rabbits. Gore Place's fantastic backpack program for kids is called Take A Walk and is offered year-round and changes with the seasons. For $5, you have use of a backpack that contains binoculars, a magnifying glass, and seasonal activities that take kids around the property for an hour. Backpacks for kids ages 3 to 8 are available, as well as themed ones, such as Archaeology, Raised Garden Beds, and Math Challenge for elementary-school-aged children. The backpacks are available Mondays through Fridays 10 A.M. to 3 P.M. and Saturdays from noon to 3 P.M. In winter, you can also rent snowshoes for $5.

A small barnyard at historic Gore Place is home to sheep, goats, chickens, and rabbits.

On a 10-acre field, Gore Place grows a variety of crops; much of the food is donated to charities, but some of it is for sale. An honor-system farm stand is located behind the Farmer's Cottage next to the barns. In season, a flag with the word "open" means you can come see what's in stock. You might find squash, garlic, onions, or other produce. Bring exact change and leave it in a box provided.

Several fun events are scheduled at the property over the course of the year, including a sheep-shearing festival, a Jane Austen tour, Santa's tea, full-moon house tours, and preschool story hours. Visit the website for details.

Remember: The mansion is open only for guided tours. Call ahead to check the hours in case a special event is scheduled.

PLAN B: Habitat Education Center and Wildlife Sanctuary (Trip 25) offers a chance to see more animals in the wild.

WHERE TO EAT NEARBY: You'll find places to eat on Main Street.

Trip 25

Habitat Education Center and Wildlife Sanctuary

This property will enchant children and adults with its Turtle Pond, formal garden, and meadows and forests to explore.

Address: 10 Juniper Road, Belmont, MA

Hours: Trails: dawn to dusk daily; visitor center: 8:30 A.M. to 4:30 P.M. weekdays, 10 A.M. to 4 P.M. weekends

Fee: Adults, $4; children ages 2–12, $3; Mass Audubon members, free

Contact: habitat@massaudubon.org; 617-489-5050

Bathrooms: At the visitor center

Water/Snacks: Water fountain and some snacks for purchase in the visitor center

Map: USGS Boston North; massaudubon.org/Nature_Connection/Sanctuaries/ images/maps/habitat_trails.pdf

Directions by Car: From Boston, take I-93 North to Exit 31 and merge onto Mystic Valley Parkway/MA 16 West toward Arlington. Turn right onto Winthrop Street. At the traffic circle, take the third exit onto High Street. Stay on High Street through two more traffic circles. The street name will change to Medford Street at the third traffic circle, then to Chestnut Street. Take a left onto Mystic Street, which becomes Pleasant Street. After 1.6 miles, turn right onto Somerset Street. Take the second left to stay on Somerset; then take the second right onto Juniper Street, where you'll see the parking lot on the left. *GPS coordinates:* 42° 24.142′ N, 71° 11.017′ W.

Directions by Public Transit: Take the Red Line to Alewife and switch to the #78 bus. Get off on West Service Road at Park Avenue. The sanctuary is a 15-minute walk south.

Try to go to this toddler-friendly sanctuary when the visitor center is open— the staffers and volunteers go out of their way to be helpful and informative. In the center, you can pick up a Discovery Booklet, which has a scavenger hunt and some other activities to engage children as you hike through the 90-acre property. If your children have a Passport to Nature book from Mass Audubon (in which they can keep track of properties they visit), they can visit the stamp box outside by the parking lot or the one inside the visitor center to have their books stamped.

A young visitor explores Turtle Pond, looking for the namesake turtles and other wildlife.

Three hikes that are good for kids range from 0.5 mile to 1.6 miles; each hike has a number of side paths to explore. The property has deciduous and evergreen forests, meadows, two ponds, and a wetland containing a vernal pool. Behind the visitor center, which hosts monthly art exhibits, is a beautiful formal garden.

On one visit with my daughter and a friend of hers, we started with the 0.5-mile Turtle Loop and were rewarded with hearing first, then spotting, a great blue heron. They can be quite loud! Several turtles lounged on rocks in the sun while dragonflies flitted about. If you have toddlers, this is a perfect walk that rewards with lots to see in a short amount of time. The longer Highland Farm Loop takes you to the highest point in Belmont. If you make the longer walk to Weeks Pond, you'll find a secluded and peaceful spot to visit. The sanctuary offers several programs, including winter naturalist walks and a summer camp; ask for information at the visitor center.

Remember: It can be buggy in the woods in spring and summer. Don't forget to pack some bug spray!

PLAN B: Fresh Pond Reservation (Trip 17) is less than ten minutes away by car. Visit the butterfly meadow or tot lot playground, or stroll around the pond.

WHERE TO EAT NEARBY: Belmont Center has plenty of options from ice cream shops to sit-down restaurants.

Trip 26

Blue Hills Reservation: Great Blue Hill

The 7,000-acre Blue Hills Reservation is the largest open space within 35 miles of Boston and a vast playground for lovers of the outdoors.

Address: 1904 Canton Avenue, Milton, MA
Hours: Dawn to dusk daily
Fee: Free
Contact: mass.gov/dcr; 617-698-1802
Bathrooms: Near the parking lot and inside the Blue Hills Trailside Museum
Water/Snacks: Water fountains near the parking lot and at the Trailside Museum; snacks at the museum
Map: USGS Norwood; mass.gov/dcr/parks/trails/blueHills.gif; AMC's *Massachusetts Trail Map 4*
Directions by Car: From Boston, take I-93 South to Exit 2B. Follow MA 138 for about 1 mile and you'll see the parking lot on the right. *GPS coordinates:* 42° 13.130′ N, 71° 07.150′ W.
Directions by Public Transit: Take the Red Line to Ashmont, then board the high-speed trolley line to Mattapan. From there, take the Canton and Blue Hills bus service to the Trailside Museum and Great Blue Hill on MA 138.

I recommend starting this hike from the Mass Audubon Blue Hills Trailside Museum, which serves as the interpretive center for the reservation (though the reservation itself is run by the Department of Conservation and Recreation). There you can get oriented to the area, pick up maps, and view both indoor and outdoor exhibits that feature native wildlife. In the outdoor pens, you can see rescued injured animals, such as deer, turkey, hawks, and owls. Kids will adore watching the river otter, which seems to love performing for an audience by diving and flipping in a pool.

Take Red Dot Trail, which starts behind the museum. This 2-mile loop is great for snowshoes in winter. You'll see a signpost with maps at the trailhead. Hiking up to the summit of Great Blue Hill, which at 635 feet high is the highest point in the Blue Hills, is a moderate challenge for kids, but the payoff is worth it. They'll love first getting to the stone Eliot Tower, which they can climb for wonderful views. The picnic tables in the shade are a great spot for a

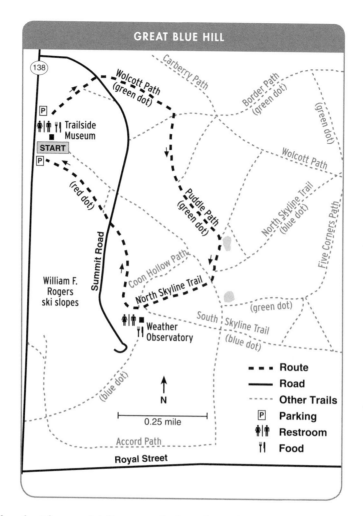

138
P
Trailside Museum
START
P
(red dot)
Wolcott Path (green dot)
Carberry Path
Border Path (green dot)
(green dot)
Wolcott Path
Puddle Path (green dot)
North Skyline Trail (blue dot)
Five Corners Path
Summit Road
William F. Rogers ski slopes
Coon Hollow Path
North Skyline Trail
Weather Observatory
South Skyline Trail (blue dot)
(green dot)
(blue dot)
N
0.25 mile
Accord Path
Royal Street

- - - Route
— Road
----- Other Trails
P Parking
Restroom
Food

snack break. Afterward, hike up to the Weather Observatory (you'll see a sign pointing the way next to the tower). The observatory is a National Historic Landmark; here, incidentally, you'll find a bathroom, a water fountain, and a gift shop selling snacks and drinks. Special programs are offered here through-out the year—check with the reservation for details. (If you have a stroller, you can take the paved Summit Road to get to the top. If you take the trail up and worry that the kids may get tired on the descent, take the road back down.) In winter, downhill skiing and sledding is allowed at the William F. Rogers ski slopes on Great Blue Hill (781-828-5070).

An interesting fact to tell the kids is that the Blue Hills were named by early European explorers who noticed the bluish hue on the slopes when viewed from a distance. Long before that, native peoples who lived here referred to themselves as Massachusett, or "people of the great hills."

A hike up Great Blue Hill, the highest point in Blue Hills Reservation, is a great outing with kids.

Remember: If you want to spend more time at the Blue Hills, why not spend the night? You can stay at the Appalachian Mountain Club cabins on Ponkapoag Pond (see Trip 27); for reservations call 781-961-7007 or visit outdoors. org/lodging. Keep your dog on a leash and clean up after it.

PLAN B: If it is a hot summer day, take a dip in Houghton's Pond (Trip 28) or walk around the pond to look for wildlife.

WHERE TO EAT NEARBY: The Trailside Museum sells a variety of snacks, drinks, and ice cream.

Trip 27

Blue Hills Reservation: Ponkapoag Pond

Kids will love walking along planks through a bog to get to Ponkapoag Pond.

Address: 2167 Washington Street, Canton, MA
Hours: Dawn to dusk daily
Fee: Free
Contact: mass.gov/dcr; 617-698-1802
Bathrooms: None
Water/Snacks: Beverage vending machine near the parking lot on Maple Avenue
Map: USGS Norwood; mass.gov/dcr/parks/metroboston/blue%20hills%20 brochure.pdf; AMC's *Massachusetts Trail Map 4*
Directions by Car: From Boston, take I-93 to Exit 2A onto Washington Street. Turn left into the DCR/Ponkapoag Golf Club parking lot. *GPS coordinates:* 42° 11.524′ N, 71° 07.012′ W.

Lovers of the outdoors flock to the 7,000-acre Blue Hills Reservation, the largest open space within 35 miles of Boston. Trekking to the 230-acre Ponkapoag Pond is one of the adventures here kids will enjoy. From the golf course parking lot, head down Maple Avenue through the course to get to the trailhead, which is to the left of the pond (yield to golfers).

You can walk all the way around the pond, but be aware that this hike is 4 miles. The walk directly to the pond (see map) is much shorter but offers a lot of opportunity for wildlife sightings. The trail here is entirely on a "floating boardwalk," which is actually a series of planks over a bog leading to the pond. Children find the boards, which tilt this way and that as people step on and off, a source of much hilarity. This Atlantic white cedar bog is unusual for New England and is home to the carnivorous pitcher plant and a variety of protected plants and animals. When you get to the pond, look for great blue herons and osprey, which like to fish here.

Be sure to visit Blue Hills in winter for great snowshoeing or cross-country skiing opportunities. The snowy scenery is spectacular.

Remember: For those wanting to stay overnight, the Appalachian Mountain Club has cabins and tent sites on the other side of the pond. Advance

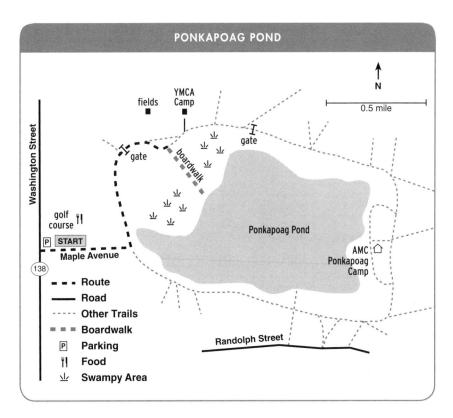

PONKAPOAG POND

fields
YMCA Camp
0.5 mile
N
Washington Street
gate
boardwalk
gate
golf course
START
P
Ponkapoag Pond
AMC Ponkapoag Camp
Maple Avenue
138

- - - Route
—— Road
---- Other Trails
▦▦▦ Boardwalk
P Parking
⑂ Food
↙ Swampy Area

Randolph Street

registration is required; call 781-961-7007 or visit outdoors.org/lodging for information. Keep your dog on a leash and clean up after it.

PLAN B: Visit the Mass Audubon's Trailside Museum (Trip 26) to check out exhibits about the wildlife found in the Blue Hills.

WHERE TO EAT NEARBY: The golf course has a grill and snack bar.

Trip 28

Ages 5–8

Blue Hills Reservation: Houghton's Pond Recreation Area

This family favorite features an easy trail, a shallow swimming area, a large playground, and a scenic setting to enjoy.

Address: 840 Hillside Street, Milton, MA
Hours: Dawn to dusk daily
Fee: Free
Contact: mass.gov/dcr; 617-698-1802
Bathrooms: At the visitor center
Water/Snacks: Water fountain in the center of the playground; concessions at snack bar during warm weather
Map: USGS Norwood; mass.gov/dcr/parks/metroboston/maps/ houghtonsbrochure-map.pdf; AMC's *Massachusetts Trail Map 4*
Directions by Car: From Boston, take I-93 South to Exit 3. Turn right on Blue Hill River Road, then take a right on Hillside Street. Follow the signs to the pond. Two huge parking lots are available, one on Blue Hill River and one on Hillside. The latter is closer to the pond. *GPS coordinates: 42° 12.544′ N, 71° 05.791′ W.*

Houghton's Pond is part of the 7,000-acre Blue Hills Reservation; in summer, it offers Boston residents a nice alternative to the more distant Walden Pond. The 24-acre pond is a spring-fed kettle hole formed by receding glaciers about 10,000 years ago. It reaches 42 feet deep in some parts.

A roped-off swimming area is supervised by lifeguards in July and August. Before or after your swim, take an easy 1-mile hike around the pond (the yellow trail) and look for wildlife. On one hike we saw a snake and an egg very close to the trail. Close to the beach area, two spurs (green and red) lead to other parts of the reservation. Fishing is popular here, as the pond is stocked, so bring along a rod if your kids want to try their luck.

When the seasons change and the weather turns cold, visit Houghton's Pond to spot meadowhawks, hardy dragonflies that can be seen as late as December. After snow falls, have the kids try snowshoeing the loop, enjoying continuous views across the pond.

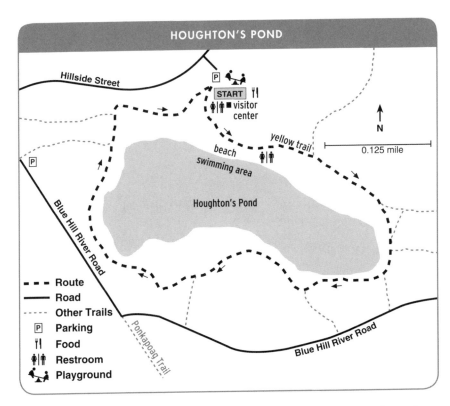

Remember: Be warned that the rules for swimming in Houghton's Pond are fairly strict. Leave balls, floats, and water toys at home; none are allowed in or near the water. The lifeguards frown on horseplay. Keep your dog on a leash and clean up after it.

PLAN B: The Mass Audubon's Trailside Museum (Trip 26) offers displays and descriptions of the wildlife found in the Blue Hills.

WHERE TO EAT NEARBY: A concession pavilion with snacks and drinks is by the Hillside parking lot and open in season.

Boston-area residents are lucky to have several farmers markets to choose from for at least half of the year, usually May through October. Get your kids excited about visiting a market by making it into an adventure for them. If you visit weekly, start a tradition: Put them in charge of finding vegetables to use as pizza toppings. Dessert can be fruit smoothies or pie made with berries that are in season. When kids get invested in what they are eating and figure out how delicious all that fresh food is, they're more likely to make healthy food choices as they grow up.

The following are some suggested markets and one farm to visit, which all happen to be close to a trip in this book in case you want to combine adventures. For more information or to find other markets around the state, the Federation of Mass Farmers Markets is a good resource (massfarmersmarkets.org). Every market has different days and hours. Check in advance for details.

Allandale Farm

Boston's last working farm, at 250 years old, boasts of certified naturally grown crops using organic methods. It sells its produce on-site at an indoor farm stand, as well as at a few other spots around town. *Near Arnold Arboretum (Trip 7) and Allandale Woods (Trip 8).*

Boston Public Market at Dewey Square

In addition to produce, this market offers a lot of great gourmet spreads, sauces, granola, and jams. *Near Boston Harbor Islands (Trips 1 and 2).*

Copley Square Farmers Market

If you are touring the city, you can pick up picnic items at this Back Bay market, which sells lots of ready-to-eat food as well as fruits, vegetables, and other goods. *Near Boston Common (Trip 3).*

Dedham Farmers Market

Besides fresh vegetables and fruits, you can pick up fresh seafood at this market. Just make sure to pack a cooler in your trunk to take it home. *Near Wilson Mountain Reservation (Trip 29).*

Haymarket

This 200-year-old market, open year-round, is more than a tourist attraction; it's also a staple for inexpensive fruits, vegetables, and seafood. *Near Boston Harbor Islands (Trips 1 and 2).*

Roslindale Farmers Market

Many local shops—including a cheese specialty store, a bakery, and a deli—sell their foods at this market, as do many regional farms, which offer produce, meats, and seafood. *Near Arnold Arboretum (Trip 7).*

Ages
9–12

Wilson Mountain Reservation

Wilson Mountain offers Boston views, rocky ledges, and paths over marshes and through the woods for a rural experience in an urban setting.

Address: 435 Common Street, Dedham, MA
Hours: Dawn to dusk daily
Fee: Free
Contact: mass.gov/dcr; 617-333-7404
Bathrooms: None
Water/Snacks: None
Map: USGS Medfield
Directions by Car: From Boston, take the Mass Pike (I-90 West) to Exit 15 (MA 128 South). Take MA 128 South to Exit 17 (MA 135 East). Turn right on MA 135 East and drive for less than 1 mile. The parking lot will be on the right with room for about a dozen cars. *GPS coordinates: 42° 15.634′ N, 71° 11.900′ W.*

The pine-needled woods at Wilson Mountain invite investigation by curious kids.

Wilson Mountain, at 213 acres, is the largest remaining piece of open space in Dedham and offers a variety of habitats to explore, from woods and wetlands to swamps and rocky ledges. Two trail options start from the parking lot: Red Dot Trail is a short hike, less than 1 mile, whereas Blue Blaze Trail is 2 miles long and offers a lot more variety.

Along Blue Blaze Trail, you'll come to an irresistible formation of boulders (begging to be climbed by most kids) and boardwalks crossing over marshes. Various trees make up the mixed woods: pine, birch, ash, maple, oak, hemlock, and more. A few sections of the hike are challenging, with some steep hills, but overall the trail is easy enough for older kids, and is good for snowshoeing in winter.

Along the trail, some forest birds you may spot are tufted titmice, chicka-dees, nuthatches, and flickers. At the summit of Wilson Mountain, you can en-joy great views of Boston. This hike is so close to the highway that sometimes you can hear cars rushing by, but rather than disturbing the peace of the hike, the sound is a reminder of how lucky we are that places like this are so acces-sible to urban dwellers.

Remember: Keep your dog on a leash and clean up after it.

PLAN B: Stony Brook Reservation (Trip 15) in Hyde Park is less than 5 miles away and offers hiking trails, playgrounds, swimming, fishing, and much more on 475 acres.

WHERE TO EAT NEARBY: A variety of dining establishments are in Dedham Center, on High Street, and on Boston–Providence Turnpike.

Trip 30

Mystic River Reservation

Minutes from Boston, the Mystic Lakes offer a quiet and beautiful setting for family gatherings and bike riding.

Address: Mystic Valley Parkway, Winchester, MA
Hours: Dawn to dusk daily
Fee: Free
Contact: mass.gov/dcr; 617-727-5380
Bathrooms: Portable toilets near the beach
Water/Snacks: None
Map: USGS Lexington; mass.gov/dcr/parks/metroboston/maps/mystl.gif
Directions by Car: From Boston, take I-93 North to Exit 31 and merge onto Mystic Valley Parkway. Turn right on Winthrop Street and at the traffic circle, take the third exit onto MA 60. Drive 1.5 miles and take a right onto Mystic Valley Parkway. Continue about 2 miles until you see the parking lot on the left. *GPS coordinates: 42° 26.443′ N, 71° 8.6876′ W.*
Directions by Public Transit: Take the Lowell commuter rail train from North Station to Wedgemere. Walk south along Mystic Valley Parkway to Upper Mystic Lake (about ten minutes).

Parks, playgrounds, bike paths, and scenic views make Mystic Lakes popular with families.

The Mystic River Reservation runs through Arlington, Medford, and Winchester and is a Department of Conservation and Recreation property. Mystic Lakes, both Upper and Lower, connect to the Mystic River; visitors can enjoy various parks and outdoor activities along the shores.

Tennis courts, playgrounds, grassy areas, boat landings, bike paths, soccer fields, and picnic tables make this a family-friendly place to visit. In Winchester, Shannon Beach, formerly named Sandy Beach, located at the northern end of Upper Mystic Lake, is popular for swimming and does indeed have a sandy beach. Kids can visit the playground here or ride bikes along the paved paths. Only nonpowered boats are allowed at the Upper Lake, but motorized boats with no wake are OK at the Lower Mystic Lake.

Remember: You can't always swim at the beach due to water-quality issues; call ahead to check. Keep your dog on a leash and clean up after it.

PLAN B: The Middlesex Fells Reservation (Trip 31), in Stoneham, is about 5 miles away and has an extensive trail system.

WHERE TO EAT NEARBY: At MA 60 near the traffic circle and before you turn onto Mystic Valley Parkway, you'll spot a couple of places to eat.

Trip 31

All Ages

Middlesex Fells Reservation

Middlesex Fells runs through six towns and, with more than 2,000 acres, offers plenty of room for a multitude of outdoor activities.

Address: 698 Fellsway West, Stoneham, MA (Sheepfold Entrance)
Hours: Reservation: dawn to dusk daily; parking lot at Sheepfold entrance: 9 A.M. to dusk
Fee: Free
Contact: mass.gov/dcr; 617-727-5380; fells.org
Bathrooms: None
Water/Snacks: None
Map: USGS Boston North; mass.gov/dcr/parks/metroboston/maps/fells.gif; fells.org/visit/map.cfm
Directions by Car: From Boston, take I-93 North to Exit 33. Merge onto MA 28 North; in about 1.5 miles, the Sheepfold entrance gate is on the left. *GPS coordinates:* 42° 27.184′ N, 71° 6.433′ W.
Directions by Public Transit: Take the Orange Line to Wellington Station, then the #100 bus to Fellsway West opposite Elm. From there, walk north on MA 28 about 1 mile to the Sheepfold entrance.

With 2,575 acres, Middlesex Fells Reservation has more than enough room and a variety of terrains to appeal to hikers, mountain bikers, horseback riders, rock climbers, cross-country skiers, and paddlers. "Fells" is a Saxon word for rocky, hilly tracts of land, and the name fits the area perfectly. Rocky outcroppings, open water, dense woods, diverse plants, and a variety of mammals, birds, and reptiles can all be found at this beloved Boston-area resource.

More than 100 miles of trails crisscross the reservation. Joining an organized hike (such as one with AMC's Boston Chapter) offers a great introduction to the Fells, which has so many options that knowing where to start may feel a bit overwhelming.

As a start, begin at the Sheepfold entrance, where you'll find sledders in winter. A 10-acre open field here is used by dog walkers and picnickers, and hikers can choose from several trails in this area. For a short, easy hike with kids, look for Soap Box Derby Road (behind the lot to the right) and signs pointing to Bear Hill Tower, which is less than 0.2 mile away. Dark Hollow Pond Trail, an easy 1-mile hike, leads to the pond through the woods.

*More than 100 miles of trails cover changing terrain,
including this path beneath an old bridge.*

Bellevue Pond is surrounded by trails and wide fire roads, some leading up to Wright's Tower, which kids will enjoy climbing. Virginia Wood, the site of an old mill village, has an interpretive history trail. Lawrence Woods also has wide fire roads, views, and vernal pools. You can rent canoes and kayaks at Spot Pond for a lovely paddle and even take sailing lessons. Don't forget your snowshoes in winter.

Remember: The Friends of the Middlesex Fells (fells.org) has a lot of information and suggested hikes on its website and runs guided hikes and programs, many especially for families and kids.

PLAN B: Stone Zoo in Stoneham (see page 37) is north of the Fells and guarantees that the kids will get to see animals!

WHERE TO EAT NEARBY: Head north on MA 28 and you'll find lots of places to eat in Stoneham.

Trip 32

Minuteman Bikeway

This tree-lined bike path runs from the end of the Red Line subway in Cambridge to picturesque, small-town Bedford.

Address: Alewife Station, Alewife Brook Parkway, Cambridge, MA

Hours: 5 A.M. to 9 P.M. daily

Fee: Free

Contact: minutemanbikeway.org; 781-862-0500 ext. 208

Bathrooms: At Depot Park in Bedford; at the Lexington visitor center; at Alewife Station

Water/Snacks: Water fountains at Depot Park, the Lexington visitor center, and Alewife Station

Map: USGS Lexington: minutemanbikeway.org/Media/bikeway_map.pdf

Directions by Car: From Boston, take Massachusetts Avenue/MA 2A across the bridge into Cambridge. Follow Mass Ave for 3 miles, then turn left onto Rindge Avenue. Follow to the end, and turn right onto Alewife Brook Parkway. The station will be on the left. *GPS coordinates:* 42° 23.692′ N, 71° 8.477′ W. (The bikeway's endpoint is in Bedford at Depot Park on South Street.)

Directions by Public Transit: Take the Red Line to Alewife. Once out of the station, look for the access road, which leads to the bike path.

The Minuteman Bikeway, an 11-mile-long, 12-foot-wide paved path, is built on a former rail line. It runs through Cambridge, Arlington, Lexington, and Bedford, passing playing fields, ponds, neighborhoods, bakeries, bike shops, and more. You can gain access to the bikeway at several locations, but the end points are Alewife Station in Cambridge and Depot Park in Bedford. Lexington is at the trail's midpoint; this site of Revolutionary War history hosts a reenactment of the "shot heard round the world" on Patriots' Day every April.

In addition to cyclists, the path is popular with parents pushing strollers, kids trying out their first training wheels, 9-to-5-ers walking during their lunch hour, and people on inline skates with leashed dogs. In winter, cyclists often swap their bikes for cross-country skis. Portions of the trail coincide with the Bay Circuit Trail (see page 100).

A wonderful stop along the way is the beautiful wetland area called Great Meadows in Lexington. You can take a side trail on foot to see bees and drag-

The Lexington portion of the Minuteman Bikeway offers a paved path perfect for young riders.

onflies in summer. All of a sudden, instead of cars zipping by on Mass Ave just a few hundred yards away, you'll hear creatures singing and buzzing.

Remember: Two shops along the Minuteman Bikeway in Arlington rent bicycles—one on Dudley Street and the other on Massachusetts Avenue near the Lexington border. At numerous places, the path crosses streets; though these places are well marked, do watch your little ones. Also at all times, pay attention and keep to the right. Helmets are required by state law for children under 13. Keep your dog on a leash and clean up after it.

PLAN B: For a less-crowded bike adventure, Fresh Pond Reservation (Trip 17) has a great bike path.

WHERE TO EAT NEARBY: The bike path passes through Lexington Center, Arlington Heights, and Arlington Center, each with many child-friendly restaurants.

Trip 33

Breakheart Reservation

Breakheart Reservation has dozens of trails and opportunities to do activities from biking to swimming to fishing.

Address: 100 Hemlock Road, Wakefield, MA (Hemlock Road Gate entrance); 177 Forest Street, Saugus, MA (main entrance)
Hours: Dawn to dusk daily
Fee: Free
Contact: mass.gov/dcr; 781-233-0834
Bathrooms: Portable toilets by Pearce Lake and at the visitor center
Water/Snacks: Water fountain at the visitor center; ice cream truck by Pearce Lake during summer
Map: USGS Lynn and Boston North; saugus.org/FOBR
Directions by Car: From Boston, take I-93 North to the Tobin Bridge. Merge onto US 1 North, drive for about 8 miles, then exit onto Main Street toward Wakefield. Drive about 3 miles and take a right into the Northeast Metro Tech High School parking lot (parking spaces are marked with signs for reservation visitors). More parking is located at the main entrance as well. *GPS coordinates:* 42° 29.662′ N, 71° 2.587′ W (Hemlock Road); 42° 28.781′ N, 71° 1.550′ W (Forest Street).

Breakheart Reservation has more than two dozen trails on its 700-plus acres, but one that's especially great for younger kids is Eagle Rock Trail, which you can combine with a swim at Pearce Lake (also called the Lower Pond). In winter, you can snowshoe or search for coyote, fisher, deer, otter, and other animal tracks.

Park at the high school lot and take a left on the quarter-mile paved road to Pearce Lake, where you'll find a playground, climbing structures, and picnic tables. In the lake, three areas of varying depths are roped off for swimmers and supervised by lifeguards. A fishing platform is to the right, and that's where you can pick up the trail that leads to Eagle Rock, an easy hike of less than 0.5 mile that gives you a commanding view over the lake.

If you decide to walk to the visitor center from Pearce Lake, take Fox Run Trail, which is about 1 mile long. A 5-mile paved loop around the park offers a wonderful and safe place for kids to ride their bikes. (At one point, the roads were open to cars, but only rangers can use cars now.) Various rich habitats

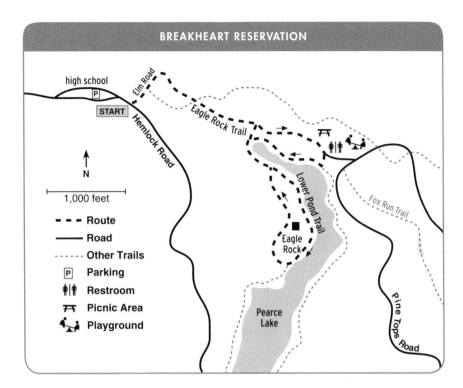

are at Breakheart, with two freshwater lakes, marshes, rivers, and seven hills that are more than 200 feet high. Year-round programs offered by rangers are a great way to learn about the reservation's wildlife. Check the website or the visitor center for details.

Remember: If you go swimming at Pearce Lake, make sure kids stay within the roped boundaries. There is a dog park within the reservation called Bark Place, where dogs can run free; on the trails, however, keep your dog on a leash and clean up after it.

PLAN B: Lynn Woods Reservation (Trip 34), less than ten minutes away, offers an adventurous spin to an outing if you visit the famous Dungeon Rock, supposedly the location of a buried pirate treasure.

WHERE TO EAT NEARBY: Restaurants for every taste and budget are along US 1.

Trip 34

Lynn Woods Reservation: Dungeon Rock

Pirates, buried treasure, spirits, and a long, dark tunnel make for a great story and an adventurous hike.

Address: Pennybrook Road, Lynn, MA
Hours: Reservation: dawn to dusk daily; Dungeon Rock tunnel: 9 A.M. to 2:30 P.M. Tuesday through Saturday, May through October
Fee: Free
Contact: flw.org; 781-477-7123
Bathrooms: At the ranger station by the main parking lot
Water/Snacks: None
Map: USGS Lynn and Boston North; flw.org/pdf_files/lwmap.pdf
Directions by Car: From Boston, take I-93 North to the Tobin Bridge. Merge onto US 1 North, drive for about 10 miles, and take the Walnut Street exit. In 1.9 miles, turn left onto Menlo Avenue and then take the second left onto Pennybrook Road. The parking lot is at the main entrance. *GPS coordinates:* 42° 28.587′ N, 70° 59.163′ W.

Lynn Woods Reservation is the second-largest municipal park in the United States, offering 30 miles of trails and three reservoirs in a 2,200-acre forest park. Bring your cross-country skis or snowshoes in winter. With so much space, you will feel like it is your own private winter wonderland. While all this makes Lynn Woods a beautiful place to visit, what will get the kids most excited is the story of Dungeon Rock and how it came to be called that.

To head to Dungeon Rock, start from the main entrance at Pennybrook Lane and take Jackson Path. (If you see picnic tables, then you know you are heading in the right direction.) Along the way, tell the kids the legend about the area, which goes like this: In 1658, a pirate ship sailed into Lynn Harbor and lowered a boat into the water with a chest onboard. British soldiers set off after the four pirates. Three were caught, but one escaped. The escapee, Thomas Veale, hid out in these woods, living in a cave for some time. One day, a rare earthquake hit the area and a piece of rock sealed up the cave, trapping Veale and the treasure. That was that for 200 years, until treasure hunters in the 1830s tried to blow up the rock to find the supposed loot. They had no

Kids love searching for treasure near the Dungeon Rock cave.

luck. Then, in 1852, Hiram Marble, a spiritualist who believed he received a message from Veale's ghost telling him to come to Dungeon Rock, bought 5 acres surrounding the cave. He and his family dug for years looking but also had no luck. Today, you can climb down the dark, slippery stairs into part of the tunnel that Marble blasted as he looked for the treasure.

There's more to the story, which you can read about on the Friends of Lynn Woods website (flw.org). You will definitely need a flashlight to go down into the 174-foot-long tunnel. It's cold, damp, slippery, wet, and spooky—in the best way. Tell kids to hold on to the railing, and remind all those more than 5 feet tall to watch their head.

Remember: If you miss visiting the cave during the set times it is open, you can still climb on top and around it! Keep your dog on a leash and clean up after it.

PLAN B: Breakheart Reservation (Trip 33) is nearby and, in summer, is a perfect place for a pond swim.

WHERE TO EAT NEARBY: A few pizza places and convenience shops are on Walnut Street in Lynn.

Trip 35

Lynn Shore and Nahant Beach Reservation

Strolling along the shore is great in every season, while swimming and paddling are summertime favorites.

Address: Lynn Shore Drive and Nahant Road, Lynn, MA
Hours: Dawn to dusk daily
Fee: Free
Contact: mass.gov/dcr; 781-485-2803
Bathrooms: At the Ward Memorial Bathhouse
Water/Snacks: Water fountains near the bathhouse
Map: USGS Lynn; mass.gov/dcr/parks/metroboston/maps/LynnShoreMap.pdf
Directions by Car: From Boston, take MA 1A North and at the traffic circle, follow signs to stay on 1A North. At the second traffic circle, take the second exit to stay on 1A North (North Shore Road). At the next traffic circle, take the exit onto Nahant Road. Find metered street parking, or follow signs for beach parking (fee). *GPS coordinates:* 42° 26.620′ N, 70° 56.237′ W.
Directions by Public Transit: Take the Newburyport/Rockport commuter rail train from North Station. The beach is a 15-minute walk from the Lynn station.

This 4-mile stretch of park is a combination of two reservations along the water—Lynn Shore and Nahant Beach. A paved promenade runs 2 miles, spanning the two reservations, at the edge of Nahant Bay. The area is quite busy, especially in summer, and with good cause—families can find a ton to do here. Ball fields, racquetball and tennis courts, and a tot lot near the park headquarters at Ward Bathhouse are just the beginning.

Of course, most people come to swim at Long Beach and King's Beach, but kids also enjoy checking out the tide pools at Red Rock Park at low tide. Considering how developed the area is, it is surprising that a 1-mile-long system of fragile sand dunes runs parallel to Long Beach. Visit in colder months for a wintry walk that will give you an entirely different beach experience.

Interpretive programs and beach-related events are offered occasionally, so check at the park headquarters to see what's going on. Concerts are held at Red Rock Park once or twice a week in summer.

Four miles of sand beach stretch along Nahant Bay.

Remember: In summer, the lot fills fast and parking is difficult to find. Plan to arrive early in the morning or late in the afternoon.

PLAN B: Lynn Woods Reservation (Trip 34) is less than 4 miles away and is much farther off the beaten path than the beach is.

WHERE TO EAT NEARBY: Some restaurants are near the last traffic circle and on the Lynnway.

Section 3

West of Boston

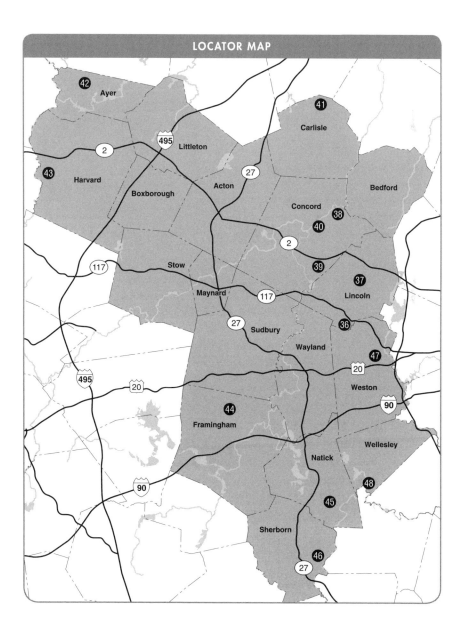

Trip 36

Drumlin Farm Wildlife Sanctuary

If your kids want to see what Old MacDonald's farm might look like, this Mass Audubon sanctuary will fit the bill, plus offer some surprises.

Address: 208 South Great Road, Lincoln, MA

Hours: 9 A.M. to 5 P.M., March through October; 9 A.M. to 4 P.M., November through February; closed on Mondays, except federal holidays

Fee: Adults, $6; children ages 2–12, $4; Mass Audubon members, free

Contact: drumlimfarm@massaudubon.org; 781-259-2200

Bathrooms: At the visitor center; at a picnic area near the farmyard

Water/Snacks: Water fountains at the visitor center and at a picnic area near the farmyard; fresh, in-season produce at a farm stand near the entrance

Map: USGS Maynard; massaudubon.org/Nature_Connection/Sanctuaries/ Drumlin_Farm/maps.php

Directions by Car: From Boston, take the Mass Pike (I-90 West) to Exit 15 to I-95/MA 128 North. Take Exit 29B onto MA 2 West. At the third set of lights, turn left onto MA 126 South. Follow it for 2.5 miles and turn left onto MA 117 East. The parking lot is 1 mile ahead on the right. *GPS coordinates: 42° 24.592′ N, 71° 19.908′ W.*

Directions by Public Transit: Take the Fitchburg/South Acton Line from North Station to Lincoln. The farm is just over 0.5 mile southwest from the station.

Drumlin Farm is always a kid favorite. After all, kids can visit pigs, cows, sheep, goats, and chickens; plus, real farmers work in the garden and take care of the animals. A hay ride ($2 for adults, $1 for kids) is the crowning touch on a quintessential farm visit. At the poultry house, sheep shed, pig barn, and red barn, interpretive signs offer up facts about the animals.

But you'll find more to see here than at a typical farm. Various wild animals that have been injured or disabled also call the farm home. Rescued animals that live here include skunks, rabbits, owls, hawks, deer, and fox. Signs describe what happened to the animals and how they came to the farm.

After you have explored the farmyard, you can take several trails on the 232-acre property. The most popular one is probably Drumlin Loop, which on clear days offers views of Mount Monadnock and Mount Wachusett.

The farm offers excellent drop-in discovery activities run by naturalists; these are free with admission. The activities run several times a day through-

A sow and her piglets take a nap at Drumlin Farm.

out the year. Special family programs, such as planting and harvesting crops, are also offered, as well as summer and holiday camps, a community preschool, community-supported agriculture (CSA) farm shares, and a farm stand that is open to the public. Visit in winter and kids can learn how wildlife survives the cold months. Check with the sanctuary for details.

Remember: It's against U.S. Department of Agriculture regulations to feed the animals on the farm, so eat in the picnic area only.

PLAN B: Walden Pond (Trip 39) is close by if you feel like a swim or a walk in the woods.

WHERE TO EAT NEARBY: Take MA 126 to Concord Center, which is less than ten minutes away by car and offers plenty of dining options.

deCordova Sculpture Park and Museum

At deCordova's outdoor sculpture park, kids will love to explore the modern artworks, some of which they can touch or even climb on.

Address: 51 Sandy Pond Road, Lincoln, MA

Hours: Sculpture park: dawn to dusk daily; museum: 10 A.M. to 5 P.M. Tuesday through Sunday

Fee: When the museum is closed: free; when the museum is open: adults, $12; children ages 6–12, $8; children under age 5, free

Contact: decordova.org; 781-259-8355

Bathrooms: At the museum store (by the parking lot) and at the museum

Water/Snacks: Water fountain in the museum; vending machine in the museum shop

Map: USGS Concord

Directions by Car: From Boston, take the Mass Pike (I-90 West) to Exit 15 to I-95/MA 128 North. After about 6 miles, take Exit 28B to merge onto Trapelo Road. Follow this for about 3 miles. The road name changes to Sandy Pond. The deCordova site will be on the right. If the museum is open, stop at the gate and pay. If the museum is closed, just drive into the parking lot. *GPS coordinates: 42° 25.832′ N, 71° 18.610′ W.*

DeCordova Sculpture Park and Museum is a fantastic place to start your kids on the road to appreciating art, in a setting that allows outside voices and (for the most part) hands-on exploration.

Set amid 35 acres of woodlands and lawns, it is the largest park of its kind in New England. Large-scale artworks include modern and contemporary sculpture and site-specific installations, some permanent and some that rotate through. Children can roam around to discover artworks hidden beneath tree branches or use sticks to make sounds on the Musical Fence. Picnicking on the grounds is a lot of fun if you settle close to some artwork that can spark conversation. If you feel like taking a longer walk or want a more secluded picnic spot, you can gain access to trails from the museum to neighboring Sandy Pond, which is Lincoln Conservation Land. The pond is a drinking-water reservoir.

Kids can interact with the art at deCordova Sculpture Park and Museum.

Throughout the year, the museum offers several outdoor programs, including snowshoe tours, yoga sessions, birding tours, curator and artist conversations, and screenings. If you don't want to spend all your time outside, head indoors for the rotating exhibits of contemporary art. Truly a museum that thinks about future artists, deCordova is the only contemporary art museum in the United States that hosts a preschool.

Remember: Make sure you read signs located near the artworks before your kids get to them; some should not be touched. Keep your dog on a leash and clean up after it.

PLAN B: Nearby Drumlin Farm Wildlife Sanctuary (Trip 36) is a picture-perfect farm, with animals galore and several trails to hike.

WHERE TO EAT NEARBY: A café is in the museum, or you can head into Lincoln (go back to Sandy Pond Road and turn right on Lincoln Road) to find pizza places and bistros.

Trip 38

Great Meadows National Wildlife Refuge

Opportunities abound for wildlife sightings at Great Meadows, which make this a wonderful place for kids.

Address: 1 Monsen Road, Concord, MA
Hours: Dawn to dusk daily
Fee: Free
Contact: fws.gov/northeast/greatmeadows; 978-443-4661
Bathrooms: At a comfort station near the parking lot
Water/Snacks: None
Map: USGS Maynard; fws.gov/northeast/greatmeadows/refuge_brochure.html
Directions by Car: From Boston, take I-93 North to Exit 37B to I-95 South. Go 7 miles to Exit 31B to MA 225 West. After about 3 miles, make a slight left onto MA 62 West and follow for about 3 miles to Monsen Road. Take a right and follow signs to the refuge. Pass a small lot, then park in the larger lot next to the tower. *GPS coordinates: 42° 28.508′ N, 71° 19.777′ W.*

The Great Meadows National Wildlife Refuge is composed of 3,800 acres, which may sound daunting when planning your visit, but families who want an almost-guaranteed sighting of wildlife along easy trails should head to the Concord Unit. (There is a unit in Sudbury as well.)

About 2.5 miles of trails—great for hiking, snowshoeing, or cross-country skiing—are on the property. A dike that runs between the Upper and Lower Pools (also called impoundments) is the main path. The dike separates the "meadow" from the river, and it's an easy walk. Start your visit at the observation tower to check out views of the property, then head down the 1.7-mile Dike Trail. If you have young kids and want a shorter walk, you can take this trail straight to the Concord River, stopping along the way at a wildlife observation platform, and then turn around. Otherwise you can take the trail all the way around the Lower Pool. The impoundments are drained into the river in summer, turning into mudflats and becoming a haven for birds, such as red-winged blackbirds and great blue herons.

Birds aren't the only creatures happy to be here, especially in summer. On one hot, sunny day, my group lost count of how many black northern water

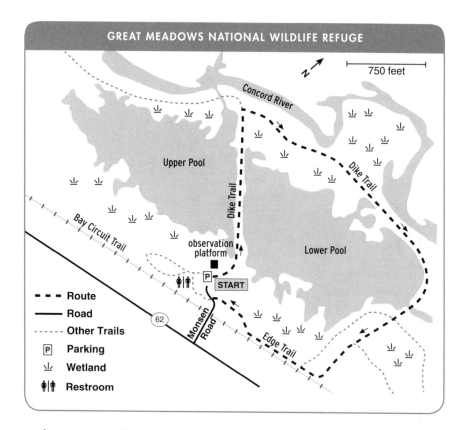

Legend:

- - - Route
—— Road
----- Other Trails
P Parking
⅄ Wetland
♦♦ Restroom

snakes we spotted lounging on rocks. In addition, we saw numbers of leopard frogs, bullfrogs, dragonflies, and turtles.

Remember: This is a carry-in, carry-out property, so plan accordingly. The 4-mile Reformatory Branch Rail Trail passes by the property and follows the roadbed of the Boston & Maine's old Reformatory Branch between Railroad Avenue in Bedford and Lowell Road in Concord. Portions of the Bay Circuit Trail also pass through Great Meadows (see page 100).

PLAN B: To switch from nature trails to a bit of history, head west on MA 62 to the Battle Road Trail and the Old Manse (Trip 40) in Concord.

WHERE TO EAT NEARBY: A number of restaurants are in Concord Center.

Picture a scalloped letter *C* circling Boston in a 300-degree arc that swings from Plum Island and Ipswich on Massachusetts's North Shore, through Lowell, Acton, and Framingham, all the way to the Duxbury and Kingston beaches of the South Shore. This 200-plus-mile arc connects green spaces and passes through, or near, eleven of the destinations featured in this guide. Through woods, farmlands, cranberry bogs, vernal pools, and busy suburbs, the Bay Circuit Trail links parks and open spaces in 57 Boston-area communities and offers a path to nature open to everyone.

The Bay Circuit Trail and Greenway was conceived in the late 1920s by green space visionaries of the time, including Benton MacKaye, founder of the Appalachian Trail. The idea was to create a greenbelt to provide open space to Boston's ever-expanding population. While the plan was not realized for many years, in the 1990s the Bay Circuit Alliance, a nonprofit volunteer organization, was formed. In the years since, the Alliance has overseen the designation of 86 percent of the trail and 5,000 acres of new conservation land has been added to the corridor. In 2011, a new era for the trail began when the Appalachian Mountain Club and The Trustees of Reservations partnered to lead the Bay Circuit Alliance to protect and promote the trail and greenway, making it available to future generations. (More information and maps can be found at baycircuit.org.)

Throughout this book, I've made note of where the Bay Circuit Trail connects to one of the adventures I've described, but these are just the beginning—there's so much more of the trail to explore. While using this book, look for the Bay Circuit Trail at:

- Minuteman Bikeway, Lexington and Concord (Trip 32)
- Great Meadows National Wildlife Refuge, Concord (Trip 38)
- Walden Pond State Reservation, Concord (Trip 39)
- Battle Road Trail and the Old Manse (Trip 40)
- Rocky Narrows: Southern Section, Sherborn (Trip 46)
- Moose Hill Wildlife Sanctuary, Sharon (Trip 55)
- Moose Hill Farm, Sharon (Trip 56)
- Borderland State Park, Easton (Trip 59)
- Harold Parker State Forest, North Andover (Trip 74)
- Crane Beach, Ipswich (Trip 76)
- Appleton Farms and Grass Rides, Ipswich (Trip 77)

Trip 39

Walden Pond State Reservation

Walden Pond, inspiration and onetime home to author Henry David Thoreau, is still an oasis of beauty and peace.

Address: 915 Walden Street (MA 126), Concord, MA
Hours: Dawn to dusk daily
Fee: Parking lot: $5 per vehicle; season passes available
Contact: mass.parks@state.ma.us; 978-369-3254
Bathrooms: At the park headquarters and at the changing station by the pond
Water/Snacks: Water fountains at the park headquarters and at the changing station by the pond
Map: USGS Maynard; mass.gov/dcr/parks/walden/brochures.htm
Directions by Car: From Boston, take the Mass Pike (I-90 West) to Exit 15 to I-95/MA 128 North. Take Exit 29B onto MA 2 West. At the third set of lights, turn left onto MA 126 South. The parking lot is 0.25 mile down the road on the left. *GPS coordinates:* 42° 26.454′ N, 71° 20.117′ W.

When my daughter was a baby, come summer, we'd make our way to the small roped-off beach patrolled by lifeguards at Walden Pond, where we'd join dozens of other families with the same idea. It's a lovely little beach, but it can get really crowded.

Now that she's older, we go farther afield; finding little private inlets for swimming is a favorite activity. The pond, 103 feet deep in some places, is a kettle hole that formed more than 12,000 years ago. Canoeing, kayaking, and fishing are all allowed. Hiking or snowshoeing around the pond is a wonderful way to get a new perspective on the park, which, with 462 acres, has more to offer than just summer fun. In fall and winter, the park takes on a different feel, with far fewer crowds and a quiet kind of beauty. Fall foliage here is nothing short of spectacular, and looking for animal tracks in the snow is a wonderful winter activity with kids. Pond Path, less than 3 miles around, is easy to navigate, but make sure you stay on the path; the area is a victim of its own popularity, and erosion is an ongoing issue. The Bay Circuit Trail (see page 100) passes through the reservation.

Henry David Thoreau lived and worked at Walden Pond for two years beginning in 1845. *Walden*, his book about his time spent here, was published in

Fog rolls over Walden Pond, a peaceful place to hike in late fall.

1854. Kids will enjoy visiting the replica of Thoreau's home (next to the parking lot), where they can contemplate how he could live in such a tiny one-room house for two years! On the hike around the pond, look for the site of Thoreau's actual home. A plaque commemorates the site, and visitors have made a tradition of stacking rocks on a pile there.

The reservation offers interpretive programs, including seasonal children's activities such as nature crafts, storytime, and a Junior Ranger series. Poetry readings, tracking programs, and Thoreau walks are also offered. Call the park or visit the website for more information.

Remember: In summer, the parking lot fills up quickly and the park rangers will close it. Get there early or go later in the day when the crowds start to clear out. Always call ahead to see if you can get in.

PLAN B: Drumlin Farm Wildlife Sanctuary (Trip 36) is in the neighboring town of Lincoln. Visiting the goats, pigs, and other farm animals should make up for any disappointment if you can't get into the lot at Walden.

WHERE TO EAT NEARBY: Take MA 126 (across MA 2) and follow it to Concord Center, which is less than ten minutes away by car and offers plenty of options.

Trip 40

All Ages $ 🍼 🚶 🚲

Battle Road Trail and the Old Manse

Combine hiking and biking with visits to famous Revolutionary-era sites.

Address: 269 Monument Street, Concord, MA
Hours: Trail: dawn to dusk daily
Fee: Trail: free; Old Manse: adults, $8; children ages 6–12, $5; Trustees of Reservations members, free
Contact: nps.gov/mima; 978-369-6993; trustees.org; 978-369-3909
Bathrooms: At the visitor center
Water/Snacks: Water fountain at the visitor center
Map: USGS Maynard; nps.gov/mima/planyourvisit/upload/MIMA%20Park%20Map.pdf
Directions by Car: From Boston, take I-93 North to Exit 37B onto I-95 South. Go 7 miles, then take Exit 31B to MA 225 West. Follow about 3 miles and make a slight left onto MA 62 West. After 4 miles, make a right on Monument Street. After about 0.5 mile, the parking lot will be on the right across the street from the Old Manse. *GPS coordinates:* 42° 28.182′ N, 71° 20.929′ W.

At some point or another, most New England kids will probably visit Concord and Lexington on a school field trip, but the beautiful area is worth more than one visit and may be more fun when a lesson isn't the only agenda.

The Battle Road Trail is a 5.5-mile pathway that follows a part of the route taken by the British regulars in 1775 on their march from Boston to Concord and back. Along the route are historic houses and significant landmarks as well as farmlands, wetlands, and fields.

If walking or biking the entire route is not an option, park across from the Old Manse, built in 1770 by minister William Emerson. The house became a central meeting place for transcendentalists in the mid-nineteenth century. Both Ralph Waldo Emerson (grandson of William) and Nathaniel Hawthorne lived here at various times. Paddlers on the Concord River can tie up their boats at the small boathouse dock on the property, but launching is not allowed. If the house is not open when you visit, you can still walk or snowshoe around the property, then head to the North Bridge next to it. The first effective resistance to British rule in the American colonies occurred here. Rangers are usually stationed near the bridge to answer any questions you may have.

Climbing trees is a perennial favorite.

Concord and Lexington celebrate Patriots' Day on the third Monday in April with a parade, reenactments, and music.

Continue up the trail to the North Bridge visitor center, which was the former mansion of Major John Buttrick of the Concord Minutemen. You can see exhibits of clothing, uniforms, and gear of colonial militia and British regulars. There's a bookstore and replica colonial toys for sale. Outside, beautiful gardens offer a peaceful place to relax.

Remember: The Minute Man National Historical Park visitor center in Lincoln has exhibits, information, and ranger programs.

PLAN B: Great Meadows National Wildlife Refuge (Trip 38) is a wonderful place to see wildlife and offers a pleasant walk to the Concord River.

WHERE TO EAT NEARBY: Head back on Monument Street to Concord's center to find a variety of restaurants and cafés.

Great Brook Farm State Park

Explore a big network of wide, flat trails and visit the animals at this working dairy farm in summer; visit for skiing in winter.

Address: 984 Lowell Street, Carlisle, MA
Hours: Dawn to dusk daily
Fee: Parking lot: $2 per vehicle
Contact: mass.gov/dcr; 978-369-6312
Bathrooms: At the interpretive center near the parking lot
Water/Snacks: Water fountain near restrooms; ice cream shop at farm
Map: USGS Billerica: mass.gov/dcr/parks/trails/greatbrook.pdf
Directions by Car: From Boston, take I-93 North to Exit 37B onto I-95 South. Take Exit 31B and follow MA 225 West/MA 4 North for 8 miles to the Carlisle center traffic circle. Turn right onto Lowell Street. The park entrance is 2 miles ahead on the right; the office is just beyond the entrance. Turn right onto North Road to the parking lot. *GPS coordinates: 42° 33.373′ N, 71° 21.175′ W.*

Gravel trails at Great Brook Farm wind around grassy hills and through the woods.

Great Brook Farm is definitely a favorite with toddlers, who will enjoy seeing the farm animals, but 20 miles of trails also offer hiking, biking, and skiing as well. From the parking lot, walk up the grassy hill to the farm buildings. Trails branch off from here. Look for signs of seventeenth-century cellar holes along the trails in the 1,000-acre park. Meadow Pond has a canoe launch, and you can fish there. One of the farm buildings has been converted to a ski rental concession.

The active dairy farm operates year-round, and guided barn tours are available from May to October. For the last 60 years, Holstein cattle have been raised at the farm. You can feed the sheep and goats through fences (bring quarters to buy feed), or you can go into the pens when part of a tour. Right next to the barnyard is the seasonal ice cream shop, which looks onto the old milking area of the barn. The farmers now use a more modern milking system, which you can see as part of a tour. A beehive and lots of information about cows and milk are inside the shop.

The number and variety of trails (many groomed for biking and skiing) in combination with farm animals and ice cream for the littler kids make this a unique property. Once they outgrow the farm, the kids are probably ready to hit the trails.

Remember: Bring cash if you want to indulge the kids with ice cream—the shop doesn't accept credit cards.

PLAN B: Head to Concord to enjoy historic sites, such as the North Bridge and the Old Manse (Trip 40).

WHERE TO EAT NEARBY: Some chain restaurants are along MA 4. A few other food options are in Bedford's town center on MA 4.

Trip 42

All Ages

Nashua River Rail Trail

The 11 miles of this former railroad turned trail offer easy walking or bicycling with scenic views.

Address: Groton Street and MA 2A, Ayer, MA
Hours: Dawn to dusk daily
Fee: Free
Contact: mass.gov/dcr; 978-597-8802
Bathrooms: Portable toilets at the trailhead in Ayer
Water/Snacks: Water fountain in front of the Groton Town Hall, close to the trail on Station Avenue
Map: USGS Pepperell; mass.gov/dcr/parks/images/nashCampMap.gif
Directions by Car: From Boston, take I-93 North to Exit 44B (I-495 South). After 18 miles, take Exit 30 for MA 2 West/MA 110 West. Turn left and drive to a traffic circle, where you'll follow the signs to stay on 2A West. After Ayer Center, take the first right onto Groton Street to the trail parking lot on the right, with room for 60 cars. Other parking lots with access to the trail are located in Groton and Dunstable. *GPS coordinates:* 42° 33.747′ N, 71° 35.415′ W.
Directions by Public Transit: Take the Fitchburg/South Acton commuter rail train from North Station to Ayer. Walk north on Park Street to Groton Street.

The Nashua River Rail Trail is a great safe place to take kids biking, hiking, snowshoeing, or cross-country skiing. The 10-foot-wide paved trail—which mostly follows the lines of the river and passes through the towns of Ayer, Groton, Pepperell, and Dunstable—is used by walkers, bicyclists, skaters, horseback riders, and cross-country skiers.

The trail is built along the site of former railroad tracks, where trains, beginning in 1848, ran between Worcester and Nashua, New Hampshire. Starting in 1929, the tracks began to be dismantled; finally, in 1982, the last freight train ran on the line. In 2002, the rail trail was built. Along the route, you'll see wetlands, ponds, woods, swamps, and farms as well as plenty of resting stops. Kids will enjoy exploring along the river.

Remember: Tell your kids not to be surprised to see horses on the trail. Yield the right of way to riders, and never pass horses without giving a voice warning. Keep your dog on a leash and clean up after it.

A group of bike riders prepares to cycle the wide, paved Nashua River Rail Trail.

PLAN B: The Oxbow National Wildlife Refuge (Trip 43) has great hiking along the Nashua River. It's about a ten-minute drive south of the rail trail in Ayer.

WHERE TO EAT NEARBY: You can make a stop in any of the towns along the route for a snack. A café is in Groton and ice cream is available in Pepperell.

Trip 43

Oxbow National Wildlife Refuge

This remote hike offers ample opportunities to spot wildlife and marvel at the industrious work of beavers.

Address: Still River Depot Road, Harvard, MA
Hours: Dawn to dusk daily
Fee: Free
Contact: fws.gov/northeast/oxbow; 978-443-4661
Bathrooms: Compost toilets at the back of the parking lot
Water/Snacks: None
Map: USGS Ayer; fws.gov/northeast/oxbow/refuge_brochure.html
Directions by Car: From Boston, take the Mass Pike (I-90 West) to Exit 15 and merge onto I-95 North. Take Exit 29B onto MA 2 West. Take Exit 38 (MA 110/111) south toward Harvard. At Harvard Center, bear right to stay on MA 110. At the Still River post office, turn right onto Still River Depot Road. Cross the railroad tracks and then bear right and follow the road to the end, where you'll find the parking lot. *GPS coordinates: 42° 29.792′ N, 71° 37.531′ W.*

Oxbow (1,700 acres) is one of eight refuges in the Eastern Massachusetts National Wildlife Refuge Complex. The hike described here takes you through three different habitats, where the chances of seeing wildlife are great. Pick up an interpretive trail guide at the parking lot to read text that corresponds with the numbered posts you'll see as you walk.

Just to the right of the parking lot is the start of Riverside Trail. Follow this along the Nashua River, and then turn onto Turnpike Trail, which leads to Tank Road (a dirt road sometimes used by the neighboring Army Training Area) and back to the parking lot. The whole hike is about 2 miles long and pretty easy going. It will take you through wetlands, forests, and fields; it also passes two beaver lodges. The area can be buggy in spring and summer, so I highly recommend wearing pants. In winter, the trails are perfect for snowshoeing or cross-country skiing.

On one visit, when my group crossed over the boardwalk on one section of Turnpike Trail, we saw a magnificent beaver dam. Along the trail, we saw evidence of busy beavers: felled trees with telltale teeth marks. Though we didn't

Hikers will likely spot evidence of beavers along the secluded trails at Oxbow.

see the beavers themselves last time we went, we almost tripped over a painted turtle that had decided to lay eggs in the middle of the path!

Remember: This probably sounds scarier than it is, but the park does warn visitors that the area was once used for military training and that there's a remote possibility of unexploded ordnance. Tell kids that, in the unlikely event they see unusual metallic objects, not to touch them. And, as always, stick to the trail.

PLAN B: You can jump on the Nashua River Rail Trail (Trip 42) in nearby Ayer for a great bike ride.

WHERE TO EAT NEARBY: If you head back to MA 110/111, restaurants are on Ayer Road, north of MA 2.

Trip 44

Garden in the Woods

Garden in the Woods is an outdoor botanical garden with whimsical touches that appeal to kids.

Address: 180 Hemenway Road, Framingham, MA

Hours: Trails: 9 A.M. to 5 P.M., with last admissions at 4:30 P.M., Tuesdays through Sundays and holiday Mondays, April 15 through October 31

Fee: Adults, $10; children ages 3–17, $5; children under age 3, free

Contact: newfs.org; 508-877-7630

Bathrooms: At the garden shop and at the education center

Water/Snacks: Water fountain outside the education center; some snacks and drinks for sale at the garden shop

Map: USGS Natick; newfs.org/visit/Garden-in-the-Woods/garden-map.html

Directions by Car: From Boston, take the Mass Pike (I-90 West) to Exit 15 onto MA 128. Take MA 128 to US 20 West, drive 8 miles to Raymond Road, and take a left. Go about 1 mile to Hemenway Road and bear right up the hill to the entrance. Plenty of parking spots are available in three lots. *GPS coordinates: 42° 20.426' N, 71° 25.584' W.*

Garden in the Woods, part of the New England Wild Flower Society, is New England's premier wildflower garden, with more than 1,000 native plant species. The paths and trails found here can seem magical to kids. The main trail, Curtis Path, is about 1 mile long. If you're looking for a longer, more rugged walk, try one of the woodsy trails. Either way, pick up a scavenger hunt at the garden center when you arrive. Two versions of the hunt are available: one for younger kids, one for older.

Near the beginning of Curtis Path is Lily Pond, a main attraction for kids. The pond is shallow and has little floating islands with tons of frogs, turtles, and dragonflies in lots of bright colors, all surrounded by wildflowers. It is hard to drag kids away from the pond. On one visit, we saw a big green frog swallow a worm about a foot away from where we stood! The wildlife is transfixing, but if you are participating in the scavenger hunt, you'll probably be able to move on.

It's worth leaving the main loop to see the flowers on Hop Brook Trail in summer. The exhibits change each year, so visiting never gets stale. Sections

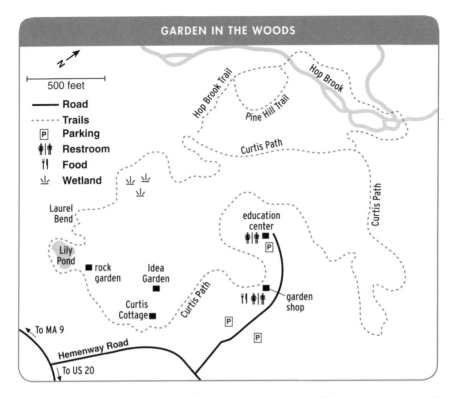

GARDEN IN THE WOODS

500 feet

— Road
---- Trails
P Parking
Restroom
Food
Wetland

Hop Brook Trail

Hop Brook

Pine Hill Trail

Curtis Path

Curtis Path

Laurel Bend

Lily Pond

education center

rock garden

Idea Garden

Curtis Path

garden shop

Curtis Cottage

To MA 9

Hemenway Road

To US 20

may include the Idea Garden, with container gardens, edible plants, and a roof garden. Interpretive signs describe the garden and habitats in depth.

Remember: Guided walking tours are offered every day Garden in the Woods is open. Weekday tours are offered at 10 A.M., and weekend tours are at 2 P.M. Special events include full-moon walks and winter solstice celebrations. The trail is well kept and smooth, but a baby pack would probably work better than a stroller here because of a few steps.

PLAN B: The Danforth Museum of Art, also in Framingham, has a great collection of contemporary art and offers family-friendly programs.

WHERE TO EAT NEARBY: Several restaurants are on MA 9 in Framingham.

Trip 45

Broadmoor Wildlife Sanctuary

Over the brook and through the woods, 9 miles of trails at Broadmoor will enchant kids with boardwalks, waterfalls, and wildlife.

Address: 280 Eliot Street, Natick, MA
Hours: Trails: dawn to dusk Tuesday through Sunday; nature center: 9 A.M. to 5 P.M. Tuesday through Friday, 10 A.M. to 5 P.M. weekends and Monday holidays
Fee: Adults, $5; children ages 3–12, $4; Mass Audubon members, free
Contact: broadmoor@massaudubon.org; 508-655-2296
Bathrooms: At the nature center
Water/Snacks: Water fountain in the nature center
Map: USGS Framingham; massaudubon.org/Nature_Connection/Sanctuaries/ Broadmoor/maps.php
Directions by Car: From Boston, take the Mass Pike (I-90 West) to Exit 16 (West Newton/Wellesley). Follow MA 16 West for 8.8 miles; you'll see the sanctuary on the left and a large parking lot. *GPS coordinates:* 42° 15.324′ N, 71° 20.445′ W.

Your kids probably won't want to leave the boardwalk sections of Broadmoor's trails after spotting turtles, geese, frogs, and other wildlife. The promise of a waterfall should do the trick, though. From the Mass Audobon's nature center, where you have to check in, start with All Persons Trail, a 430-foot-long accessible boardwalk along Indian Brook and over marsh, then head to Mill Pond/ Marsh Trail to see the waterfall. The water gushing down the chute was used for powering a wheel at the former mill site.

Though this is just a mile-long trek, be prepared for slow going because there's so much to see. This is a hike not to get somewhere, but rather to enjoy the journey. You may want to explain to the kids that you have to return the same way so that they know they will get a chance to explore the same territory again.

The various habitats—wetlands, fields, woods, brooks, vernal pools—attract all sorts of animals, including beaver, otters, turtles, and more than 150 varieties of birds. A gristmill was once on the property, which you'll see evidence of by the cascading waterfall that powered the saw for the mill. Other trails lead to the Charles River, open fields, and a drumlin (an elongated hill formed by glacial drift). The sanctuary is also a great place to snowshoe in winter.

Two friends look for turtles, frogs, and fish from the 430-foot-long boardwalk along Indian Brook.

Remember: Don't skip the nature center, where you can learn about its green features, including solar panels for electricity and composting toilets.

PLAN B: Elm Bank Reservation (Trip 48) is in Wellesley, less than 3 miles away.

WHERE TO EAT NEARBY: Natick's Main Street offers a variety of places to eat.

Trip 46

Ages 5–8

Rocky Narrows: Southern Section

The southern section of Rocky Narrows offers easy trails and short loops perfect for younger hikers.

Address: South Main Street (MA 27), Sherborn, MA
Hours: Dawn to dusk daily
Fee: Free
Contact: thetrustees.org; 508-785-0339
Bathrooms: None
Water/Snacks: None
Map: USGS Medfield; thetrustees.org/assets/documents/places-to-visit/
   trailmaps/Rocky-Narrows-Trail-Map.pdf
Directions by Car: From Boston, take the Mass Pike (I-90 West) to Exit 16. Take
   MA 16 West. After about 5 miles, this road turns into MA 135 West. Follow
   this for 3 miles. Take a left on MA 27 South. Follow this for about 5 miles to
   the small lot (room for four cars) on the right. (Alternate parking is available
   on Forest Street off Snow Street at the northern edge of the property.) *GPS
   coordinates:* 42° 12.872′ N, 71° 21.626′ W.

Rocky Narrows has several different trails to explore, and the Bay Circuit Trail (see page 100) passes through the reservation. The southern section, a 77-acre parcel of land, is part of the 249-acre property but is separated from the rest of the reservation by an active railroad track. This section doesn't allow access to the Rocky Narrows Overlook or King Philip's Overlook, which you may have heard of and are certainly worth visiting, but this area offers its own charms and is easier than the northern section for younger kids.

White Trail, which you'll find at the end of the parking lot, is the only blazed trail here and takes you through woodlands and wetlands on a fairly easy path. We had fun on one visit counting the tiny brown frogs that seemed to be everywhere that day and seeing who could spot the most. Eventually you get to a split at Marker 1; you can choose to go right on a path that leads to the tracks and back, or you can go to the left for a shorter loop trail, with a couple of spurs to make it even shorter. This is also a great trail for when you don't have a lot of time but want to get the kids out to stretch their legs. It's also perfect for a short snowshoe trek.

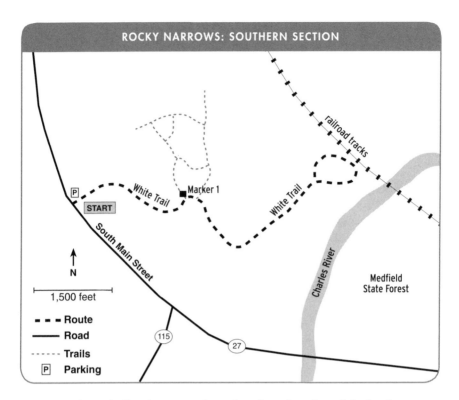

Remember: It's illegal to cross the railroad tracks. If you hike by them, stay on your own side.

PLAN B: For a very different and more challenging hike, go to the northern section of Rocky Narrows. Paddling is also available there.

WHERE TO EAT NEARBY: Places to dine are in Sherborn along MA 27, north of the reservation.

Trip 47

Ages 0–4

College Pond

This short and pretty hike around College Pond is perfect for younger kids.

Address: 269 Concord Road, Weston, MA
Hours: Dawn to dusk daily
Fee: Free
Contact: westonforesttrail.org
Bathrooms: Next to the tennis courts
Water/Snacks: Next to the bathrooms
Map: USGS Concord; westonforesttrail.org/interactiveMap.html
Directions by Car: From Boston, take the Mass Pike (I-90 West) to Exit 15 and follow signs to MA 30 West. Take a right onto Newton Street and drive about 2 miles, where the road will change names to Ash Street. Almost immediately, take a slight right onto School Street and then in 0.5 mile, take a left onto Boston Post Road. Go 0.5 mile and make a left onto Concord Road. The Burchard Park parking lot will be on the right in about 1 mile. *GPS coordinates: 42° 22.885′ N, 71° 19.036′ W.*

Weston has about 100 miles of hiking trails, many of which, like this one, start behind parks or schools. The nonprofit Weston Forest and Trail Association helps maintain and protect open spaces in the town and offers a large trail map for sale at the town hall. You can also look up trails on the association's website.

To hike around College Pond, which is behind Burchard Park, walk behind the tennis courts to the right and then pass the ball fields. You'll see glimpses of the pond and then finally come to it. Pushing a stroller is easy enough here, as the path is mostly wide and flat. After you pass by the pond, you'll come to a small orchard, a lovely place for a picnic if it's nice out. In short order the trail leads to Concord Road—a paved path runs beside the road—where you turn right and then come to the entrance of the park and the parking lot. In all, this hike takes only about 30 to 40 minutes, so it's great for younger kids. In winter, this is a good, short snowshoe hike.

On the association's website are posted several Weston hike descriptions, written by members of a local Girl Scout Troop. The hike descriptions are quite detailed, and the troop also posted sketches and poems. Your kids might be inspired to do the same if you show these to them.

Great green lily pads blanket much of College Pond.

Remember: From October through May, the Weston Forest and Trail Association meets on the first Sunday of the month at 2 P.M. for a hike in a different part of town. It's a great way to get acquainted with the area.

PLAN B: The Drumlin Farm Wildlife Sanctuary (Trip 36), just about 2 miles to the north, is a favorite for families with younger kids.

WHERE TO EAT NEARBY: Take Concord Road south into Weston Center for a variety of restaurants and cafés.

Trip 48

Elm Bank Reservation

Elm Bank Reservation, home to the Massachusetts Horticultural Society's Gardens at Elm Bank, offers natural beauty both wild and planned.

Address: 900 Washington Street, Wellesley, MA
Hours: Dawn to dusk daily; gates open to cars at 8 A.M.
Fee: Free
Contact: mass.gov/dcr; 617-333-7404
Bathrooms: At the Hunnewell Building
Water/Snacks: At the Hunnewell Building
Map: USGS Natick
Directions by Car: From Boston, take MA 9 West to MA 16 West. Follow MA 16/Washington Street through Wellesley. The reservation and several parking areas are near the intersection of Washington and Forest streets, 1 mile past Wellesley College on the left. *GPS coordinates:* 42° 16.456′ N, 71° 18.230′ W.

Elm Bank Reservation, run by the Department of Conservation and Recreation, has 182 acres of woodlands, fields, and old estate lands to explore. The property is surrounded on three sides by the Charles River; head to the canoe launch if you want to paddle. The easy trails here are stroller-friendly, the paved paths are great for biking, and the fields are perfect for kicking a soccer ball around.

What families—especially those with toddlers—will enjoy tremendously are the Massachusetts Horticultural Society's gardens, which occupy 36 acres on the reservation. The nonprofit organization, founded in 1829, is dedicated to encouraging the science and practice of horticulture and developing the public's enjoyment, appreciation, and understanding of plants and the environment. You can visit several different types of gardens. A $5 donation is suggested, which can be left in the box at the gate.

Once inside, head straight to the utterly charming Weezie's Garden for Children, which has a sand play area shaded by banana trees, a wooden tower to climb, an enormous chair fit for a giant (or for small kids to scramble up), and plants that kids are allowed and encouraged to smell and touch.

Other gardens include an Italianate Garden, a Garden-to-Table Chef's Garden and its Food Pantry Garden, an educational New England Trial Garden,

Kids are delighted by the oversized chair in Weezie's Garden at the Massachusetts Horticultural Society's gardens at Elm Bank.

and a Goddess Sculpture Garden. If you have a phone with you, you can listen to a free audio tour describing the gardens. In winter, a steep hill behind the horticultural building is popular for sledding.

Remember: Dogs are allowed only in sections of the reservation; look for signs marking where they are forbidden to go. Keep your dog on a leash and clean up after it.

PLAN B: Just 2 miles farther west on MA 16, the Mass Audubon's Broadmoor Wildlife Sanctuary (Trip 45) has a wonderful 1-mile hike that traverses boardwalks over marshes and a pond.

WHERE TO EAT NEARBY: Wellesley Square, at the corner of Washington and Grove streets, has several places to eat.

Section 4

South of Boston

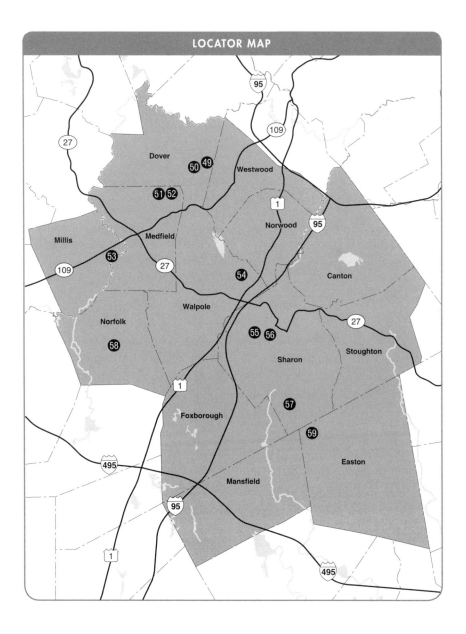

Trip 49

Ages 9–12

Noanet Woodlands

This hike leads to a former mill site with a waterfall and ponds that will enchant kids.

Address: Dedham Street, Dover, MA
Hours: Dawn to dusk daily
Fee: Free
Contact: thetrustees.org; 508-785-0339
Bathrooms: Portable toilet next to parking lot
Water/Snacks: Near the playground to the right of the parking lot
Map: USGS Framingham, Medfield; thetrustees.org/assets/documents/places-to-visit/trailmaps/Noanet-Woodlands-Trail-Map.pdf
Directions by Car: From Boston, take I-95 North to MA 128 South and take Exit 17 (MA 135 West). In less than 1 mile, turn left onto South Street. Drive 1.1 miles and turn left onto Chestnut Street, which turns into Dedham Street. Follow for 2 miles to the Caryl Park parking lot on the left. *GPS coordinates: 42° 14.863′ N, 71°16.157′ W.*

Noanet Woodlands is a Trustees of Reservations property adjacent to Caryl Park, which is run by the Town of Dover. If you have younger kids who spot the large playground to the right of the parking lot, your walk might end right there. However, you should direct them to the trails on Noanet, where they'll be rewarded with a waterfall and ponds to check out.

The property encompasses a former mill site, a great goal to reach on your hike. From the left side of the parking lot, pick up a laminated map at the trailhead of the 1.6-mile Caryl Loop Trail (marked by red blazes). This leads to the old mill site, which has a waterfall and the Upper and Lower Mill Ponds. The first interesting landmark you come to on the trail is the Boulder, which is named as such on the map. Kids love to stop here for a short climb. When you get to the mill site, make sure you take a short detour around the Lower Mill Pond to look over the waterfall and to see Upper Mill Pond. You can have a snack or eat lunch at the picnic table here.

If your kids are feeling energetic, push on to Noanet Peak Trail (marked by yellow blazes), which takes you to the top of the 387-foot-hill called Noanet Peak for views of the Boston skyline. You can pick up this trail at the Lower

New parents enjoy a shaded hike through Noanet Woodlands with their baby.

Mill Pond. It will add at least 1 mile to your hike. For a longer trek, choose from more than 17 miles of trails and other ponds. The extensive trail network makes for great cross-country skiing in winter.

Remember: Parking is restricted in April and May when athletic games are being played at Caryl Park between 3 and 8 P.M., Monday through Friday. Keep your dog on a leash and clean up after it.

PLAN B: Powisset Farm (Trip 50) offers a pastoral scene and farm animals.

WHERE TO EAT NEARBY: Head north to Needham Center for a variety of dining options near the intersection of Highland and Great Plain avenues.

Trip 50

Powisset Farm

Powisset Farm features a gentle trail that takes you around the farm through fields, woods, and wetlands.

Address: 37 Powisset Street, Dover, MA
Hours: Dawn to dusk daily
Fee: Free
Contact: charlesrivervalley@ttor.org; 508-785-0339
Bathrooms: None
Water/Snacks: None
Map: USGS Medfield; thetrustees.org/assets/documents/places-to-visit/
  trailmaps/Powisset-Farm-Trail-Map.pdf
Directions by Car: From Boston, take I-95 North to Exit 16B (MA 109 West).
  Follow for about 1 mile, then take a right on Dover Road. The farm is 2.5
  miles ahead on the left. Parking spaces are found beside the barn. If they are
  all taken, you can park on the grass on the right side of the driveway. *GPS
  coordinates: 42° 13.52' N, 71° 15.647' W.*

If you have any would-be farmers in your family, Powisset Farm is a great place to let them get their hands dirty. This Trustees of Reservations property operates a popular community-supported agriculture (CSA), program: members pay for shares of fruits and vegetable that the farm produces, but you don't have to be a member to visit the farm or volunteer to work in the fields.

The farm dates back more than 300 years. In the 1600s, colonists claimed the land and farmed it steadily until the 1800s. Eventually, Amelia Peabody, a great believer in public access to open spaces, purchased the land; later, it came into the Trustees' hands. After you oink at the pigs and cluck at the chickens, you can take the 1-mile loop trail through fields, checking out what is growing, then head to an oak forest, passing two brooks, vernal pools, and wetlands on the 108.5-acre property. If you feel like a longer walk, a trail spur leads into the adjacent 1,200-acre Hale Reservation.

Every Saturday afternoon from May through September, the farm has drop-in volunteer hours, where you can help with a variety of farm projects. Kids are welcome to come with a parent.

Programs at Powisset Farm include a how-to workshop about building bee boxes, bat houses, and bluebird boxes (seen here).

Another program option for kids ages 3 to 6 is the Children's Farm Fun workshop, which runs several times in summer. Activities may include making a children's flower garden, doing farm crafts, or exploring the farm geared with shovels, trowels, and magnifying glasses. Check the farm's website (thetrustees.org/places-to-visit/csas/powisset-farm-csa/our-csa) or call for details.

The public can buy some of what the farm produces on Tuesdays, June through October, from 1:30 to 6:30 P.M. You can also pick your own flowers and herbs from gardens found next to the main barn daily during the same months for a donation.

Remember: Warn kids that the fence around the cultivated fields is electric (to keep away deer), so they should stay away from it.

PLAN B: Noanet Woodlands (Trip 49) is just across the street from the farm.

WHERE TO EAT NEARBY: Return to MA 109 and go west to Westwood Center, where you can find a variety of restaurants and convenience stores.

Trip 51

Fork Factory Brook

Look for signs of a former nineteenth-century pitchfork mill as you hike through wetlands, around hay fields, and down wooded hillsides.

Address: Hartford Street and MA 109, Medfield, MA
Hours: Dawn to dusk daily
Fee: Adults, $4; children under age 12 and Trustees of Reservations members, free (fees collected by rangers on weekends and holidays; honor system other times)
Contact: thetrustees.org; 508-785-0339
Bathrooms: Portable toilet near the pavilion
Water/Snacks: None
Map: USGS Medfield; thetrustees.org/assets/documents/places-to-visit/ trailmaps/Rocky-Woods-Fork-Factory-Brook-Trail-Map.pdf
Directions by Car: From I-95 South, take Exit 16B to MA 109 West. Follow for 5.7 miles through Westwood. Take a right hairpin turn onto Hartford Street in Medfield. Follow for 0.6 miles to the Rocky Woods parking lot on the left. *GPS coordinates:* 42° 12.359′ N, 71° 16.632′ W.

The former Long Acre Farm offers 1.5 miles of trails to explore, through wetlands to hay fields to wooded hillsides. The area has a long history of agriculture, dating back 300 years. Throughout the eighteenth century, workers on this quintessential New England farm kept livestock, grew crops, and harvested hay. They also made butter, cheese, rope, candles, and boots, and processed flax and wool.

Hiking around, you'll see remnants of a nineteenth-century pitchfork mill, which is how the property got its name. In the late 1700s and into the 1800s, there were both a gristmill along the Mill Brook and a cut-nail mill. These were eventually combined to create a factory that made pitchforks, shovels, spades, and hoes for area farmers. In 1927, the town of Medfield widened Main Street (MA 109) and demolished the mill. All that's left to see is the earthen dam and stone raceway at the southern end of the property. This is most clear when you cross over a small bridge over the brook. The trails through the woods are quite twisty and feature lots of hills and switchbacks. The route is also a bit overgrown in parts, so long pants are recommended.

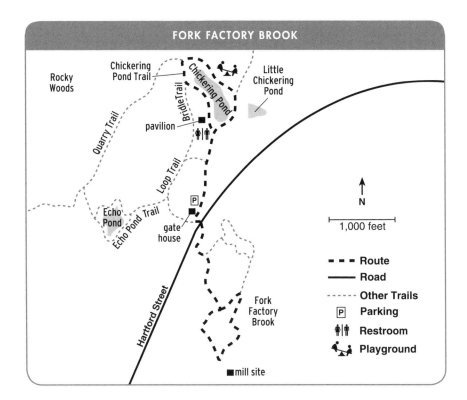

FORK FACTORY BROOK

Rocky Woods

Chickering Pond Trail

Little Chickering Pond

Chickering Pond

Bridle Trail

Quarry Trail

pavilion

Loop Trail

Echo Pond

Echo Pond Trail

gate house

N

1,000 feet

Hartford Street

Fork Factory Brook

mill site

- - - Route
— Road
- - - - - Other Trails
P Parking
Restroom
Playground

Remember: You can bring a dog if you have registered for the Trustees of Reservations' Green Dogs program, which is free for members. At Rocky Woods next door, dogs can run free in some sections.

PLAN B: For some easier hiking, with clearer paths, a playground, and picnic tables around a pond, explore Rocky Woods next door (Trip 52).

WHERE TO EAT NEARBY: If you head west on MA 109, you will find a number of cafés and stores.

Trip 52

Rocky Woods

Five ponds, a playground, and easy walking make Rocky Woods a great destination for families.

Address: Hartford Street and MA 109, Medfield, MA
Hours: Dawn to dusk daily
Fee: Adults, $4; children under age 12 and Trustees of Reservations members, free (fees collected by rangers on weekends and holidays; honor system other times)
Contact: thetrustees.org; 508-785-0339
Bathrooms: Portable toilet near the pavilion
Water/Snacks: None
Map: USGS Medfield; thetrustees.org/assets/documents/places-to-visit/ trailmaps/Rocky-Woods-Fork-Factory-Brook-Trail-Map.pdf
Directions by Car: From I-95 South, take Exit 16B to MA 109 West. Follow for 5.7 miles through Westwood. Take a right hairpin turn onto Hartford Street in Medfield. Follow for 0.6 miles to the parking lot on the left. *GPS coordinates:* 42° 12.359′ N, 71° 16.632′ W.

Rocky Woods has 6.5 miles of trails to explore, with a variety of options perfect for families. As you wander the trails, you'll see the rocks in the woods that give the property its name, but the 491-acre reservation also offers many easy, clear trails. Some lead around ponds, while others lead up to the 420-foot-high Mine Hill ridge.

The 0.75-mile loop around Chickering Pond is probably the best for families with little ones. Look for bullfrogs and painted turtles that make their home here. About half-way around the pond, a small playground and a few picnic tables on the shores are perfect for a lunch break. Visitors are allowed to catch-and-release fish here. For a longer walk, the Hemlock Knoll Loop to Whale Rock is a 1-mile hike that you can pick up from Chickering Pond and that leads to a rock that looks like the back of a whale.

Other trails include Bridle Trail and Loop Trail, which go through wetlands and are quite flat. Echo Pond Trail, a half-mile route, features a narrow footbridge that loops around the large pond. The wide path with small slopes is fun for cross-country skiers.

A trail at Rocky Woods leads to a large pond—a favorite for kids ready to explore.

Rocky Woods has a playing field and a large pavilion that groups can reserve for events. From mid-June through October, a farm stand with produce from Powisset Farm (Trip 50) is open from 9 A.M. to 1 P.M. on Saturdays.

Remember: You can bring a dog if you have registered for the Trustees of Reservations' Green Dogs program, which is free for members. Dogs can roam leash-free on some trails (marked).

PLAN B: For a more challenging hike to the site of a former mill, cross the street to Fork Factory Brook (Trip 51).

WHERE TO EAT NEARBY: If you head west on MA 109, you can find a number of cafés and stores.

Cedariver

A cart path trail at this former farm on the Charles River offers a lovely scenic walk. Afterward, paddle your canoe or kayak along the river.

Address: 161 Forest Road, Millis, MA
Hours: Dawn to dusk daily
Fee: Free
Contact: thetrustees.org; 508-785-0339
Bathrooms: None
Water/Snacks: None
Map: USGS Medfield; printed map available at trailhead
Directions by Car: From Boston, take I-93 South to I-95 North. Take Exit 16B to MA 109 West into Medfield Center. Pass MA 27, then turn left onto Causeway Street. Go to the end and turn right onto Orchard Street. The entrance will be on the left. Look for a big Trustees of Reservations sign; park at the trailhead on the grass. *GPS coordinates: 42° 9.447′ N, 71° 20.104′ W.*

A 1-mile hike along a cart path by the Charles River leads through an oak pine forest.

The Baker family operated a small farm here on the Charles River through the mid-twentieth century and donated the land to The Trustees of Reservations in 2004. Today, you can take a leisurely stroll on a 1-mile trail that takes you through meadows and an oak pine forest. While the forest is mostly pine, some cedar trees are on the property as well, which may be why the Bakers named it Cedariver. Bring a picnic; if you take a short detour on the loop about halfway around the trail, you can enjoy lunch at a picnic table right on the river.

But the best way to enjoy this area might be by canoeing down the Charles River. Far from the busy sections of riverfront in Boston, this quiet area will give you a different perspective of the Charles. The Department of Conservation and Recreation has a boat landing across the street where you can launch canoes and kayaks. In winter, you can go sledding on a hill that overlooks the river.

Remember: A couple of private residences are on the property, so respect the owners' privacy and stay on the trail. Keep your dog on a leash and clean up after it.

PLAN B: Rocky Narrows (Trip 46), another Trustees of Reservations property, is 20 minutes away in Sherborn, and has an extensive trail system with longer hikes.

WHERE TO EAT NEARBY: Medfield Center, on and around MA 109, has a few restaurants.

Trip 54

Francis William Bird Park

Stone bridges, ponds, a playground, and paved paths make this park a family favorite, especially for those pushing strollers.

Address: Washington Street and Polley Lane, Walpole, MA
Hours: Dawn to dusk daily
Fee: Free
Contact: thetrustees.org; 508-668-6136
Bathrooms: Portable toilets by the playground (spring and summer only)
Water/Snacks: None
Map: USGS Norwood; thetrustees.org/assets/documents/places-to-visit/
   trailmaps/Bird-Park-Trail-Map.pdf
Directions by Car: From Boston, take I-95 South to Exit 10 (Coney Street,
   Sharon, Walpole) and turn right onto Coney Street. Turn left onto Pleasant
   Street, and then take a right onto Polley Lane. The main parking area is on
   the left, three lots are around the perimeter of the park, and street parking is
   often available. *GPS coordinates:* 42° 9.201′ N, 71° 12.996′ W.

This park was designed for city dwellers to have a peaceful retreat.

This park was created in 1925 to be a breathing space for the community. Industrialist Charles Sumner Bird Sr. and his wife, Anna, commissioned it in memory of their oldest son, Francis William Bird, who died during the influenza epidemic of 1918, at the age of 37.

The couple hired John Nolen, a disciple of landscape architect Frederick Law Olmsted, who believed landscape design could be a tool for societal improvement. While your kids might not be thinking about its history, the park is a fine example of the trend at the time to make sure urban areas offered outdoor opportunities to enjoy nature.

Today, you'll find a tot lot, tennis courts, a basketball backboard, and plenty of places to sit in the shade or enjoy a picnic. Most of the 3 miles of walking paths are paved, and are good for cross-country skiing and snowshoeing.

Remember: You can pick up the pamphlet titled "Over the Bridge and Through the Years Quest" next to the tot lot. Clues and a map lead to a hidden treasure box, where you can sign your name or get a stamp. Keep your dog on a leash and clean up after it.

PLAN B: Moose Hill Wildlife Sanctuary (Trip 55) is less than 4 miles to the south if you'd like to experience more varied, vigorous trails.

WHERE TO EAT NEARBY: Head to Washington Street, which forms one boundary of the park, to find restaurants.

Trip 55

Moose Hill Wildlife Sanctuary

Explore 25 miles of hiking trails and numerous habitats at Mass Audubon's oldest sanctuary.

Address: 293 Moose Hill Street, Sharon, MA

Hours: Trails: 7 A.M. to 7 P.M. spring and summer; 8 A.M. to 5 P.M. fall and winter; nature center: 9 A.M. to 5 P.M. weekdays, 10 A.M. to 4 P.M. weekends

Fee: Adults, $4; children ages 2–12, $3; Mass Audubon members, free

Contact: moosehill@massaudubon.org; 781-784-5691

Bathrooms: At the nature center

Water/Snacks: Water fountain near the bathrooms

Map: USGS Norwood; massaudubon.org/Nature_Connection/Sanctuaries/Moose_Hill/maps.php

Directions by Car: From Boston, take I-95 South to Exit 10 (Coney Street, Sharon, Walpole). Take a left off the exit and take the first right onto MA 27 North (Walpole). Take the first left onto Moose Hill Street. You'll pass Moose Hill Farm. Continue to the top of the hill and turn left onto Moose Hill Parkway. The parking lot is on the left. *GPS coordinates: 42° 7.430' N, 71° 12.436' W.*

Directions by Public Transit: Take the Providence/Stoughton commuter rail train from South Station to Sharon. The sanctuary is a 2-mile walk from the station, but you can arrange for pickup by calling the sanctuary in advance.

Moose Hill has an embarrassment of riches for outdoors lovers. Do your kids want to look for frogs in a vernal pool? Check out the sugar shack? Snowshoe past an old barn and enormous maple trees? Climb the summit to the highest point (534 feet) on the property? Cross a swamp over a 700-foot-long boardwalk? Decisions, decisions. The good news is that whatever you decide, you won't be disappointed. With almost 2,000 acres of protected space (when combined with the neighboring Trustees of Reservations property, Moose Hill Farm), the sanctuary offers a welcome habitat for all sorts of animals. Deer, foxes, and turtles as well as turkeys, owls, and any number of other birds can be found here. Inside the nature center, art exhibits rotate through a dedicated gallery.

Probably the most popular hiking trails are the 1-mile Billings Loop, which takes you by the sugar shack through fields and the forest; Vernal Pool Trail,

A downed tree at Moose Hill Wildlife Sanctuary gives young visitors a new vantage point.

which is an easy walk that starts right behind the nature center; and Summit Trail, which is a bit of a rigorous hike. The fire tower at the summit is usually locked, so prepare your kids for that likely possibility if they think they can climb up. You can also explore some of the Bay Circuit Trail (see page 100), which passes through Moose Hill.

Remember: Ask at the nature center desk for advice on what trails to take. People there can tell you which ones offer the most sights depending on the season. Check out the art gallery and other exhibits while you're there.

PLAN B: Moose Hill Farm (Trip 56), a Trustees of Reservations property, is just next door.

WHERE TO EAT NEARBY: Take MA 27 back to Walpole, where you'll find a number of restaurants and take-out spots near the intersection of MA 27 and Main Street.

New England winters can be long and cold, but when March rolls around and the sap starts flowing in maple trees, anyone who's a fan of maple syrup has something to celebrate. The Mass Audubon Society does so in style at several of its properties, as do many farms and sugarhouses in the region.

The Moose Hill Wildlife Sanctuary (Trip 55) has an annual maple sugaring festival that usually runs the last three Sundays in March. Each day, reenactors in period garb lead 90-minute tours about American Indian and colonial sugaring techniques.

No one really knows for sure who first discovered that sap could be made into syrup, but you might hear a storyteller relate one legend about an American Indian chief who hit a sugar maple tree with his tomahawk, causing the sap to flow out. According to the legend, his wife then used the liquid in cooking and discovered that it was delicious. A more likely theory is that the native peoples observed animals drinking from open cuts in trees

Visitors at Moose Hill can also see a modern operational sugarhouse where sap is made into syrup, and even sample the final product. Kids can enjoy arts and crafts inside the nature center and probably talk their parents into buying pancakes with syrup, "sap dogs," or maple popcorn. If you sample too much, walk it off on one of the numerous trails on the property.

In Milton, Maple Sugar Days are held the second weekend in March at Brookwood Farm. The Mass Audubon Blue Hills Trailside Museum and Department of Conservation and Recreation team up with Brookwood Farm to offer a variety of activities, including making maple syrup in the traditional way. Details about this event can be found on the Mass Audubon website (massaudubon.org), where you can also find information about other properties with maple sugaring events.

A fun and delicious project to do with the kids is to make "sugar on snow." All you need is maple syrup and a container of snow. Heat the maple syrup in a saucepan on the stovetop until it reaches 234 degrees Fahrenheit. As soon as the syrup reaches the proper temperature, pour or drizzle it immediately over packed snow (shaved ice works too). Because it cools so rapidly, the maple syrup turns into a taffy-like string over the snow. Use a fork or a Popsicle stick to twirl it up, and enjoy.

To find a sugarhouse near you, visit the Massachusetts Maple Producers Association website (massmaple.org), which has a directory and map of sugarhouses in the state.

Trip 56

All
Ages

Moose Hill Farm

Moose Hill Farm has about 5 miles of trails ranging from meadows to pastures to woodlands. The farm's highest point offers unbeatable views of Boston.

Address: 396 Moose Hill Street, Sharon, MA
Hours: Dawn to dusk daily
Fee: Adults, $4; children under age 12 and Trustees of Reservations members, free
Contact: thetrustees.org; 781-784-0567
Bathrooms: None
Water/Snacks: None
Map: USGS Norwood, Brockton; thetrustees.org/assets/documents/places-to-
visit/trailmaps/Moose-Hill-Farm-Trail-Map.pdf
Directions by Car: From Boston, take I-95 South to Exit 10 (Coney Street,
Sharon, Walpole). Take a left off the exit and take the first right onto MA 27
North (Walpole). Take the first left onto Moose Hill Street, and you'll see the
parking lot. *GPS coordinates:* 42° 7.660′ N, 71° 12.632′ W.

A fun way to explore this Trustees of Reservations property with kids is by doing the Rooms in Time quest (available at the information box at the parking
lot). Rhyming clues and a map lead to a hidden treasure box and tell the story
of Moose Hill Farm, which served as an agricultural site as early as the 1600s.
The farm was the Kendall family estate for generations. At one point, fields
were cleared by ox, then were home to sheep and, later, dairy cows. The quest
takes a little over an hour and covers the entire property.

Today as you hike about, you'll see evidence of the property's past—cellar
holes, stone walls, and open fields. Many of the trails link to the adjacent Mass
Audubon Moose Hill Sanctuary. From the parking lot, take Old Farm Trail
(red blazes). You'll see a sign directing you to branch off to the left to get to the
Moose Hill fire tower, where the elevation is 466 feet. If you stay on Old Farm
Trail, it will lead to hillside hay fields for the great view of Boston. Visit when
snow covers the ground and you'll find peaceful snowshoeing opportunities.

If you're lucky, you might see wild turkeys and white-tailed deer, which
feed on the few American chestnut trees present here. This tree, once ubiquitous in the east, was nearly wiped out by a black fungus blight, which began in
the early 1900s.

Two girls are off and running on a Trustees of Reservations nature quest.

Remember: You can bring a dog if you have registered for the Trustees of Reservations' Green Dogs program, which is free for members.

PLAN B: Moose Hill Wildlife Sanctuary (Trip 55), a Mass Audubon property, is just next door.

WHERE TO EAT NEARBY: Take MA 27 back to Walpole, where restaurants and take-out spots are near the intersection of MA 27 and Main Street.

Trip 57

King Philip's Rock and Cave

Giant boulders, perfect for climbing, will entice kids on this short hike in the woods.

Address: 81–93 Mansfield Street, Sharon, MA
Hours: Dawn to dusk daily
Fee: Free
Contact: sharonfoc.org; 781-784-4533
Bathrooms: None
Water/Snacks: None
Map: USGS Brockton; sharonfoc.org/maps.html
Directions by Car: From Boston, take I-93 South to I-95 South to Exit 10 and turn left onto Coney Street. After about 1.5 miles, make a left turn onto MA 27 South/Upland Road and then turn right onto Pond Street. At the traffic circle, take the first exit onto Massapoag Avenue. Turn right onto Mansfield Street, and look for the small gravel driveway (room for four cars) and sign. *GPS coordinates: 42° 04.461′ N, 71° 10.801′ W.*

It's always fun to have a good story to go along with a hike, and King Philip's Rock and Cave offer more than just one. First, an Eagle Scout built the bulletin board shelter at the entrance on Mansfield Street as a service project, and Boy Scouts help maintain the trails.

The history of the rock and cave is a little mysterious. The site is thought to be an American Indian meeting place and is named for the Wampanoag leader Metacomet (also known as King Philip). American Indians might have met here to plan strategy during King Philip's War (1675–76). Some people surmise that ancient peoples observed the solstices and made other astronomical observations from the large rock formation now called King Philip's Rock.

Whatever the case, kids will love the easy hike to the large rocks formed by receding glaciers long ago. Trails extend from Sharon into Foxborough conservation land and entice bikers and cross-country skiers with wide, relatively flat paths. Start your hike by visiting the cave, then loop around to the rock. If you want an abbreviated hike, take only the 0.25-mile trail to the rock.

Remember: At the Mansfield parking area, you are between two houses. Be respectful of the neighbors.

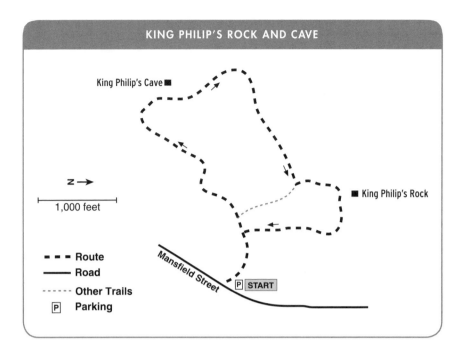

PLAN B: At Borderland State Park (Trip 59) you can hike, fish, paddle, ice-skate, and sled.

WHERE TO EAT NEARBY: Restaurants are in Sharon, where MA 27 crosses Main Street.

Trip 58

All Ages

Stony Brook Wildlife Sanctuary

Walking along boardwalks that cross over marshland, you are likely to see lots of wildlife here, from swans to great blue herons to turtles to frogs.

Address: 108 North Street, Norfolk, MA
Hours: Trails: dawn to dusk daily; nature center: 10 A.M. to 4 P.M. Tuesday through Saturday, 12:30 P.M. to 4 P.M. Sunday, 10 A.M. to 4 P.M. Mondays in July and August
Fee: Adults, $4; children ages 3–12, $3; Mass Audubon members, free
Contact: massaububon.org; 508-528-3140
Bathrooms: At the nature center
Water/Snacks: Water fountain in the nature center
Map: USGS Franklin
Directions by Car: From Boston, take I-93 South to I-95 South to Exit 9, where you merge onto US 1 South/Boston–Providence Turnpike toward Foxborough/Wrentham. Stay on US 1 for about 4 miles, then turn right onto Pine Street. In less than 0.5 mile, turn right onto MA 115 North/Pine Street. After 2.5 miles, take a left onto North Street. The sanctuary and parking lot will be on the right. *GPS coordinates:* 42° 6.466′ N, 71° 19.046′ W.

Much of this hike involves walking along boardwalks over and around Teal Marsh, Kingfisher Pond, and Stony Brook Pond. Take Pond Loop Trail, which starts at Sensory Trail (which is a wheelchair-accessible loop), and make sure you take the short detour along Beech Grove Loop. (You'll also be crossing through some woods and fields along the way.) The whole trip is just over 1 mile and is suitable for snowshoeing.

On a recent visit, we searched in vain for otters that we were told swim here, but we were rewarded with a pair of swans that came to eat right below a section of the boardwalk. We watched quietly while the gorgeous creatures fished at a shallow part of the Kingfisher Pond and then swam off. Later, as we ate lunch at a picnic table near the nature center, we also spotted a great blue heron flying overhead. Clearly, the ponds and marsh are rich feeding grounds for birds at this Mass Audubon sanctuary.

Remember: Don't forget binoculars and a camera when you visit. You're bound to want a closer look at all the birds here.

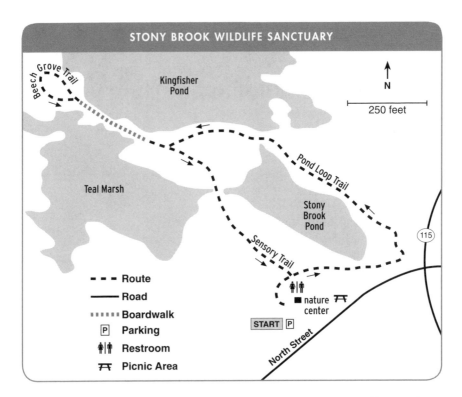

PLAN B: Moose Hill Wildlife Sanctuary (Trip 55) and Moose Hill Farm (Trip 56) are both about 20 minutes away by car.

WHERE TO EAT NEARBY: The town of Norfolk is north of the sanctuary on MA 115 and its main street offers a few options for dining. US 1 has plenty of mainstream chain restaurants too.

Trip 59

Borderland State Park

This former country estate has more than 20 miles of trails, six ponds, and a historic property to explore.

Address: 259 Massapoag Avenue, North Easton, MA
Hours: Park: 8 A.M. to sunset daily; mansion tours: third Sunday of the month, April through November, from 1 to 3 P.M., $3
Fee: Parking lot: $2 per vehicle
Contact: mass.gov/dcr; 508-238-6566
Bathrooms: At the visitor center
Water/Snacks: Water fountains inside and in front of the visitor center
Map: USGS Mansfield; mass.gov/dcr/parks/borderland/brochures.htm
Directions by Car: From Boston, take MA 128 North to I-95 South. Take Exit 10 (Sharon, Walpole, and Coney Street) and make a left. Drive about 2.5 miles and bear right onto Pond Street. Follow Pond Street for 1.5 miles until you come to a traffic circle. Go halfway around and continue onto Massapoag Avenue. The park will be 3 miles ahead on your left. Pay at the self-service station at the entrance, then park in the lot. *GPS coordinates: 42° 3.739′ N, 71° 09.896′ W.*

The 1,800-acre Borderland State Park offers a recreational smorgasbord of activities. From fishing on one of six ponds to hiking or biking on extensive trails to picnicking on the perfectly manicured lawn of the historic mansion, outdoor enthusiasts can't fail to find something fun to do.

The property was once a country estate in the 1900s and got its name from its location straddling the towns of Sharon and Easton. The Ames home, a three-story stone mansion built in 1910, is the centerpiece of the park. In 1971, the state of Massachusetts acquired the estate and opened it as a state park.

The 3-mile Pond Walk, which starts next to the visitor center and loops around Leach Pond, is a good walk for families. The path follows old farm roads and goes through hay fields. If 3 miles seems too long, you can go down to the pond to skip rocks and then take a spur onto either Swamp Trail or Quiet Woods Trail. Both trails lead back to the lawn of the estate. If you bring your own disc, you can play disc golf at Borderland, which has 18 "holes." In winter, you can ice skate on the ponds and sled behind the mansion.

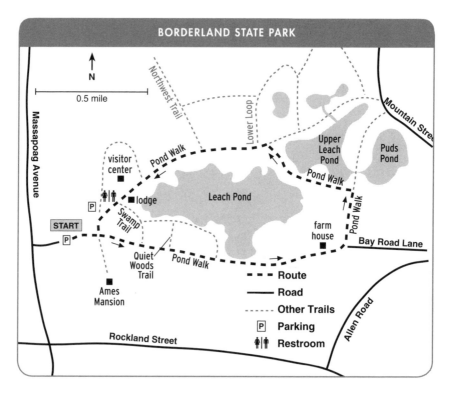

BORDERLAND STATE PARK

Choose from more than 20 miles of hiking trails in total, including a section of the Bay Circuit Trail (see page 100). Trails range from moderate to difficult, and the rangers are happy to offer advice on which trail to take. Anytime you visit, you're bound to see kids on mountain bikes, people walking their dogs, and usually someone on horseback.

Remember: You can visit the mansion only on tours offered by the Friends of Borderland on the third Sunday of the month between April and November. Call the park to confirm hours.

PLAN B: Nearby Moose Hill Wildlife Sanctuary (Trip 55), a Mass Audubon property, has another 25 miles to hike and explore.

WHERE TO EAT NEARBY: A few cafés and pizza places are on Pond Street in Sharon.

Section 5

Southern Massachusetts and Cape Cod

LOCATOR MAP

Trip 60

All Ages

Quincy Shores Reservation:
Wollaston Beach

Minutes from Boston, Wollaston Beach is a summertime family favorite.

Address: Quincy Shore Drive, Quincy, MA
Hours: Dawn to dusk daily
Fee: Free
Contact: wollastonbeach.org; 617-727-5290
Bathrooms: At the bathhouse (located opposite the beach, open July through September)
Water/Snacks: Water fountains along Quincy Shore Drive
Map: USGS Boston South
Directions by Car: From Boston, take I-93 South to take Exit 12 toward Neponset/Quincy. Take a slight left onto Quincy Shore Drive. Plenty of parking is along Quincy Shore Drive and in the lot between Rice Road and Fenno Street. *GPS coordinates:* 42° 16.607′ N, 71° 0.636′ W.
Directions by Public Transit: Take the Red Line to Wollaston, then walk northeast about 20 minutes to the shore.

Wollaston Beach is part of the Quincy Shore Reservation. The 2.3-mile beach, which is supervised by lifeguards in summer, is a family favorite. You can easily spend all day here. If you need a break from the beach, it's definitely worth checking out Caddy Memorial Park and Moswetuset Hummock, also part of the reservation.

Caddy Park, on the southern end of the beach, has a play area, a lookout tower, picnic tables, and 15 acres of fields and marsh. Around the play area, large rocks engraved with interesting nature facts offer impromptu lessons. Kids can learn about estuaries, salt marshes, gray squirrels, and more. On the northern end, Moswetuset Hummock, a National Historic Site, is the former summer campsite of American Indians during the 1600s. A short loop trail here leads to the beach.

The Friends of Wollaston Beach (wollastonbeach.org) hold a number of events, such as kite-flying contests and ice cream socials. Visit their website for a schedule.

Kids love digging in the sandy Wollaston Beach,
building sand castles before the tide comes in.

Remember: If you plan to stay on the beach, bring an umbrella and plenty of water.

PLAN B: Castle Island (Trip 6) is just minutes away and is a great place to watch planes taking off from and landing at Logan Airport.

WHERE TO EAT NEARBY: Several clam shacks are along Quincy Shore Drive.

Trip 61

Quincy Quarries Reservation

Visit the place where the granite for the Bunker Hill Monument was quarried.

Address: 77 Ricciuti Drive, West Quincy, MA
Hours: Dawn to dusk daily
Fee: Free
Contact: mass.gov/dcr; 617-727-4573
Bathrooms: None
Water/Snacks: None
Map: USGS Boston South; mass.gov/dcr/parks/metroboston/quincyquarries.pdf
Directions by Car: From Boston, take I-93 South to Exit 8 toward Furnace Brook Parkway and turn onto Ricciuti Drive. The parking lot has plenty of spaces. *GPS coordinates: 42° 14.549′ N, 71° 2.137′ W.*
Directions by Public Transit: Take the Red Line to Ashmont and switch to the #214 bus toward Quincy Station. Get off at Willard Street near California Avenue and walk south to Ricciuti Drive.

The granite quarry is a good place for kids to learn some Boston history. Park rangers offer programs year-round.

This reservation is managed by the Department of Conservation and Recreation, and park rangers offer programs year-round detailing its history. Serious rock climbers enjoy the quarries, but you don't need to be one to climb here. Kids will like scrambling over some of the smaller granite outcroppings.

If your child has visited the historic Bunker Hill Monument in Charlestown, he or she may be interested to know that its materials came from here, the birthplace of America's large-scale granite quarrying industry. In its heyday, there were more than 50 quarries here. Granite from Quincy was used in buildings across the country. The last active quarry closed in 1963.

The Granite Railway Quarry, one of the more important quarries here, opened in 1830 and was active into the 1940s. Abandoned, it began to fill with water and eventually had depths of up to 300 feet. It was a popular yet very unsafe diving and swimming hole, so it was drained and filled; it now makes up part of the 22-acre park.

Remember: Long pants and sturdy footwear, such as hiking boots or sneakers, are recommended for rock climbing. Keep your dog on a leash and clean up after it.

PLAN B: If the kids would rather play in the sand than on granite, visit Wollaston Beach (Trip 60) only about 10 minutes away.

WHERE TO EAT NEARBY: Get back on Furnace Brook Parkway and take a left onto Adams Street, where you'll find lots of dining options in West Quincy.

Geocaching is a treasure hunt of sorts, using a global positioning system (GPS) device to find a hidden container, or cache. Inside the cache you might find anything from trinkets for trading to a logbook in which you sign your name to show that you were there. The terms "letterboxing" and "questing" are often used interchangeably with geocaching, but they are different. Letterboxing, for one, has a much longer history, dating back to the 1800s, and usually involves solving puzzles or elaborate clues. Participants use rubber stamps to record their discoveries. Geocaching came about when the technology evolved to allow everyday people to pinpoint destinations with precision. However, the principle is the same with both: Find the hidden box. The Mass Audubon Society offers some quests at several of its properties. Other public spaces, such as the Arnold Arboretum, call their treasure hunt a letterboxing adventure.

Geocache.com is the largest website dedicated to the outdoor sport, and it's free to join. If your child needs motivation to get outside other than enjoying a nature walk, this might be the ticket for you. You can search for geocaches by general location, degree of difficulty, or when the cache was last found. An amusing one I discovered was a toy car cache, for which you bring toy cars to trade. This was one of more than 600 geocaches listed within 10 miles of my house!

You may think that finding a box with GPS is a no-brainer, but hiders often go to extremes to disguise their boxes. Some may be camouflaged, hidden in holes in tree trunks, or covered by rocks and leaves. Other hikers may have found them and not put them back precisely. A suggestion by Geocache.com should be taken to heart: Plan on looking for several caches in the same region in case you can't find one or, better yet, because your kids love finding them so much, they want to continue.

Letterboxing.org, also free to join, has a specific children's page describing how to make personalized rubber stamps. Letterboxing can be really appealing to younger children because many like to use rubber stamps and ink pads. Make sure your child brings a journal or a logbook because usually the letterbox has a unique stamp, as well as a logbook, inside. The idea is to stamp your journal to record your visit and leave an imprint of your personal stamp in the letterbox journal to say you were there.

Before setting out, you should make it clear to your child that sometimes you won't be able to find a box, for any number of reasons, and the point of the activity is the adventure. A final note: Geocaches are not supposed to be located in wilderness areas. Geocache hiders, and seekers, should respect the environment and follow Leave No Trace principles (see page xxvii).

Trip 62

World's End

Saved time and again from development, World's End is a wonderful place to stroll, picnic, and enjoy spectacular views of Boston.

Address: 250 Martin's Lane, Hingham, MA
Hours: 8 A.M. to sunset daily
Fee: Adults, $5; children and Trustees of Reservations members, free
Contact: thetrustees.org; 781-740-7233
Bathrooms: Portable toilets by the entrance
Water/Snacks: Water fountain near the entrance
Map: USGS Hull; thetrustees.org/assets/documents/places-to-visit/trailmaps/World-s-End-Trail-Map.pdf
Directions by Car: From Boston, take I-93 South to Exit 7. From MA 3, take Exit 14 to MA 228 North for 6.5 miles. Turn left onto 3A and follow for less than 1 mile and turn right onto Summer Street. Cross over Rockland Street and continue across onto Martin's Lane, which leads to the entrance and parking area. *GPS coordinates: 42° 15.493′ N, 70° 52.435′ W.*

As the crow flies, World's End is just 15 miles away from Boston. The amazing views of the city's skyline from this 250-acre Trustees of Reservations property are one of the payoffs of visiting.

The area, however, was almost lost to the public, having narrowly escaped becoming a 163-house residential subdivision in the late nineteenth century. Wealthy Boston businessman John Brewer bought a farming estate in the 1880s and hired landscape architect Frederick Law Olmsted in 1890 to plan and design a community of residences. The homes were never built. Later, in 1945, the property was short-listed for the site of the United Nations headquarters, which ultimately found a home in New York City. Twenty years later, it was looked at as a possible site for a nuclear power plant. Finally, in 1967, the land was bought by the nonprofit and saved for us to enjoy.

Olmsted's 4 miles of carriage roads remain to this day and are perfect for walking and snowshoeing, and cross-country skiers in particular enjoy the gentle slopes. Habitats here include saltwater marshes, meadows, and woodlands. Kids will enjoy exploring the rocky beach along the sandbar that con-

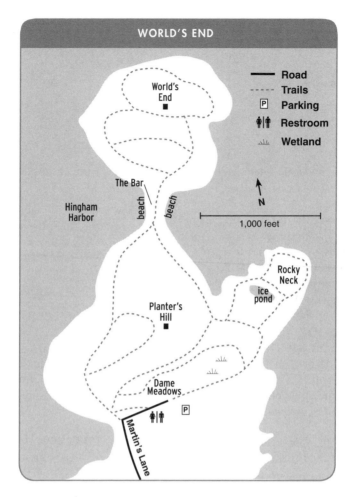

WORLD'S END

World's End

The Bar

Hingham Harbor

beach · beach

Road
Trails
P Parking
Restroom
Wetland

N

1,000 feet

Rocky Neck

ice pond

Planter's Hill

Dame Meadows

Martin's Lane

P

nects the Planter's Hill drumlin (an elongated hill formed by glacial drift) to the World's End drumlin.

Remember: Keep your dog on a leash and clean up after it.

PLAN B: Wompatuck State Park (Trip 64) is a great place to go bike riding.

WHERE TO EAT NEARBY: Head to the center of Hingham, where you can find restaurants on North Street.

Trip 63

Weir River Farm

Weir River Farm, one of the last working farms in Hingham, is a charming attraction for kids.

Address: Turkey Hill Lane, Hingham, MA
Hours: Trails: dawn to dusk daily; barnyard: seasonal
Fee: Trails: free; Barnyard: small admission fee for nonmembers of The Trustees of Reservations
Contact: thetrustees.org; 781-740-7233
Bathrooms: Portable toilet at the barnyard available when the barnyard is open
Water/Snacks: None
Map: USGS Weymouth; thetrustees.org/assets/documents/places-to-visit/trailmaps/Weir-River-Farm-Trail-Map.pdf
Directions by Car: From Boston, take I-93 South to Exit 7. Merge onto MA 3A South, then take Exit 15. Turn right onto Derby Street, then left onto Cushing Street. After 1.6 miles, turn right to stay on Cushing Street. Turn left onto MA 228 North, then turn right onto Leavitt Street just before the Hingham Town Library. Follow for 0.6 mile and bear left onto Turkey Hill Lane to the parking lot. Another lot is beyond this one, with room for five cars. *GPS coordinates:* 42° 41.896′ N, 71° 06.628′ W.

Although you can visit Weir River Farm all year long, if you have fans of farm animals in your group, make sure to check the website of this Trustees of Reservations property to see when the barnyard is open. The 10-acre working farm is one of the last farms in Hingham, home to horses, pigs, cows, chickens, and sheep as well as an easy 1.5-mile loop trail. The farm gets its name from the Weir River, which passes through the property. Last time we visited, we found out that all the cows in the field had names that started with the letter Q. (It's a tracking system; each year, newborn calves are all named with the same letter).

Every Saturday from May through October, Weir River hosts Open Barnyard hours, when the public is invited to visit the animals and watch the farmers at work. On Wednesdays from June through September, the farm hosts an outdoor story hour. Several other family-friendly activities are held year-round, including school vacation camps and after-school programs.

Besides fields and pastures, the grounds include oak and red cedar woodlands and grasslands. If you'd like to take a longer trek, you can get to the

One of Hingham's last working farms offers a glimpse of grazing belted Galloway cows.

adjacent Whitney and Thayer Woods on trails at the farm. The trails also connect to Wompatuck State Park and the Triphammer Conservation Area. Altogether, at nearly 5,000 acres, the trail network is the largest contiguous tract of open space on the South Shore.

Remember: If the barnyard isn't open, you may still see grazing animals. Just warn kids there's no guarantee.

PLAN B: For an oceanside adventure, head to nearby Nantasket Beach Reservation (Trip 65).

WHERE TO EAT NEARBY: Hingham has a variety of dining options, from upscale restaurants to clam shacks.

Trip 64

Wompatuck State Park

Wompatuck offers miles of fantastic trails for biking, hiking, or cross-country skiing. Visitors can also turn a day trip into an overnight at one of the park's wooded campsites.

Address: 1 Union Street, Hingham, MA
Hours: Dawn to dusk daily
Fee: Free
Contact: mass.gov/dcr; 781-749-7160
Bathrooms: At the visitor center
Water/Snacks: Water fountain next to the bathrooms
Map: USGS Weymouth; mass.gov/dcr/parks/trails/wompatuck.pdf
Directions by Car: From Boston, take I-93 South to Exit 7 onto MA 3 South. Take Exit 14 to the intersection of MA 228. Follow MA 228 North about 5 miles, turn right onto Free Street, and follow it 1 mile to the park entrance. Parking is on the right. *GPS coordinates:* 42° 13.002′ N, 70°51.778′ W.

Wompatuck State Park is a fantastic place to take kids bike riding. Twelve miles of paved bicycle trails, in addition to miles of wooded bridle paths and hiking trails, offer lots of riding options. The park is popular with campers and has more than 250 wooded campsites (some with electricity). In winter, the trails are perfect for cross-country skiing.

The park is named after an American Indian chief whom the local colonists knew as Josiah Wompatuck. In 1665, Chief Wompatuck deeded the park and the surrounding land to the English settlers. During World War II, the park was used as an ammunition depot by the U.S. military.

Kids will love to visit Mount Blue Spring, a source of fresh drinking water where you can fill up your water containers for free. It's near the campground. Stop at the visitor center for a map, and check in advance about special programs. Rangers lead hikes, discuss insects and animals that live in the park, and hold Junior Ranger programs on topics such as fire safety and preparing a campsite.

Remember: Fishing is allowed in the Cohasset Reservoir, but only car-top (nonmotorized) boats are allowed. Keep your dog on a leash and clean up after it.

Kids love searching for creatures large and small, such as this frog hiding among lily pads.

PLAN B: World's End (Trip 62) is quite close by and has stunning views of the Boston skyline and easy carriage paths to hike, as well as a rocky beach where kids can comb for sea glass or flat rocks for skipping.

WHERE TO EAT NEARBY: Hingham has a variety of dining options, from upscale restaurants to casual clam shacks.

Trip 65

Nantasket Beach Reservation

This beach has been a popular spot for beach lovers since the nineteenth century.

Address: Route 3A, Hull, MA
Hours: Dawn to dusk daily
Fee: Free
Contact: mass.gov/dcr; 617-727-5290
Bathrooms: At the comfort station
Water/Snacks: Water fountains along the promenade
Map: USGS Hull
Directions by Car: Take I-93 South to MA 3 South and get off at Exit 14 (MA 228). Take a left at the bottom of the ramp and cross over MA 53 to stay on MA 228. Parking is along the beach and in a garage. *GPS coordinates: 42° 16.031' N, 70° 50.996' W.*

Nantasket Beach Reservation is a 26-acre ocean playground. From the late 1800s, Hull (known by the Wampanoags as Nantasket, meaning "at the straight" or "low-tide place"), was the place to see and be seen. It had the largest summer hotel in the nation, and in its golden age, luminaries such as President Grover Cleveland and President Calvin Coolidge visited. At one point, there was an amusement park—the historic Paragon Carousel is a landmark to that era and still brings thrills to small kids.

Today, besides swimming, sunbathing, and building sandcastles, you can enjoy concerts and public dance lessons in summer. The 1.5-mile promenade trail along the shore is great for people-watching and enjoying the views.

Remember: Lifeguards are on duty from late June to early September. At other times, swimming is at your own risk.

PLAN B: Visit the Hull Lifesaving Museum, where you can learn about the region's lifesaving tradition and maritime history.

WHERE TO EAT NEARBY: A number of options for dining are along the beach.

Trip 66

South Shore Natural Science Center

Address: 48 Jacobs Lane, Norwell, MA

Hours: Trails: dawn to dusk daily; science center: 9:30 A.M. to 4:30 P.M. Monday through Saturday

Fee: Trails: free; science center: adults, $7; children ages 2–15, $3

Contact: ssnsc.org; 781-659-2559

Bathrooms: At the science center

Water/Snacks: Water fountain in the center

Map: USGS Cohasset

Directions by Car: From Boston, take I-93 South to Exit 7 and merge onto MA 3 South. After 10 miles take Exit 13 to MA 53 North toward MA 123. Turn left onto MA 53, then make a right onto MA 123 North. In less than 0.5 mile, turn left on Jacob's Lane. The center and parking lot will be on the left. *GPS coordinates: 42° 9.645' N, 70° 50.6' W.*

An employee shows off Hedwig, the Natural Science Center's resident barred owl.

The South Shore Natural Science Center is located on 30 acres of land surrounded by 200 acres of town conservation/recreation land consisting of meadows, woodland, and a pond. You can hike six trails, but the main attraction here is the EcoZone museum.

Interactive exhibits in the museum focus on southeastern Massachusetts's wetlands, woodlands, and meadows ecosystems. Kids will love to see the live turtles and frogs, and a tunnel underneath the turtle pond exhibit allows kids to crawl through, peer up at turtles from below, and watch them swimming.

Other animals to visit include snakes and spotted salamanders, and a favorite is the barred owl, Hedwig, who lives behind the building. At the small working greenhouse, you can see a Venus flytrap as well as a variety of other plants; there is also a rainforest section. Jacob's Pond, behind the center, offers a fun boardwalk trek leading to a bench overlooking the pond and marsh. Smaller children will delight in following the storybook trail behind the center, which is a short trail marked with pages from a book about a city mouse and a country mouse.

Remember: The center offers extensive programming throughout the year, from walks to animal education to archaeology, for families and kids. Call ahead or visit the website for dates and details.

PLAN B: Wompatuck State Park (Trip 64) is just north of the center and offers camping and lots of trails for bike riding.

WHERE TO EAT NEARBY: Take MA 123, which turns into Main Street, into Norwell to find places to eat.

Duxbury Beach Reservation

A beautiful barrier beach offers miles of sand and surf to play in or stroll along.

Address: 435 Gurnet Road, Duxbury, MA
Hours: 9 A.M. to 8 P.M. daily
Fee: Parking lot: $15 per vehicle
Contact: duxburybeachpark.com; 781-837-3112
Bathrooms: At the bathhouse (seasonally)
Water/Snacks: Water available at the bathhouse (seasonally); snack bar open from Memorial Day through Labor Day
Map: USGS Duxbury
Directions by Car: From Boston, take I-93 South to MA 3 South to Exit 11. Take a right off the ramp and go straight onto MA 14/MA 139. Follow signs for MA 139 and bear right on Canal Street, which turns into Gurnet Street. Signs will lead to the park and parking lot. *GPS coordinates:* 42° 3.030′ N, 70° 38.667′ W.

Duxbury Beach is a 6-mile-long barrier beach that extends from Marshfield in the north to Gurnet Point and Saquish in the south. The nonprofit Duxbury Beach Reservation owns about 4 miles of the beach and leases most of it to the Town of Duxbury for use by local residents and the general public.

The beach is a bit rocky in parts, so bring water shoes for children's tender feet. It never really gets overcrowded at this beach, so you'll have plenty of room to spread out, play games, and build sandcastles. Besides people, piping plovers also like to visit the beach. When it is low tide, kids will enjoy being able to walk quite far out to collect shells and rocks.

Remember: Make sure to go to the public parking area; the reservation parking area is for Duxbury residents only.

PLAN B: The Mass Audubon Society's North Hill Marsh, also in Duxbury, is an 823-acre property that has lots of trails around a 90-acre pond.

WHERE TO EAT NEARBY: A snack bar sells sandwiches and ice cream, while a restaurant serves dinner Thursday through Sunday. Both are open Memorial Day through Labor Day.

Trip 68

Myles Standish State Forest

This 14,000-acre park, popular with campers and bicyclists, has miles of trails to explore.

Address: 194 Cranberry Road, South Carver, MA
Hours: Dawn to dusk daily
Fee: Trails: free; College Pond day use: $5
Contact: mass.gov/dcr; 508-866-2526
Bathrooms: At the interpretive center
Water/Snacks: Water available at the interpretive center and campsites
Map: USGS Wareham; mass.gov/dcr/parks/trails/mssf1.pdf
Directions by Car: From Boston, take I-93 South to Exit 7 onto MA 3 South. Take Exit 5 and turn right onto Long Pond Road. Continue for about 3 miles to the main park entrance. The parking lot is on the right. *GPS coordinates:* 41° 50.360′ N, 70° 41.456′ W.

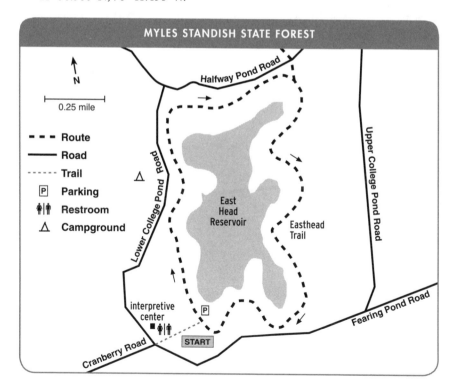

This enormous state park, which reaches across the southern sections of Plymouth and Carver, is the largest publicly owned recreation area in southeastern Massachusetts. It is popular with campers, who have a choice of five camping areas in the forest or next to four of the park's sixteen ponds.

Overall, 15 miles of bicycle trails, 35 miles of equestrian trails, and 13 miles of hiking trails go deep into the forest, which is one of the largest pitch pine–scrub oak forests in New England. This is a great place to teach kids to ride a bike and for families to enjoy a safe ride together. Throughout the forest are several coastal-plain kettle ponds. In summer, rangers lead interpretive programs, pond shore walks, and cranberry bog explorations. In winter, the trails are perfect for cross-country skiing and snowshoeing.

At the main park office, pick up a nature trail guide, then take a 3-mile hike around the East Head Reservoir, which is behind the interpretive center. The reservoir was made in 1868 and is still used to irrigate nearby cranberry bogs in fall.

Remember: A day-use area at College Pond offers picnicking, swimming, fishing, and canoeing. The fee is $5.

PLAN B: Plimoth Plantation, a wonderful seventeenth-century living history museum, is about 10 miles northeast of the park.

WHERE TO EAT NEARBY: Along Plymouth's main drag on Water Street, you'll find numerous restaurants.

Trip 69

All Ages

Scusset Beach State Reservation

Set along the Cape Cod Canal, Scusset Beach State Reservation is popular for swimming, fishing, and biking.

Address: 140 Scusset Beach Road, Sandwich, MA
Hours: 8 A.M. to 6 P.M. daily
Fee: Parking lot: $7 per vehicle
Contact: mass.gov/dcr; 508-888-0859
Bathrooms: At the park headquarters and at the bathhouse
Water/Snacks: Water fountain at the bathhouse; concession stand in summer
Map: USGS Sagamore
Directions by Car: From Boston, take I-93 South to Exit 7 onto MA 3 South. Take Exit 1A for US 6 West. Keep left at the fork and follow signs for Scusset Beach Road. Turn left at the Scenic Highway and continue on Meetinghouse Lane to Scusset Beach Road, where you'll find several parking lots. *GPS coordinates:* 41° 46.490′ N, 70° 31.068′ W.

Scusset Beach, located on Cape Cod Bay at the east end of the Cape Cod Canal, has a beautiful sandy beach and a long stone jetty that extends from the end of the service road into Cape Cod Bay, separating the canal from Scusset Beach. Kids will love to climb the rocks and walk down to the end. The jetty is also a popular area to fish, and a fishing pier is at the first parking lot. You can gain access to the Cape Cod Canal Bikeway (see below) from the beach.

The 98-site camping area at the beach is usually filled to capacity in summer, and some people camp here well into winter. Reservations are accepted six months in advance. The majority of sites are for RVs ($20 per night), but five are tent sites ($15 per night). For a family vacation on a Cape Cod beach, this is a great deal. A 0.7-mile trail to the left of the first parking lot goes to Sagamore Hill, where you can visit an area that was once an American Indian meeting ground. Later, it was the site of a World War II coastal fortification.

Nearby, the U.S. Army Corps of Engineers runs the Cape Cod Canal Visitor Center, where you can learn about the area's history, the operation of the Cape Cod Canal, and the U.S. Army Corps of Engineers (60 Ed Moffitt Drive, Sandwich; 508-833-9678). It's open May through October.

Tidal pools, offering a chance to spot sea life, fascinate kids.

Remember: The parking fee is enforced from 9 A.M. to 5:30 P.M. If you arrive earlier, stop at the park office to pay, as the gate is unattended until 9 A.M.

PLAN B: The Cape Cod Canal Bikeway follows the Cape Cod Canal for about 7 miles through sections of Bourne and Sagamore.

WHERE TO EAT NEARBY: Several places to eat are along Scusset Beach Road.

Trip 70

Wellfleet Bay Wildlife Sanctuary

This sanctuary on Cape Cod is a magnet for wildlife with its salt marsh, sandy beach, pine woods, freshwater pond, and rare heath land.

Address: 291 State Highway, South Wellfleet, MA
Hours: Trails: 8 A.M. to dusk daily (8 A.M. to 8 P.M. daily in summer); nature center: 8:30 A.M. to 5 P.M. daily, Memorial Day through Columbus Day, 8:30 A.M. to 5 P.M. Tuesday through Sunday, Columbus Day to Memorial Day
Fee: Adults, $5; children ages 3–12, $3; Mass Audubon members, free
Contact: massaudubon.org; 508-349-2615
Bathrooms: At the nature center
Water/Snacks: Next to the bathrooms
Map: USGS Wellfleet; massaudubon.org/Nature_Connection/Sanctuaries/Wellfleet/maps.php
Directions by Car: From Boston, take I-93 South to MA 3 South, and cross the Sagamore Bridge to Cape Cod. Follow US 6 East for 45 miles. The sanctuary entrance and parking lot are on the left (after the Wellfleet Drive-in Theater). *GPS coordinates: 41° 53.006′ N, 69° 59.701′ W.*

Five miles of trails on the sanctuary's 1,100 acres offer a variety of habitats to explore—that is, if you can get your kids out of the nature center, which has two 700-gallon aquariums with displays revealing the underwater worlds of the salt marsh and the tidal flats, plus animal and plant exhibits, puzzles, and books about the Cape. You can also learn about green architecture, as the LEED-certified building features composting toilets, solar panels, and sustainable materials, all documented on display boards. An excellent gift shop offers books and fun nature items such as observation jars and hand lenses.

Outside are five main trails and a butterfly garden. Take Goose Pond Trail (part of which is wheelchair accessible) on foot or on snowshoes through pine and oak woodlands, by two ponds, past a coastal heath (low-growing shrubs and plants), and along the edges of a salt marsh. To get to the sandy beach, take Boardwalk Trail across the salt marsh to see what's going on at the tidal flats. Kids will enjoy watching hundreds of fiddler crabs crawling about the flats near the boardwalk. An amazing 260-plus species of birds have been recorded at the sanctuary, so chances are good you'll encounter some on your walk. Five species of turtles live here, so keep an eye out in the marsh and pond.

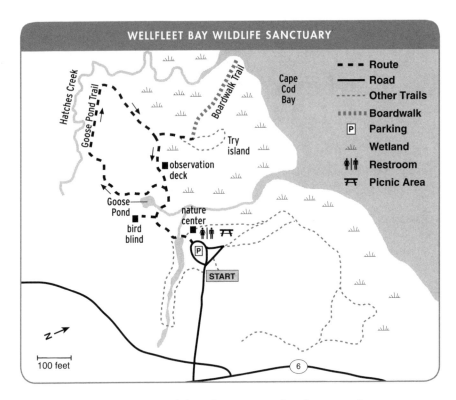

WELLFLEET BAY WILDLIFE SANCTUARY

If you've been a Mass Audubon Society member for more than a year, you can camp at one of twenty sites (tents only, no fires) the sanctuary maintains from Memorial Day to Columbus Day, but be sure to book well in advance.

Remember: Every Tuesday at 10 A.M., you can join naturalists and birders at the nature center for coffee and pastries to view birds at the feeding station and learn more about the many birds that visit the sanctuary. Check out the recent sightings board where animals that have been seen are listed to help you decide which trail to take. A number of naturalist programs are offered for younger children.

PLAN B: The Cape Cod National Seashore, farther east on US 6, offers many trails, beaches, and historic lighthouses to visit. The refuge is a short drive from the Wellfleet trailhead of the Cape Cod Rail Trail (Trip 71).

WHERE TO EAT NEARBY: Lobster shacks and other eateries are along US 6.

Trip 71

Cape Cod Rail Trail

This 22-mile trail is idyllic for bicyclists, with scenic beach views and easy riding.

Address: 50 Doane Road, Eastham, MA
Hours: Dawn to dusk daily
Fee: Free
Contact: mass.gov/dcr; 508-896-3491
Bathrooms: At the visitor center
Water/Snacks: Water fountain at the visitor center
Map: USGS Orleans; mass.gov/dcr/parks/trails/print/ccrt.pdf
Directions by Car: The Cape Cod Rail Trail is located in the mid-Cape area, in southeastern Massachusetts. You can start from multiple points, but to get to Cape Cod National Seashore at the Salt Pond Visitor Center in Eastham, where you can pick up maps, take MA 3 South to the Sagamore Bridge in Bourne. Follow US 6 eastward to Eastham and Provincetown. *GPS coordinates: 41° 50.274′ N, 69° 58.404′ W.*

For bikers and beach lovers, it doesn't get much better than the Cape Cod Rail Trail. The 22-mile paved trail on a former railroad right-of-way has few hills, is great for kids learning to ride or parents with kids in tow, and passes by multiple stopping points for food, beaches, and historic sites. If you pack a picnic, you can stop at one of the great spots to enjoy the view while you eat. Along the route, you'll pass through or by woods, marshes, cranberry bogs, and ponds. When snow covers the trail, take out your cross-country skis and experience the route on a different self-powered mode of transit.

The trail, open to walkers, runners, and horseback riders, passes through the towns of Dennis, Harwich, Brewster, Orleans, Eastham, and Wellfleet. Public restrooms can be found at Nickerson State Park in Brewster, Salt Pond Visitor Center at Cape Cod National Seashore in Eastham, and the National Seashore Headquarters in Wellfleet.

Since there are several places to gain access to the trail, you can consider your riding companions and plan accordingly. Is a short trek to a beach your best bet? A long ride with a picnic at the end? Or would you like to play it by ear? All are easy enough to do, and several places where you can stop to rest or refuel are available along the way. A number of side trails lead off the main

Leave time for detours to historic lighthouses near the Cape Cod Rail Trail.

trail. Nickerson State Park, near the trail's midpoint, is a great base for cyclists who want to spend more time in the area. The park offers 400 campsites, swimming, paddling, and fishing.

Remember: The trailhead for the rail trail is 0.5 mile away from the visitor center. A 1.6-mile bike trail also starts at the visitor center and goes to Coast Guard Beach. Several places to rent bikes are near the trail. Visit capecodbike guide.com for a list.

PLAN B: The Wellfleet Bay Wildlife Sanctuary (Trip 70), a Mass Audubon property right along the seashore, offers lovely trails and wildlife exhibits.

WHERE TO EAT NEARBY: A number of casual beach shack restaurants are along US 6. The trail also passes through downtown Orleans, where you can find a nice ice cream shop.

Section 6

North of Boston

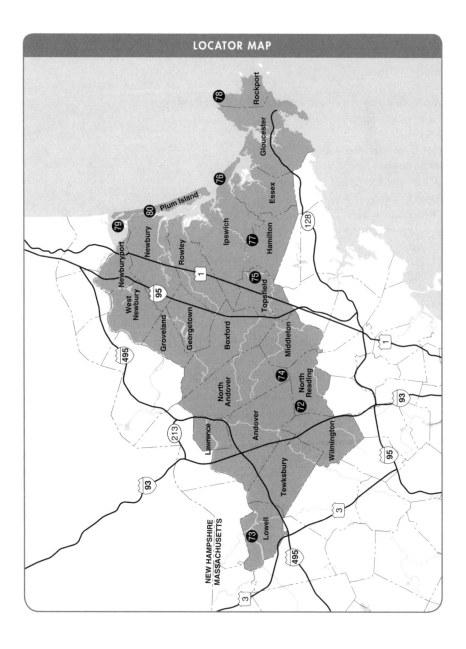

LOCATOR MAP

Trip 72

Martins Pond

Martins Pond, with a small beach and playground, is a popular place to bring young children.

Address: Burroughs Road (off MA 28), North Reading, MA
Hours: Dawn to dusk daily
Fee: Free
Contact: martinspond.org
Bathrooms: None
Water/Snacks: None
Map: USGS Reading
Directions by Car: From Boston, take I-93 North to Exit 40 to MA 62 East. Turn right onto MA 62, then after 1.6 miles, take a left onto North Street. In about 0.5 mile, take the second left onto MA 28 and then turn left again onto Burroughs Road. Clarke Park, which has a parking lot, is located about 0.25 mile down on the right. *GPS coordinates:* 42° 35.461′ N, 71° 7.498′ W.

Martins Pond is a 92-acre freshwater pond located just off a busy highway. The pond is about 2,000 feet across and about 3,050 feet long, with an average depth of less than 5 feet. The deepest point is only 7.25 feet deep. A small unsupervised public beach and a large playground are at Clarke Park, the main parking area for the pond. Grills, picnic tables, and sun shelters make this a great place for a cookout or family gathering.

At the small park you'll find Turtle Trail, a paved loop painted with numbered turtles and named for the snapping turtles that live around the pond. A pamphlet at the information box next to the parking lot is written for kids and describes the history of the area. The Martins Pond Association holds a few events at the pond during the year, including a haunted playground event at Halloween and a fishing derby.

Remember: Nonmotorized public boating is allowed, so bring a canoe or kayak to paddle around.

PLAN B: Head to the Harold Parker State Forest (Trip 74) for an off-the-beaten path adventure.

WHERE TO EAT NEARBY: Main Street in either direction has a variety of restaurants, grocery markets, and convenience stores.

Trip 73

Lowell National Historical Park

Downtown Lowell offers a glimpse into where America's Industrial Revolution began, as well as great opportunities for biking and paddling.

Address: 246 Market Street, Lowell, MA
Hours: Visitor center: 9 A.M. to 5 P.M.
Fee: Free
Contact: nps.gov/lowe; 978-970-5000
Bathrooms: At the visitor center
Water/Snacks: Water fountains near the bathroom
Map: USGS Lowell; nps.gov/pwr/customcf/apps/maps/showmap.cfm?alphacode =lowe&parkname=Lowell%20National%20Historical%20Park
Directions by Car: From Boston, take I-93 North to I-495 South to Exit 39 onto MA 133 West. Go about 5 miles and turn right onto MA 3A North. In less than 0.5 mile, turn right onto Market Street and to a small free parking lot at the visitor center lot at 304 Dutton Street. GPS coordinates: 42° 38.613′ N, 71° 18.883′ W.
Directions by Public Transit: Take the Lowell commuter rail train from North Station. The park is a 0.5-mile walk from the Lowell station.

Visitors can enjoy boat tours of the historic Lowell Canal system.

Lowell National Historical Park, in the heart of downtown Lowell, is a mix of museums, historic sites, and canals. The visitor center is inside Market Mills, the former Lowell Manufacturing Company mill complex. The city, with its textile mills, was the first large-scale planned industrial city in American history.

Take a tour at the center, pick up maps, explore exhibits, and watch the video "Lowell: The Industrial Revelation" to learn about the city and its history. Afterward you can ride on historic replica trolleys, cruise on the city's canals aboard a tour boat, or walk along 5.6-mile paved paths next to the canals. Interpretive signs give information about historic buildings along the way and the town's history.

The Concord River Greenway (CRG) is a multiuse trail that runs through the heart of Lowell. Amazingly, in spring, the Concord River transforms into a class 3/4 rapids, great for whitewater rafting. Along the trail, you can bike, walk, and fish. Pick up the trail east of the Lowell National Historical Park on Lawrence Street.

Remember: The annual Lowell Folk Festival in July is a popular family-friendly event.

PLAN B: Western Avenue Studios is a brick mill building with six floors of 143 studios filled with artists working in all disciplines, media, and styles. Visitors are welcome, and it is great place to bring kids to see art being created.

WHERE TO EAT NEARBY: A number of places to dine are on and around Market Street.

Tending a large garden or an orchard is not an option for many people, but you can still pick flowers, apples, pumpkins, blueberries, strawberries, and other produce at pick-your-own farms. Many families make picking apples or visiting a pumpkin patch an annual tradition.

To make even more out of your visit, preplan a project to do with the kids. If you've picked flowers, press some between two pieces of waxed paper and use an iron to seal the paper. Depending on the shape of the petals, you can make bookmarks, sun catchers, or greeting cards. If you've gone apple picking, teach your kids that applesauce doesn't just come from a jar; simmer a few pounds of cut-up apples with water, lemon, cinnamon, and sugar; mash the mix, then let it cool before serving. The process of picking the apples and then making something delicious with them will be satisfying for everyone.

Listed below are a few farms near some of the hikes in this book. To find more, look at the Massachusetts Farm and Orchard Guide (mass.gov/agr/massgrown), which lists pick-your-own farms as well as food tips, recipes, and events such as agricultural fairs.

Belkin Family Lookout Farm

Besides pick-your-own fruit—peaches, apples, and pumpkins—there's a play area, a "train" (actually a trolley of sorts) that takes you around the farm, pony rides, and other activities. *In South Natick; lookoutfarm.com. Near Broadmoor Wildlife Sanctuary (Trip 45).*

Berlin Farms

You can pick blueberries, raspberries, pumpkins, and corn here, and purchase fresh eggs or visit the heritage barnyard. *In Berlin; berlinorchards.com. Near Oxbow National Wildlife Refuge (Trip 43).*

Dowse Orchards

This 200-year-old family farm operation has 25 varieties of apples to pick as well as Christmas trees. *In Sherborn; dowseorchards.com. Near Rocky Narrows (Trip 46).*

Land's Sake Farm

Pick beans, peas, cherry tomatoes, strawberries, herbs, raspberries, blueberries, and flowers. *In Weston; landssake.org. Near College Pond (Trip 47).*

Parlee Farms

Parlee has pumpkins; 14 acres of apple trees; and gladioli, zinnias, sunflowers, and dahlias to pick, plus a petting zoo with goats, sheep, rabbits, and chickens; a play area; and a demonstration beehive. *In Tyngsboro; parleefarms.com. Near Lowell National Historical Park (Trip 73).*

Trip 74

Harold Parker State Forest

This state forest comprises more than 3,000 acres where visitors can hike, mountain bike, fish, hunt, cross-country ski, horseback ride, camp, and picnic.

Address: 305 Middleton Road, North Andover, MA
Hours: Dawn to dusk daily
Fee: Free
Contact: mass.gov/dcr; 978-686-3391
Bathrooms: At the park headquarters
Water/Snacks: None
Map: USGS Reading; mass.gov/dcr/parks/trails/harold.pdf
Directions by Car: From Boston, take I-93 North to Exit 41 and follow MA 125 North (toward Andover) for about 4 miles to Wildwood Road. Take a right there and go about 0.5 mile to Wethersfield Road and take another right. In less than 1 mile, turn right onto Salem Road, which turns into Middleton Road. You'll see the Berry Pond parking lot on the right, where this hike starts. (To get to the park headquarters, continue down Middleton.) *GPS coordinates: 42° 37.243′ N, 71° 5.078′ W.*

Once you visit Harold Parker State Forest, which lies in Andover, North Andover, North Reading, and Middleton, you'll be making plans to come back. With 3,500 acres, numerous trails, eleven ponds, and a variety of activities, one day or even a weekend is not enough time to enjoy all the forest offers.

For a first-time visit, start at Berry Pond, where you can hike to the site of an old quarry and mill, then circle around to end at the pond. Look for the Healthy Trail sign and white blazes near the parking lot to start this hike, which quickly leads to a boardwalk, then a gravel path, and finally a dirt path. You'll come to large granite rocks where kids will want to stop and climb. This is not the old quarry, but if you have younger kids, this is a good stopping point; you can shorten the trip here and head to Berry Pond.

Another option is to take a paved, accessible path from the parking lot, which makes getting to the pond easy with a stroller. At one point, the state forest allowed swimming here and built a large open shelter and a bathhouse with bathrooms, but the pond is now off-limits for swimming due to bacteria and the bathhouse is locked up. But that doesn't mean it's not fun to fish for bass or skip rocks at the pond, or throw a ball in the field.

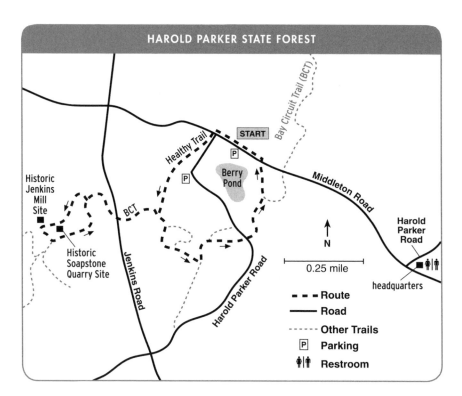

Overall, more than 35 miles of logging roads and trails are in the forest, including portions of the Bay Circuit Trail (see page 100). Nonmotorized boating is allowed on any of the ponds. The area was once inhabited by Pentacook Indians until it was settled by English farmers around 1650. According to park materials, many of the homes surrounding the forest were used as Underground Railroad hideouts in the 1850s, and Frederick Douglass, Harriet Beecher Stowe, and William Lloyd Garrison were frequent visitors to families in the area.

Remember: If you want to make a weekend trip, the Lorraine Park Campground on the property has 89 campsites with picnic tables and grills; camping is allowed late May to early September; reservations are accepted six months in advance. The fee is $12 per night. Only camp visitors are allowed to swim at Frye Pond.

PLAN B: Martins Pond in North Reading (Trip 72) offers a more urban and easily accessible outing.

WHERE TO EAT NEARBY: A few places to eat are south of MA 125 on MA 28.

Trip 75

Ipswich River Wildlife Sanctuary

Cool rock tunnels, a pond, and boardwalks make Ipswich River Wildlife Sanctuary a favorite with kids.

Address: 87 Perkins Row, Topsfield, MA

Hours: Trails: dawn to dusk Tuesday through Sunday and Monday holidays; visitor center: 9 A.M. to 4 P.M. Tuesday through Friday, 9 A.M. to 5 P.M. weekends and Monday holidays (November through April, visitor center closes at 4 P.M.)

Fee: Adults, $4; children ages 3–12, $3; Mass Audubon members, free

Contact: massaudubon.org; 978-887-9264

Bathrooms: Next to the parking lot

Water/Snacks: Water fountain by the parking lot; snacks in the visitor center

Map: USGS Salem; massaudubon.org/Nature_Connection/Sanctuaries/Ipswich_River/maps.php

Directions by Car: From Boston, take I-93 North to the Tobin Bridge and merge onto US 1 North. Go about 21 miles to MA 97. Turn right onto MA 97 South and follow for about 0.5 mile. Take a left onto Perkins Row and drive less than 1 mile to the sanctuary and its large parking lot on the right. *GPS coordinates:* 42° 37.899′ N, 70° 55.288′ W.

Within minutes of hiking or snowshoeing along Rockery Trail at this Mass Audubon sanctuary, you get a surprise that kids will love: huge rocks that were brought in to form part of an arboretum built in the 1900s. Tunnels, staircases, and bridges await exploration, and kids will happily spend their time climbing around and on them as long as you let them.

Once you move on, more than 10 miles of trails take you through forests, meadows, and wetlands. Rockery Trail goes around Rockery Pond, where you might see painted turtles basking in the sun as you wander past. Part of the trail is on a boardwalk, another kid-pleaser. Instead of heading directly back to the visitor center, take a left on Waterfowl Pond Trail to the Stone Bridge, where you can see evidence of beavers hard at work in the pond. Take Innermost Trail back to the visitor center. For an added exploration, cross the parking lot to the short Bunker Meadows Trail, which leads to an observation tower that kids will want to climb. (You could also start your hike here to get a lay of the land before setting out.)

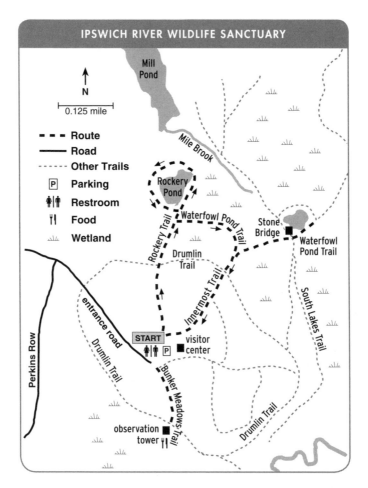

Volunteer docents are on duty on Sundays and Monday holidays between Labor Day and Memorial Day and offer information on all sorts of nature topics. Also, at 1 P.M. on Sundays, docents lead hour-long nature hikes. In the nature center, check out various exhibits and spend time watching birds at the outside feeders through a giant glass window.

Remember: Mass Audubon members can rent a canoe to paddle along the Ipswich River, spend the night at the sanctuary's one cabin, or camp on Perkins Island from May through October.

PLAN B: Nearby Appleton Farms and Grass Rides (Trip 77) is a charming seventeenth-century farm still in operation, also run by The Trustees of Reservations.

WHERE TO EAT NEARBY: Retrace your steps to MA 97 and head north into Topsfield. Along Main Street, you'll find a few options for dining.

Trip 76

All Ages

Crane Beach

White sand beaches, gorgeous views, and trails for hiking, snowshoeing, and cross-country skiing make Crane Beach a family favorite.

Address: 290 Argilla Road, Ipswich, MA
Hours: 8 A.M. to sunset daily
Fee: Admission fees vary depending on vehicle and time of day; Trustees of Reservations members receive a discount
Contact: thetrustees.org; 978-356-4354
Bathrooms: At the bathhouse
Water/Snacks: Water fountain near the bathhouse; snack bar open seasonally
Map: USGS Ipswich and Rockport; thetrustees.org/assets/documents/places-to-visit/trailmaps/Crane-Estate-Trail-Map.pdf
Directions by Car: From Boston, take I-93 North to Exit 27 onto US 1 North. Merge onto MA 128 North. Take Exit 20A onto MA 1A North. After about 8 miles, turn right onto MA 133 East and follow for 1.5 miles. Turn left onto Northgate Road and follow for about 0.5 mile. Turn right onto Argilla Road and follow until you reach the entrance and parking lot. *GPS coordinates:* 42° 41.077′ N, 70° 45.992′ W.

A seaside scavenger hunt at Crane Beach is an exciting way to spend the afternoon.

Crane Beach is well known as one of the most gorgeous beaches on the East Coast. It lives up to its reputation, but it's more than just a beach. The property is part of the Crane Estate, a complex of more than 2,000 acres comprising the beach, the dunes, Castle Hill, a wildlife refuge, and the 59-room Stuart-style mansion called the Great House on Castle Hill, all owned by The Trustees of Reservations.

More than 5 miles of trails lead through the protected coastal dunes, which are part of the Bay Circuit Trail (see page 100). Kids, however, will most likely want to stay by the water. Pick up a scavenger hunt from the visitor center—the laminated sheets are attached to a bucket—and explore the water's edge, looking for razor clam shells, sand dollars, crab shells, and other evidence of sea creatures. Trustees employees often have special family-friendly programs running in summer, so be sure to check their schedule.

Remember: Flotation devices are not allowed. You can bring a dog October 1 through March 30 if you have registered for the Trustees' Green Dogs program, which is free for members.

PLAN B: Nearby Appleton Farms and Grass Rides (Trip 77) is a charming seventeenth-century farm still in operation, also run by the Trustees.

WHERE TO EAT NEARBY: You can eat at the snack bar or head back to MA 133 for clam shacks and ice cream spots.

Trip 77

Appleton Farms and Grass Rides

Appleton Farms, the country's oldest working farm, has historic farm buildings to check out, cows to moo at, and easy walking trails to explore.

Address: MA 1A, Hamilton and Ipswich, MA
Hours: Dawn to dusk daily
Fee: Adults and children, $3; Trustees of Reservations members, free
Contact: thetrustees.org; 978-356-5728
Bathrooms: At the carriage barn in the farmstead
Water/Snacks: None
Map: USGS Salem; thetrustees.org/assets/documents/places-to-visit/trailmaps/
    Appleton-Farms-Trail-Map.pdf
Directions by Car: From Boston, take I-93 North to Exit 27 onto US 1 North.
    Merge onto MA 128 North. Take Exit 20A onto MA 1A North. Drive about
    7 miles and turn left onto Waldingfield Road to the parking lot. (Another
    parking area is at Highland Road.) *GPS coordinates:* 42° 39.363′ N, 70° 50.760′ W.

Appleton Farms, established in 1636, is not a relic by any means. The farm is still active, and The Trustees of Reservations runs a community supported agriculture (CSA) program as well as a grass-fed beef and dairy operation. Kids will like visiting the carriage barn to see the historic carriage collection and the stables with horse statues that re-create the feel of the barn in its heyday.

You can wander along 6 miles of footpaths, bridle paths, and farm roads (some of which are part of the Bay Circuit Trail—see page 100). I recommend parking at the Waldingfield Road entrance and making your way to the farm compound. At the map station here, you can pick up a laminated quest pamphlet that teaches kids about the farm's history and eventually leads them to a treasure box with a book in which they can sign their name and a stamp they can use on a notebook or piece of paper.

If you happen to visit at a time when the cows are being led into the barns or out to pasture, watching them parade by will delight smaller children.

The Grass Rides are actually avenues that were built for horseback and carriage driving. They comprise about 5 miles, and you may be lucky enough to spot some local horseback riders out for a walk. The Grass Rides are also popular in winter with cross-country skiers.

Kids can feed cows at America's oldest working farm.

Remember: The Trustees run a number of great family-friendly programs at the farm. Call or visit their website for details.

PLAN B: Crane Beach (Trip 76), another Trustees property, is minutes away and offers a very different outdoor experience.

WHERE TO EAT NEARBY: Clam shacks and ice cream stands are on MA 133.

Trip 78

Halibut Point State Park

Scrambling over rocks and checking out the many tidal pools at Halibut Point is a thrill for sea-life-loving kids.

Address: 5 Gott Avenue, Rockport, MA
Hours: 8 A.M. to 9 P.M. daily, Memorial Day to Labor Day; dawn to dusk daily, Labor Day to Memorial Day
Fee: Parking: $2, Memorial Day to Labor Day
Contact: mass.gov/dcr; 617-626-1267
Bathrooms: At the visitor center
Water/Snacks: Water fountain outside the visitor center
Map: USGS Rockport
Directions by Car: From Boston, take US 1 North and merge onto I-95/MA 128 North. After 12 miles, merge onto MA 128 North and drive about 20 miles toward Gloucester and Rockport. At the first traffic circle, follow MA 127 North (Annisquam and Pigeon Cove). After about 6 miles, you'll see a sign for the park on the left. *GPS coordinates:* 42° 41.217′ N, 70° 37.865′ W.

Trails here lead around the former Babson Farm Quarry, head down to the ocean, and feature stunning views and a number of tidal pools to explore. Start your day at the visitor center, located in a renovated 60-foot World War II fire tower. Exhibits explain the quarry's history. Halibut Point is made of sheets of 440-million-year-old granite. Starting in the 1840s, granite was quarried from this area. When the industry collapsed in 1929, owners of the quarry gave 17 acres on the eastern side to the nonprofit Trustees of Reservations, which jointly manages the area with the Department of Conservation and Recreation today.

Any kid who's played the game Telephone can appreciate how Halibut Point probably got its name: In the 1700s, sailors were wary of the rocky shoreline and had to "haul about" to avoid wrecking the ship on the point. Eventually the two words turned into "halibut."

After checking out the view from above, head to the beach and the tidal pools below. Kids will love looking for creatures that make their home here, such as starfish, tadpoles, and barnacles. Saturday mornings in season, rang-

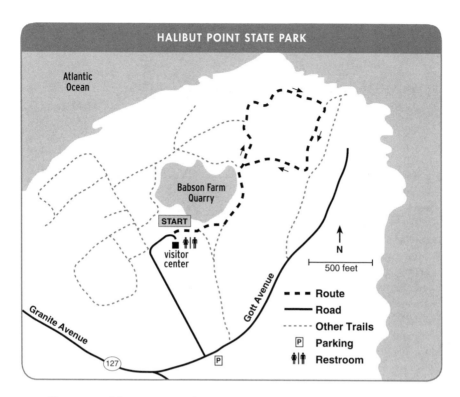

ers offer tours of the quarry and you can see a granite-cutting demonstration. Other programs include wildflower, seabird, and tide-pool walks.

Remember: The rocks can be slippery, so proper footwear is important. Keep your dog on a leash and clean up after it.

PLAN B: Rockport is a charming seaside town, and the waterfront area is fun to explore.

WHERE TO EAT NEARBY: MA 127 has classic lobster shacks along the road, and Rockport's waterfront area offers many other options.

Trip 79

Ages 5–8

Joppa Flats Education Center

Joppa Flats Education Center—with a children's education room, marine touch tanks, butterfly gardens, and interpretive displays—offers a great overview of the region.

Address: 1 Plum Island Turnpike, Newburyport, MA

Hours: 8:30 A.M. to 4 P.M. Tuesday through Sunday and Monday holidays

Fee: Suggested donation, $2; Mass Audubon members, free

Contact: massaudubon.org; 978-462-9998

Bathrooms: At the visitor center

Water/Snacks: Water fountain next to the bathrooms; vending machine; ice cream for sale and coffee and tea offered for a donation

Map: USGS Newburyport; massaudubon.org/Nature_Connection/Sanctuaries/Joppa_Flats/maps.php

Directions by Car: From Boston, take I-95 North to Exit 57 (MA 113, West, Newbury/Newburyport). At the end of the exit ramp, turn right onto MA 113 East. Drive for 3.8 miles through Newburyport to Rolfe's Lane in Newbury, where you take a left. At the end of the road, take a right and the center (and its parking lot) will be on the left. *GPS coordinates: 42° 47.934′ N, 70° 50.814′ W.*

Views from the Joppa Flats Education Center include the Merrimack River and salt marshes.

The two-story Joppa Flats Education Center sits right on the banks of the Merrimack River. The surrounding salt marshes, mudflats, rivers, bays, and coastal waters are a magnet for more than 300 species of birds, including the bald eagle and snowy owl, and many warblers, shorebirds, and waterfowl.

The education center at this Mass Audubon property offers a number of programs for children and families, such as walks and canoe trips, so it's advisable to call ahead or visit its website if you might be interested. However, the programs are not necessary for enjoying the center. Kids will like looking at the creatures in the marine tanks and peering through a telescope to see if they can spot anything outside. An excellent shop is stocked with nature guides and gifts. Outside, benches invite you to sit and watch the river go by and gardens planted to attract butterflies offer a peaceful setting.

Remember: There are no hiking trails on this property, but the visit is worthwhile for learning about the area. The knowledgeable staff is happy to talk with you and your kids and will offer advice on which trails you should take at nearby Parker River.

PLAN B: Parker River National Wildlife Refuge (Trip 80) and the Plum Island estuary are just a few minutes' drive away. Head there to explore the trails and habitats you've learned about at Joppa Flats.

WHERE TO EAT NEARBY: Quaint Newburyport offers many dining options from clam shacks to more upscale restaurants.

Trip 80

Parker River National Wildlife Refuge

This barrier island wildlife refuge is a haven for birds and people alike, with trails, beaches, and salt marshes.

Address: Sunset Drive, Newburyport, MA
Hours: Dawn to dusk daily
Fee: $5 per car; $2 if on foot or bike
Contact: fws.gov/northeast/parkerriver; 978-465-5753
Bathrooms: At Lot 1 (spring through fall); portable toilets available at other locations in the park (see map)
Water/Snacks: None
Map: USGS Newburyport; fws.gov/northeast/parkerriver/pdf/Parker%20 River%20Map.pdf
Directions by Car: From Boston, take I-95 North to Exit 57 (MA 113). At the end of the exit ramp, turn right onto MA 113 East and continue straight onto MA 1A South to the intersection with Rolfe's Lane. Turn left onto Rolfe's Lane and travel to the end, where you turn right onto the Plum Island Turnpike and cross the bridge to Plum Island. Take the first right onto Sunset Drive to the refuge entrance. You will be directed to whichever parking lot is open. *GPS coordinates: 42° 47.450′ N, 70° 48.597′ W.*

The Parker River National Wildlife Refuge was established in 1942 to provide a feeding, resting, and nesting habitat for migratory birds. Located on Plum Island, a barrier island, it is home to more than 300 species of resident and migratory birds as well as other animals. It is a critical habitat for the federally threatened piping plover.

Humans, however, can also enjoy a variety of activities at this special place, including swimming, hiking, snowshoeing, fishing, and, of course, bird-watching. In winter, this is one of the best places to spot snowy owls, which hunt in the open salt marshes.

Hellcat Interpretive Trail is a good hike for kids. The 1.5-mile trail has numbered posts that correspond to a narrative brochure (pick one up at the trailhead, refuge headquarters, or the entrance gatehouse). Take the Dune

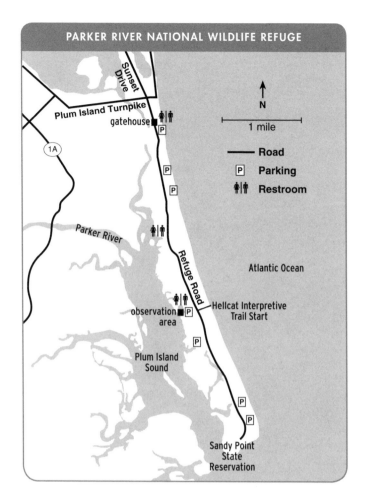

Sunset Drive

Plum Island Turnpike

gatehouse

1A

Parker River

Refuge Road

Atlantic Ocean

Hellcat Interpretive Trail Start

observation area

Plum Island Sound

Sandy Point State Reservation

N

1 mile

—— Road

P Parking

Restroom

Loop part of the trail to go up a 50-foot-tall dune for a 360-degree view of the island. If you have a canoe or kayak, you can launch across from Lot 1.

The great thing about the reservation is the small number of other visitors you'll encounter, since the refuge limits cars. Particularly in summer, plan to come early or arrive late to get in. If you can, go to the Sandy Point State Reservation beach all the way at the end of the island for fantastic views and swimming.

Remember: Greenheads, an aggressive blood-feeding horsefly, visit the refuge in large numbers from July through mid-August. Call ahead to see if they are present. If they are, don't go! They will make your visit utterly miserable. Also, sometimes the refuge closes due to crowds, weather, or special events.

PLAN B: Make sure to stop at Mass Audubon's Joppa Flats Education Center (Trip 79) for exhibits and more information.

WHERE TO EAT NEARBY: Newburyport offers many dining options.

Section 7

Central and Western Massachusetts

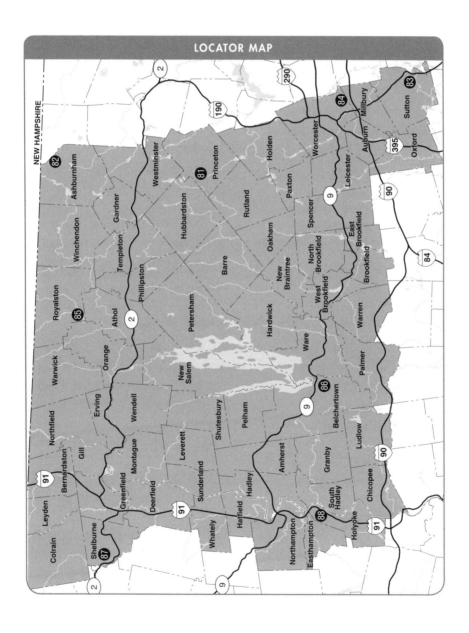

LOCATOR MAP

Trip 81

All Ages

Wachusett Meadow Wildlife Sanctuary

Otters and beavers make their home at this sanctuary, which offers a variety of habitats around its 12 miles of trails.

Address: 113 Goodnow Road, Princeton, MA
Hours: Trails: dawn to dusk daily; nature center: 10 A.M. to 2 P.M. Tuesday through Friday, 10 A.M. to 4 P.M. Saturday, 12:30 P.M. to 4 P.M. Sunday
Fee: Adults, $4; children ages 3–12, $3; Mass Audubon members, free
Contact: massaudubon.org; 978-464-2712
Bathrooms: At the nature center
Water/Snacks: Snacks sold in the nature center
Map: USGS Sterling; massaudubon.org/Nature_Connection/Sanctuaries/images/maps/wachusett_trails.pdf
Directions by Car: From Boston, take the Mass Pike (I-90 West) to Exit 10A to MA 146 North. After about 3 miles, stay right at a fork to go onto I-290 East. After 3 miles, take Exit 19 to I-190 North. After 9 miles, take Exit 5 for MA 140 North and drive 2 miles to MA 62 West. Make a left onto MA 62 West and continue to follow this road to Goodnow Road. The parking lot for the sanctuary is on the left. *GPS coordinates:* 42° 27.335′ N, 71° 54.324′ W.

This 1,200-acre Mass Audubon property has 12 miles of trails that traverse meadows, woodlands, and wetlands. Beavers and otters live here, and a hike to one of the ponds to see the handiwork of the beaver is a great choice for families. Other animals you might see throughout the year include snakes, turkeys, and sheep (the sanctuary keeps sheep to help maintain its meadows). In the nature center, you can buy yarn made from the sheep wool and nature-themed products and books.

Behind the nature center, take North Meadow Trail and head to the right to pick up Birch Trail to Brown Hill Loop and finally to the Otter Pond spur, which leads to a bench where you can sit and watch for otters. Along the way, you'll cross a stream and see stone walls, evidence of days when the property was a farm. Overall, this hike is about 1.5 miles round-trip. All the trails mentioned above loop around to various features of the property and are quite well marked. Cross-country skiing and snowshoeing are popular here in winter.

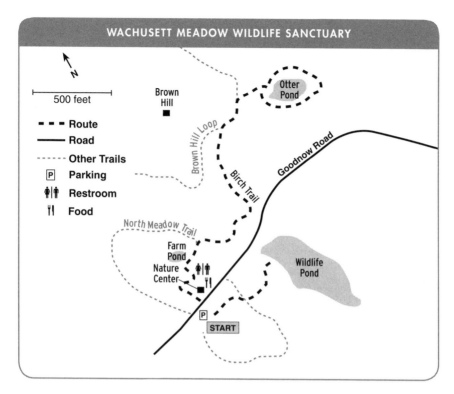

Another popular activity from May through October is to rent a canoe and paddle around Wildlife Pond, which is across the street from the sanctuary. Beavers make their home here too.

Remember: Bug spray is practically required here—the swamps and ponds attract mosquitoes.

PLAN B: Mount Wachusett is right next to the property and offers a 2.5-mile hike to its summit.

WHERE TO EAT NEARBY: On MA 62, there a few places to stop for a snack or get pizza.

Trip 82

Mount Watatic

A challenging hike to the summit of Mount Watatic (1,832 feet) is a rewarding accomplishment for kids. They'll enjoy the rocky scramble to the top, and the great views once they get there.

Address: Route 119, Ashburnham, MA
Hours: Dawn to dusk daily
Fee: Free
Contact: mass.gov/dcr; 978-597-8802
Bathrooms: None
Water/Snacks: None
Map: USGS Ashburnham
Directions by Car: From Boston, take I-93 North to I-95 South to Exit 32A and merge onto US 3 North. After 16 miles, take Exit 33 to MA 40 West. Follow MA 40 West for about 9 miles, then turn right onto MA 119 West and follow it for about 20 miles. Look for signs to the parking lot on the right. *GPS coordinates: 42° 41.805′ N, 71° 54.270′ W.*

Mount Watatic, on the Massachusetts–New Hampshire border, has an elevation of 1,832 feet, offering some steep, rocky sections to climb. From the parking lot, follow yellow blazes to hike a little bit over a mile to the summit. The hike will take about an hour, so you can plan on frequent breaks for water and rest, if needed. This is a great hike for families with older kids who are ready for a challenge.

When you reach the top, you'll be able to see the Berkshires and the Green Mountains to the west, Boston to the southeast, and the White Mountains to the north. On the way back, the trail is marked with blue blazes. As always, wear proper footgear and don't forget your water. You and the kids will need it.

If you visit from mid-September through October, you may see legions of people armed with binoculars watching thousands of hawks in the midst of migration—Watatic is one of the best places to watch the migration. The mountain is also popular for winter hikes.

Remember: While this may not be a long hike, it can be tough going. Younger children not used to hiking may have a hard time.

The hike up Mount Watatic covers varied terrain, including networks of tree roots.

PLAN B: For an easier mountain trek, visit Rhododendron State Park (Trip 96) and climb Little Monadnock Mountain.

WHERE TO EAT NEARBY: As you drive along MA 119, you'll see places to stop for food.

Trip 83

Ages 9–12

Purgatory Chasm State Reservation

Purgatory Chasm offers adventure and challenges kids will love to tackle, from climbing giant boulders to peering into dark caves.

Address: 198 Purgatory Road, Sutton, MA
Hours: Dawn to dusk daily; chasm may be closed in winter due to icy conditions
Fee: Free
Contact: mass.parks@state.ma.us; 508-243-9610
Bathrooms: At the visitor center
Water/Snacks: Water fountains at the visitor center, by the entrance to the chasm, and at one of the picnic areas; in warm weather, an ice cream cart sometimes parks by the chasm entrance
Map: USGS Milford, Worcester South; mass.gov/dcr/parks/trails/purgatory.pdf
Directions by Car: From Boston, take the Mass Pike (I-90 West) to Exit 10A to MA 146 South. Follow MA 146 South to Exit 6 in Sutton. Take a right onto Purgatory Road and follow for 0.25 mile. The entrance will be on your right. The main parking lot is at the visitor center; another lot is by the entrance to Purgatory Chasm. More parking can be found down Purgatory Road. *GPS coordinates: 42° 7.751′ N, 71° 42.824′ W.*

This 900-acre state reservation is built around a quarter-mile chasm of boulders piled up between granite walls, some parts reaching up to 70 feet high. It's a delightful natural playground for anyone who wants more than a meander through a meadow. Visit in winter to be amazed by icicles and frozen waterfalls.

The chasm has been a popular spot for decades—one historian says picnickers would spend an afternoon here as early as 1793. It was made a state reservation in 1919. While the chasm looks like a giant slammed his fist into the earth, splicing open a huge gash, it was probably created 14,000 years ago by the sudden release of dammed-up glacial meltwater near the end of the last ice age.

Chasm Loop Trail, which is 0.5 mile long, is where kids will want to go, to get climbing immediately. Chasm Loop brings you over and around giant boulders, with small caves to explore along the way. Rock formations have fanciful names such as The Coffin, The Devil's Pulpit, Lovers' Leap, and Fat Man's Misery. Even some of the caves are labeled. Look for His Majesty's Cave for a nice photo stop about a quarter of the way in.

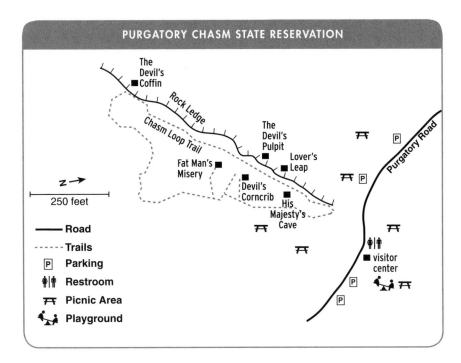

PURGATORY CHASM STATE RESERVATION

The Devil's Coffin

Rock Ledge

Chasm Loop Trail

The Devil's Pulpit

Lover's Leap

Fat Man's Misery

Devil's Corncrib

His Majesty's Cave

Purgatory Road

N

250 feet

—— Road
----- Trails
P Parking
Restroom
Picnic Area
Playground

visitor center

Once you're through the rocky part, the trail veers up so that you climb to a high vantage point and can look into the chasm. Little kids will need to be supervised at all times, especially when you are at the top. There's no guardrail. Explore numerous other trails here if you get around to it.

Remember: Wear appropriate footgear! You will be climbing and clambering over rocks. If you have adventurous kids who may want to explore some of the caves, make sure to bring a flashlight with you. You will also need your hands free, so wear a backpack.

PLAN B: If rock climbing seems too daunting or too much work, the Broad Meadow Brook Conservation Center and Wildlife Sanctuary (Trip 84), which features easy nature trails, is just about 20 minutes away.

WHERE TO EAT NEARBY: You are best off packing a lunch, because not many options are nearby. In a pinch, head to Whitinsville's Main Street, about 3 miles east, where you'll find a general store and a couple of pizza places.

Leaf peeping and apple picking are fantastic fall excursions, but you can add another activity when a snap is in the air and you want to get outside: cornfield mazes. Navigating a maze is a fun family adventure, and New England has plenty to choose from. Often the farms that create mazes also offer other activities, such as hay rides, pumpkin picking, and games.

A couple of tips: Make sure your kids are up for the challenge before you go. Sometimes mazes can feel a little claustrophobic. Stick together and make a plan should you get separated. Many places have guides stationed in the maze to help if you get stuck or lost. A few of the farms also offer smaller mazes or games for younger children.

Here are some farms that offer annual mazes:

Connors Farm

In addition to its 7-acre cornfield maze, Connors Farm has a mini-maze for smaller kids, hay rides, farm animals you can visit, and games. *In Danvers; connorsfarm.com. Near Ipswich River Wildlife Sanctuary (Trip 75).*

Davis Mega Maze

The maze at Davis can be solved in different ways, because it is designed like a game to be played at various levels. Smaller mazes, apple picking, and games will delight younger children. *In Sterling; davismegamaze.com. Near Wachusett Meadow Wildlife Sanctuary (Trip 81).*

Marini Farm

This 8-acre maze has 10 miles of pathways; to get through it, you visit 18 stations placed throughout the maze. Each station has an answer to a question on a game sheet that you are given when you enter. If you answer all the questions, you succeed. A small hay-bale maze and a hay ride for little ones are also at the farm. *In Ipswich; marinicornmaze.com. Near Appleton Farms and Grass Rides (Trip 77).*

Sauchuk Farm

You can play Maize-O-Poly in the big maze or Simon Says in a kiddie maze, then go on a hay ride. Other activities include a giant jumping pillow, duck races, and a spider-web climbing structure for kids. *In Plympton; sauchukfarm.net/maze. Near Myles Standish State Forest (Trip 68).*

West End Creamery

You can get some clues on how to get through the 5-acre maze here by answering trivia questions in a "passport" given to you when you begin. You can also enjoy a half-acre maze, hay rides, and mini-golf. *In Whitinsville; westendcreamery. com/cornmaze.html. Near Purgatory Chasm State Reservation (Trip 83).*

Trip 84

Broad Meadow Brook Conservation Center and Wildlife Sanctuary

Head to Broad Meadow Brook to visit the frogs at Frog Pond, walk through forests and wetlands, and check out interpretative exhibits.

Address: 414 Massasoit Road, Worcester, MA
Hours: Dawn to dusk daily; conservation center: 9 A.M. to 4 P.M. Tuesday through Saturday, 12:30 P.M. to 4 P.M. Sunday
Fee: Adults, $4; children ages 3–13, $3; Mass Audubon members, free
Contact: massaudubon.org; 508-753-6087
Bathrooms: At the nature center
Water/Snacks: Water fountains by the restrooms; snacks for sale and serve-yourself coffee, tea, and hot chocolate available for a donation
Map: USGS Worcester North; massaudubon.org/Nature_Connection/Sanctuaries/Broad_Meadow/maps.php
Directions by Car: From Boston, take the Mass Pike (I-90 West) to Exit 11 (Millbury) and go left onto MA 122 North. Turn left onto US 20 West. Turn right at the traffic light onto Massasoit Road, and park in a lot in front of the nature center. *GPS coordinates:* 42° 14.013' N, 71° 45.816' W.

Broad Meadow Brook is a delightful spot, with an excellent visitor center. Try to go when the nature center is open; kids will love to check out the interpretive exhibits, especially the large 3-D model of the entire sanctuary. The center has an extensive selection of gifts, books, field guides, and community resource information about the entire area.

Once outside, for a nice hike, take Holdredge Trail to Frog Pond Trail (you'll go left) to Sprague Trail, which meets up again with Holdredge in a loop to return to the center. Along the way, meander through forests, marsh, and wetlands. A stop at the tiny Frog Pond should be rewarding: seemingly dozens of frogs are content to rest on logs or swim. A sweet little play area features swings and seats cut from logs that are a big draw for kids, and you can explore further on several other trails. If you have kids who like to quest (see page 150), download the clues from the center's website before you go. Check out this Mass Audubon sanctuary's website for year-round programming, such as snowshoe lessons, naturalist walks, and winter bird-feeding workshops.

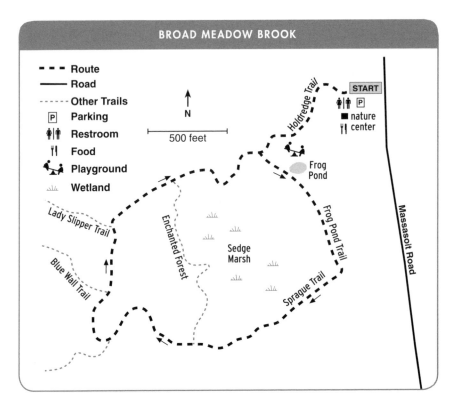

Remember: Quite a bit of poison ivy is right along some of the trails, so keep a sharp eye out.

PLAN B: For an adventurous hike nearby, try Purgatory Chasm State Reservation (Trip 83) in Sutton, about 20 minutes away.

WHERE TO EAT NEARBY: If you head back to MA 122, you'll find a few sandwich places, but you're better off packing a lunch for this visit and eating at a picnic table at the sanctuary.

Trip 85

Ages 9–12

Tully Lake

Swimming, kayaking, and hiking to waterfalls are just some of the activities available at Tully Lake.

Address: 2 Athol-Richmond Road, Royalston, MA
Hours: Dawn to dusk daily
Fee: Free
Contact: nae.usace.army.mil/recreati/tul/tulhome.htm; 978-249-9150
Bathrooms: At the recreation area
Water/Snacks: None
Map: USGS Royalston; nae.usace.army.mil/recreati/tul/Tully%20Lake%20
  Park%20Map%202009.pdf
Directions by Car: From Boston, take I-93 North to I-495 South. Take Exit 29B
  to MA 2 West. At Exit 18, take MA 2 West toward Athol. Follow signs to stay
  on MA 2 West. In about 3 miles, turn right on Crescent Street and then make
  a left onto Silver Lake Road, which turns into MA 32 North/West Royalston
  Road. Parking is located just past the dam. *GPS coordinates:* 42° 37.742′ N,
  72° 13.487′ W.

Tully Lake, located on the east branch of the Tully River, is part of a network of flood-damage-reduction dams on tributaries of the Connecticut River. The U.S. Army Corps of Engineers manages the 1,300-acre reservoir area, including the Tully Dam, which was built to reduce flood damage on the Millers and Connecticut rivers. Trails and a campground, however, are maintained by The Trustees of Reservations.

You can enjoy a multitude of outdoor activities year-round, but if you can get out on the water in summer, that would be my first recommendation. Numerous islands and inlets on the lake are a blast to explore. From the recreation area next to the dam, you can hike the 4-mile Lake Trail, which brings you all the way around the lake. Doane's Falls, a cascading waterfall, is a popular stop along the way. You can also paddle most of the way to the falls (you have to dock the boat and hike in a bit). The 22-mile Tully Trail is a popular trek for experienced hikers and leads to Tully Mountain. A 7.5-mile mountain bike trail goes along the Tully River and Long Pond.

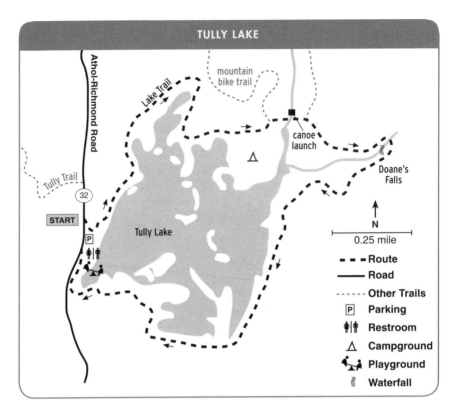

When the snow arrives, head to Tully Lake for snowshoeing or cross-country skiing on the ungroomed trails. This is also a great place to look for animal tracks in the snow.

Remember: You can rent kayaks and canoes at Tully Lake Campground even if you aren't staying overnight. Keep your dog on a leash and clean up after it.

PLAN B: Camp at the excellent campground run by The Trustees of Reservations. The tent-only campground is on the shores of the 200-acre lake and doesn't have drive-up sites—you have to carry your gear in, which makes for a very peaceful setting.

WHERE TO EAT NEARBY: Numerous spots to dine are along Athol's Main Street, south of the lake.

PADDLING GAMES

Once you and the kids are comfortable on the water, why not incorporate some games? Lots of games that work on land also work on water, particularly if you have a group of kids. Remember: Be clear and concise in your instructions, and make sure safety is a top priority (e.g., if someone flips over, stop the game or give that person immunity).

Here are some ideas:

- *Simon Says:* The Leader (Simon) calls out instructions, all preceded by "Simon says . . ." The kids can try paddling backward or in a circle, or any number of crazy combinations! But if the leader doesn't call out "Simon says . . ." and someone completes the action, that person is out.

- *Follow the Leader:* This simple game may be even more fun on water than on land. Choose a leader and have all the paddlers line up behind him or her. The followers have to mimic the leader's actions, whether it's zigzagging across the water or holding a paddle a certain way. Whoever fails to follow the leader's movements is out, and the last person in becomes the new leader.

- *Red Light/Green Light:* This playground game always gets a good laugh on the water. The leader calls out "Green light!" when the paddlers should be moving forward, and "Red light!" to have them stop. Players will quickly learn how to handle their paddles!

- *Tag:* Choose who's "it" and have him or her paddle around after the other players. Tagging should be done with the bow of the boat (not with the paddle). Whoever is tagged is out. You can also play the freeze-tag version of this game, to see how still young paddlers can remain.

Trip 86

All Ages

Quabbin Reservoir

The impressive Quabbin Reservoir is one of the largest artificial reservoirs in the country. You can hike, snowshoe, or bike its trails, or rent a canoe and paddle around.

Address: 485 Ware Road (MA 9), Belchertown, MA
Hours: Dawn to dusk daily
Fee: Free
Contact: mass.gov/dcr; 413-323-7221
Bathrooms: At the visitor center
Water/Snacks: Water fountains at the visitor center
Map: USGS Windsor Dam; mass.gov/dcr/watersupply/watershed/maphome.htm
Directions by Car: From Boston, take the Mass Pike (I-90 West) to Exit 8 (Palmer). Take a left onto MA 32 North and drive for 8 miles. In Ware, turn left at the green "Route 9 West" sign. At the next stop sign, turn left onto MA 9. Drive 5 miles, and turn right at the Quabbin Reservoir sign for the visitor center and parking lot. *GPS coordinates: 42° 16.795′ N, 72° 20.909′ W.*

The Quabbin Reservoir was created in the 1930s, when two earthen dams were built that filled gaps in the Swift River Valley to create a public water supply. It covers 39 square miles, is 18 miles long, and has 181 miles of shoreline. When it's full, the reservoir holds a staggering 412 billion gallons of water. It provides 40 percent of Massachusetts residents with their drinking water!

While this is a protected source of water, that doesn't mean you can't enjoy a visit. Since the reservoir is fed by three branches of Swift River as well as by Ware River, and the watershed land is protected, an "accidental wilderness" has been created. Wildlife thrives in this safe area, in various habitats. Wild turkeys, white-tailed deer, foxes, coyotes, and any number of bird species can be found here. In winter, bald eagles can usually be spotted from Enfield Lookout.

After you pick up a map and information at the visitor center, stop at the Quabbin Observation Tower, which has wonderful views and gives you a true perspective of how large the reservoir is. You can explore more than 20 miles of trails at the park, and biking is quite popular for all ages. On certain parts of the reservoir, you can fish or boat. Canoes and kayaks are available for rent.

The large Quabbin Reservoir has 181 miles of shoreline and is surrounded by forest.

Check at the visitor center for rules and instructions. You can purchase a one-day fishing license at the boat launch (anyone over 15 must have one).

Remember: More than 2.5 million people depend on the reservoir for their drinking water, so swimming, dog walking, or anything else that could contaminate the water supply is prohibited.

PLAN B: About 30 miles west, you can check out Dinosaur Footprints (Trip 88) to see evidence of the creatures that roamed the earth long ago.

WHERE TO EAT NEARBY: Head west on MA 9 into Belchertown to find some restaurants on and around its Main Street.

Trip 87

High Ledges Wildlife Sanctuary

Truly off the beaten path, High Ledges has lovely views of Deerfield Valley and Mount Greylock and, in spring and summer, wildflowers galore.

Address: Patten Road, Shelburne, MA
Hours: Dawn to dusk daily
Fee: Suggested donation, $3; Mass Audubon members, free
Contact: massaudubon.org; 978-464-2712
Bathrooms: None
Water/Snacks: None
Map: USGS Greenfield; massaudubon.org/Nature_Connection/Sanctuaries/
High_Ledges/maps.php
Directions by Car: At the junction of MA 2 and I-91 in Greenfield, continue west on MA 2 toward Shelburne for 6 miles. Take a right onto Little Mohawk Road and bear left at the next junction onto Patten Road. (Look for Mass Audubon signs with arrows pointing the way.) Continue on Patten Road, bear left at the next junction, and then bear right. In less than a mile, you'll see the sanctuary entrance (the second left), and the parking lots. *GPS coordinates:* 42° 37.867′ N, 72° 42.514′ W.

This 600-acre sanctuary has several trails to choose from, but probably the best one to take with kids is the 1-mile Sanctuary Road Trail, which leads to the cliffs, where you'll see why this Mass Audubon sanctuary is named High Ledges. On Sanctuary Road Trail, you'll pass by fields and a vernal pool. If you decide to go a bit farther, take Dutch and Mary Barnard Trail to find an amazing number of wildflowers in spring and summer.

Visiting High Ledges is recommended in summer or early autumn because some trails may be too muddy or washed out for hiking in spring. If you decide to visit in winter, don't forget your snowshoes. Some parts of the trails are steep, too, which is why this hike is recommended for older kids.

The sanctuary is home to a broad array of native plants and a diverse landscape, from fields to wetlands to woods. Twenty species of orchids and 30 species of ferns grow on the property, so making a game of finding as many different varieties is a good diversion as you walk. Since High Ledges was once part of a farm, you'll also see evidence of its former life: stone walls, fencing, and former pastures.

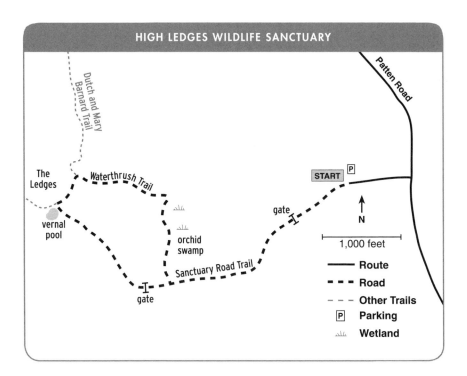

Remember: Parking areas may be inaccessible from December to May due to snow or mud. Call ahead to check conditions.

PLAN B: Head to the charming town of Shelburne Falls to visit the gorgeous Bridge of Flowers (in season) and check out the famous glacial potholes that formed in the Deerfield River more than 14,000 years ago.

WHERE TO EAT NEARBY: Numerous eateries are in Shelburne Falls.

Trip 88

Dinosaur Footprints

These slabs of sandstone are a must-visit for any dinosaur-obsessed kids who would love to see more than 100 fossilized prints.

Address: Route 5, Holyoke, MA
Hours: Dawn to dusk daily, April through November
Fee: Free
Contact: thetrustees.org; 413-532-1631
Bathrooms: None
Water/Snacks: None
Map: USGS Springfield North; thetrustees.org/places-to-visit/pioneer-valley/ dinosaur-footprints.html#t9
Directions by Car: From Boston, take the Mass Pike (I-90 West) to Exit 4 onto I-91 North toward Holyoke. Take Exit 17A to merge onto MA 141 East. Turn left onto US 5 North and follow for 2.2 miles to entrance on right. The turnout has space for about six cars. *GPS coordinates:* 42° 14.503′ N, 72° 37.415′ W.

This Trustees of Reservations property is found at a somewhat unlikely location: on the side of the road on a busy stretch of highway. What you'll find after walking on a short path are the first dinosaur prints ever to be scientifically described. More than 190 million years ago, this valley was a subtropical mix of wetlands and shallow lakes. The more than 130 tracks preserved in slabs of sandstone here are believed to have been left by small groups of two-legged carnivorous dinosaurs, perhaps some up to 15 feet tall.

According to the Trustees, the larger prints might be from ancestors of the Tyrannosaurus Rex. Other fossils present include stromatolites, fish, and plants. The dinosaur trackways found here formed the basis for the theory that dinosaurs traveled in packs or groups. Truly, there's not much hiking to be done here, but the payoff of seeing the footprints is priceless. Visiting the footprints, unless you have a rabid dinosaur fan, is probably best combined with another activity, such as visiting the Quabbin Reservoir (Trip 86).

Remember: The prints are fragile, so take off your shoes or clean them before walking around the fossils. Also, crossing the nearby railroad tracks is illegal, not to mention dangerous.

Tracks believed to have been left by two-legged dinosaurs are preserved in slabs of sandstone.

PLAN B: At the Quabbin Reservoir (Trip 86), about 30 minutes away in Belchertown, you can hike more than 20 miles of trails. On certain parts of the reservoir, you can fish and boat (canoes and kayaks are available for rent).

WHERE TO EAT NEARBY: A variety of restaurants are on US 5 in Holyoke.

Section 8

Rhode Island

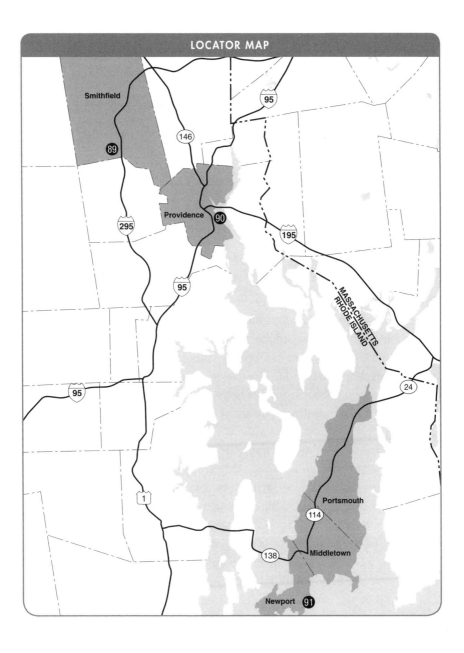

LOCATOR MAP

Smithfield

95

146

89

295

Providence

90

195

95

MASSACHUSETTS
RHODE ISLAND

95

24

1

Portsmouth

114

138

Middletown

Newport

91

Trip 89

Powder Mill Ledges Wildlife Refuge

Discover an unexpected landscape near a very busy urban area at Powder Mill Ledges.

Address: 12 Sanderson Road (RI 5), Smithfield, RI
Hours: Dawn to dusk daily
Fee: Free
Contact: asri.org; 401-949-5454
Bathrooms: At the visitor center
Water/Snacks: Water fountain next to the bathrooms
Map: USGS North Scituate; asri.org/refuges/powder-mill-ledges-wildlife-refuge. html
Directions by Car: From Boston, take I-93 South to Exit 4 for I-295 South. Take Exit 7B onto US 44 West. At the fourth set of lights, turn left onto RI 5 (Sanderson Road). Turn left at the second driveway into the parking lot. *GPS coordinates: 41° 52.103′ N, 71° 31.850′ W.*

This 120-acre wildlife refuge offers trails ranging from 0.5 mile to 1.25 miles through woods and wetlands, and beside a pond and a brook. The visitor center, which is also the Audubon Society of Rhode Island's headquarters, houses a library, where you can browse through a great selection of nature books. A gift shop and bird-feeding station are also inside. What is so striking here is that this sanctuary is just off two busy highways. Once you start walking, though, the sounds drop away and you'd never guess how close you are to civilization.

The shortest hike is along Orange Trail, which you can pick up from the center. You can either do the inner loop (0.45 mile) or the outer loop (0.85 mile). If you want to explore farther, you can connect to the 1.25-mile Blue Trail at three different points. Blue Trail then links to Yellow Trail (0.75 mile).

Visit in winter for great snowshoeing and cross-country skiing, or to take part in one of the Audubon events, such as winter wildlife wreath making or New England owl talks. Remember: When you look outside the boundaries of this property, you'll see a stark reminder of what our landscapes can turn into if we don't protect them.

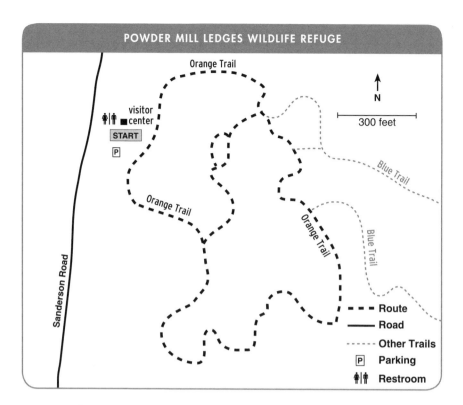

PLAN B: About 2 miles south of Powder Mill, Snake Den State Park is a 1,000-acre park with self-guided walking trails and a working farm.

WHERE TO EAT NEARBY: You'll see a lot of dining options on RI 5 and US 44.

Trip 90

All Ages

East Bay Bike Path

The East Bay Bike Path follows the route of the former Old Colony Railroad from downtown Providence to Bristol, a colonial seaside village and shipbuilding center.

Address: India Point Park, India and Gano streets, Providence, RI
Hours: Dawn to dusk daily
Fee: Free
Contact: riparks.com/eastbay.htm; 401-253-7482
Bathrooms: At Haines Memorial State Park and downtown Bristol
Water/Snacks: Water fountains in India Point Park, Haines Memorial State Park, and Colt State Park
Map: USGS Providence; greenway.org/images/RI.jpg
Directions by Car: From Boston, take I-93 South to I-95 South for 50 miles to the interchange with I-195 East. Take Exit 2 to India Street for access to the path at India Point Park or Exit 4 to Veterans Memorial Parkway, where two parking lots for the path are on the right side of the road. (Access points are in Providence, East Providence, Riverside, Barrington, Warren, and Bristol.) *GPS coordinates (India Point Park parking lot):* 41° 49.064′ N, 71° 23.446′ W.

Rhode Island's first and longest dedicated bike path is also its most beautiful. The northern end of the path begins in Providence's India Point Park, where the paved, off-street path runs along the east side of Narragansett Bay.

It's smooth going all the way to Bristol, apart from the occasional street crossing, most with pedestrian signals to stop traffic. You'll ride across an old railroad causeway (with a section of track still running alongside) and past the Pomham Rocks Lighthouse before reaching the village of Riverside, where the kids will love to detour to visit the historic Crescent Park Carousel.

In Barrington, the trail passes alongside the pretty waterfront Haines Memorial State Park. A popular fishing bridge takes you across the Warren River into downtown Warren, where alongside the path a bike shop is available for any needed repairs and a lemonade stand sells refreshing treats. Crossing the town line into Bristol, you'll find the headquarters of the Audubon Society of Rhode Island at the Powder Mill Ledges Wildlife Refuge (Trip 89). Follow the boardwalk to visit marshlands.

The path traverses the entrance road to Colt State Park before arriving in downtown Bristol, where you can explore the local shops and historic sites or

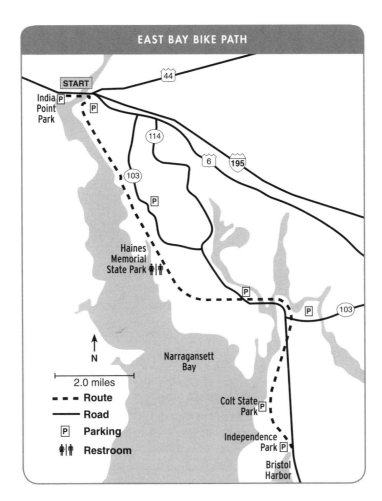

EAST BAY BIKE PATH

START

India Point Park

44

114

103

6

195

P

Haines Memorial State Park

103

N

2.0 miles

- - - Route
— Road
P   Parking
Restroom

Narragansett Bay

Colt State Park

Independence Park

Bristol Harbor

take a ferry to peaceful Prudence Island. Like many bike paths, Easy Bay is not plowed in winter, so cross-country skiers replace cyclists here in wintry months.

Remember: Visit the bike path's website to learn about any construction or detours. Rhode Island has a lot of ongoing construction projects.

PLAN B: The Blackstone River Bikeway begins in Central Falls (10 minutes from Providence) and runs 10 miles to Woonsocket along what was once a main artery during the Industrial Revolution.

WHERE TO EAT NEARBY: East Providence, Riverside, Barrington, Warren, and Bristol all have multiple restaurants—from pizza to haute cuisine—directly adjacent to the bike path or just minutes away.

Trip 91

······································

Cliff Walk

Cliff Walk takes you by Newport's famous Gilded Age mansions and along the Atlantic Ocean.

Address: Narragansett and Ochre Point avenues, Newport, RI
Hours: Dawn to dusk daily
Fee: Free
Contact: cliffwalk.com; 401-845-5802
Bathrooms: None
Water/Snacks: None
Map: USGS Newport; cliffwalk.com
Directions by Car: From Boston, take I-93 South to Exit 4 for MA 24 South. Follow MA 24 approximately 40 miles. Follow signs for I-195 West/MA 24 South and take Exit 8A to stay on MA 24 South. Exit onto RI 114. In 6.4 miles, turn right on Coddington Highway and continue onto JT O'Connell Road. At the traffic circle, take the third exit onto Admiral Kalbfus Road, then take the ramp onto RI 138 West. Turn right at America's Cup Avenue, continue onto Memorial Boulevard, turn right onto Bellevue Avenue, and turn left onto Narragansett Avenue, where you can park on the street. *GPS coordinates:* 41° 28.549′ N, 71° 17.845′ W.

Newport's famous 3.5-mile-long Cliff Walk along the eastern shore offers a glimpse into the past as well as stunning views. On one side, you have the Atlantic Ocean and on the other the amazing Newport mansions, built in the Gilded Age in the late 1800s. Several of them are open to the public for tours in summer and on holidays.

The official starting point of the trail is behind the Chanler Inn, but for this hike I've given directions to the best parking area on Narragansett Avenue. Parking can be tricky, so you might have to look around a bit, especially in summer. Visit during colder months for less crowds and to experience stunning views of the winter sun over the water. Most of the trail is easy enough to walk, but part of it goes over the rocky shoreline. If you have a stroller or small tots, you'll go about 0.5 mile before you'll have to turn back.

Just at the end of Naragansett Avenue, you'll come to Forty Steps, a staircase that leads down to the rocky shoreline. During Newport's heyday, the Forty Steps were a gathering place for servants and workers from the man-

Stunning views of the Atlantic Ocean reward visitors on Newport's Cliff Walk.

sions. They would play music and dance. If you go to the right off the steps, the onetime summer "cottages" of the rich and famous come into view. Think Vanderbilts and *The Great Gatsby* for a mental image.

Remember: As tempting as it may be, don't leave the trail! The walk is a public right-of-way over private property. Also, in some places, the drop is as much as 70 feet. Keep your dog on a leash and clean up after it.

PLAN B: Exploring Newport's historic district on foot is a great way to get to know the City by the Sea, as it is called.

WHERE TO EAT NEARBY: The historic district offers plenty of dining choices.

There's a reason Easter egg hunts are so popular: Kids love to search for things! Clue and search games are great ways to get kids to engage with their environment. With a little work on your part, you can create games in advance of your outing—or even create one ad hoc. While kids, especially younger ones, might not always reach the answers on their own, that's OK. You're there to guide them; you can incorporate helpful tips, like "You're getting hotter or colder," another way to keep them engaged.

Scavenger Hunts

Kids of all ages enjoy cracking clues to discover the world around them. To plan a hunt, visit the destination ahead of time and plot out a reasonable geographic zone—a corner of the Boston Common (Trip 3) for younger children, the whole of Mount Auburn Cemetery (Trip 19) or a stretch of the Cliff Walk (Trip 91) for older kids—and select a dozen or more things they can identify: varieties of trees, certain shapes or types of rocks, acorns, historical markers, statues—the possibilities are endless.

Once you've chosen the answers, write your clues. For example, "Mrs. Mallard leads this pack." (Answer: the *Make Way for Ducklings* statue in the Public Garden.) On-the-fly hunts—spot an object and design a leading question—are a good way to recharge and redirect kids when patience wanes; they also allow you to set kids in search of living creatures, which you can't count on being present during a planned hunt.

I Spy

This classic can be played anywhere. From the trail, "I spy with my eye something that is white." First clue not enough? "Something that is rounded on top." Still need more? "Something that is also food for animals." (Answer: a mushroom.)

Camera Seek-and-Find

Technology can sometimes enhance an outing, as is often the case with digital cameras. Hand the camera over to your child and make a list of "picture goals." Can she find a leaf that's been chewed? Can he spot a tree with pinecones? Can she shoot an image of a bird in flight? This activity will vary greatly by your child's age and interests. Give a couple of tips and suggestions, and then let him or her lead the way!

Section 9

Connecticut

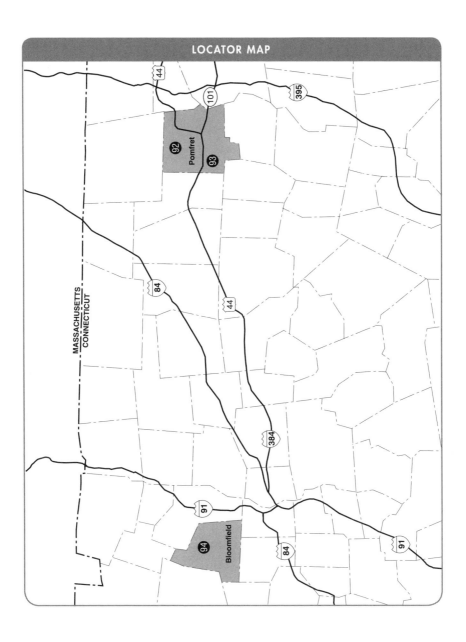

LOCATOR MAP

Trip 92

Bafflin Sanctuary at Pomfret Farms

This Connecticut Audubon Society sanctuary offers a variety of trails through different habitats.

Address: 220 Day Road, Pomfret Center, CT
Hours: Dawn to dusk daily
Fee: Free
Contact: ctaudubon.org/sanctuaries; 203-869-5272
Bathrooms: At the sanctuary
Water/Snacks: Water fountain in the sanctuary
Map: USGS Danielson; ctaudubon.org/wp-content/uploads/2011/03/BafflinMap2010.pdf
Directions by Car: From Boston, take the Mass Pike (I-90 West) to Exit 10 for I-395 South. In 25 miles, take Exit 93 to CT 101 West. Follow for about 4.5 miles to CT 169 North and turn right. In less than 0.5 mile, turn right on Day Road and follow to the parking lot. *GPS coordinates:* 41° 52.409′ N, 71° 56.728′ W.

This 702-acre Connecticut Audubon Society property was once a dairy farm, but today it offers 10 miles of walking trails (with interpretive signs) that cross beaver ponds, grasslands, a hemlock ravine, and streams. It is easy to visit and not see another soul, making for a peaceful walk. From behind the sanctuary, a lovely trail is Ravine Trail, 0.63-mile hike that takes you through a hemlock forest and next to a stream.

The property is designated an Important Bird Area, and more than 200 species have been observed here. Endangered long-eared owls come to spend the winter, while several WatchList species—including the American woodcock, blue-winged warbler, and the black-billed cuckoo—breed on the grounds.

In addition to the Bafflin Sanctuary, the Audubon Society runs the nearby Center at Pomfret, with hands-on environmental education programs, after-school and weekend programs that include hikes and bird walks, and various workshops and changing natural history exhibits.

Remember: You can hike to link up with other trails or park at other designated parking areas (see map on website) to access trails.

*This former farm's vast grasslands offer great
wildflower picking in summer.*

PLAN B: Nearby Mashamoquet Brook State Park (Trip 93) offers overnight camping and lots of trails.

WHERE TO EAT NEARBY: Head north on CT 169 to Pomfret Center for a few dining options.

Trip 93

Ages 9–12

Mashamoquet Brook State Park

This state park has a variety of outdoor attractions, from caves and rock formations to brooks and swimming.

Address: US 44, Pomfret Center, CT
Hours: Pedestrians: Dawn to dusk daily; vehicles: 8 A.M. to dusk
Fee: Parking: $15 on weekends and holidays for nonresidents
Contact: ct.goc/dep; 860-928-6121
Bathrooms: Near the parking lot as well as near the pond
Water/Snacks: Water fountains near the bathrooms
Map: USGS Danielson; ct.gov/dep/lib/dep/stateparks/maps/mashamoquet.pdf
Directions by Car: From Boston, take the Mass Pike (I-90 West) 43 miles to Exit 10 for MA 12. Keep left at the fork to merge onto I-395 South. Go 25 miles and take Exit 93 for CT 101 West toward Dayville/East Killingly. Follow CT 101 West for about 5 miles and turn left onto Wolf Den Drive. The park is on the left, with plenty of parking. *GPS coordinates:* 41° 51.071′ N, 71° 58.109′ W.

Kids will find a lot to do at Mashamoquet State Park, from hikes leading to rock formations and a cave to activities like swimming in a pond and fishing in a brook. Mashamoquet is a Mohegan word for "stream of good fishing." The region was once the domain of the Mohegan chief Uncas.

The park encompasses almost 1,000 acres and offers an excellent full-day trip as well as overnight camping. Leave your car at the park entrance, where you can visit a museum that was once a cider mill, gristmill, and wagon shop. In this area of the park, the Mashamoquet Brook rushes by and you can swim in a small pond or use the grills to cook out.

From the parking lot, you can take one of two trails—blue or red—that lead to the Putnam Wolf Den, a cave made famous when, in 1742, a man named Israel Putnam crept in and shot what was thought to be the last wolf in Connecticut. Putnam later became famous as a major general in the Continental Army during the Revolutionary War. Close to the Wolf Den, you'll find Table Rock and Indian Chair, cool natural stone formations. The trails can be a bit challenging at times for younger kids. The blue trail is longer, while the red trail is more of a direct path. They converge at one point, which is where you'll

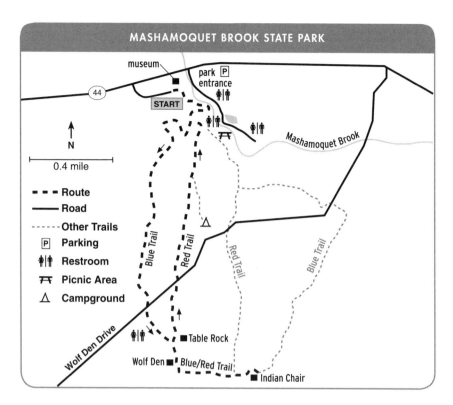

head to see the Putnam Wolf Den and Indian Chair. Painted signs on rocks point the way.

Remember: Two camping areas are open mid-April through Columbus Day—the more rustic Mashamoquet Brook Campground has 20 wooded sites, while the Wolf Den Campground has 35 sites, plus shower facilities. The overnight fee is $24 for non-Connecticut residents.

PLAN B: The Connecticut Audubon Society's Grassland Bird Conservation Center at Pomfret, just 2 miles away, features nature exhibits and is adjacent to the 700-acre Bafflin Sanctuary at Pomfret Farms (Trip 92).

WHERE TO EAT NEARBY: Drive on US 44 East and then north on CT 169 toward Pomfret Center for dining options.

Trip 94

Penwood State Park

Stroll along a paved path to beautiful Lake Louise and enjoy a picnic with a view.

Address: CT 185 and Simsbury Road, Bloomfield, CT
Hours: Dawn to dusk daily; Gate opens at 8 A.M. for cars
Fee: Free
Contact: ct.gov/dep; 860-242-1158
Bathrooms: At a comfort station at the main picnic area
Water/Snacks: Water fountain next to the bathrooms
Map: USGS Avon; ct.gov/dep/lib/dep/stateparks/maps/penwood.pdf
Directions by Car: From Boston, take the Mass Pike (I-90 West) for 54 miles to I-84 West. Drive 37 miles to Exit 61 for I-291 West. After 6 miles, take Exit 1 to CT 218 West. After about 1 mile, take a right onto Blue Hills Avenue; after about 0.5 mile, take a left onto Park Avenue (CT 178). Follow CT 178 for about 4 miles to CT 185. Take a right onto CT 185, and the park will be on your right in about 1 mile. The main parking lot is about 1 mile into the park. *GPS coordinates: 41° 51.397′ N, 72° 46.547′ W.*

The 800-acre Penwood State Park offers both challenging hikes and fields for playing. At the main picnic area, located about 1 mile into the park, you'll find tables and grills, and plenty of open space for kids to run around or toss a ball. When you're ready for a hike, you can push a stroller all the way up to Lake Louise on a 3.5-mile paved loop road (not accessible to cars) to the left of the parking area. Be prepared for a bit of a climb, as the park is on the Talcott Mountain Range.

Once at the lake, you can follow a trail around the lake or stop to fish or skip stones from a dock. A couple of picnic tables are here if you want to eat lunch or have a snack before heading back the way you came. When we visited one day, we were startled by pieces of wood falling from the trees and then we finally spotted a woodpecker high above us, working away at a tree.

You can also enjoy mountain biking and cross-country skiing on Penwood's wide trails. A section of Connecticut's blue-blazed trail system, called the Metacomet, goes through the park. Metacomet Trail is part of the New England National Scenic Trail, which runs 114 miles from the Connecticut state line to Mount Monadnock in New Hampshire. The long-distance hiking

A wooded hike to Lake Louise, in the Talcott Mountain Range, presents a nice challenge for beginner hikers.

footpath is maintained by the Appalachian Mountain Club's Berkshire Chapter Trails Committee and other volunteers. You can gain access to this trail from the first parking lot as well as at the pond.

Remember: Keep your dog on a leash and clean up after it.

PLAN B: The nearby American Legion and Peoples State Forest in Barkhamsted offers campsites if you want to spend more time in the region.

WHERE TO EAT NEARBY: Look for sandwich shops along CT 178.

Section 10

Southern New Hampshire

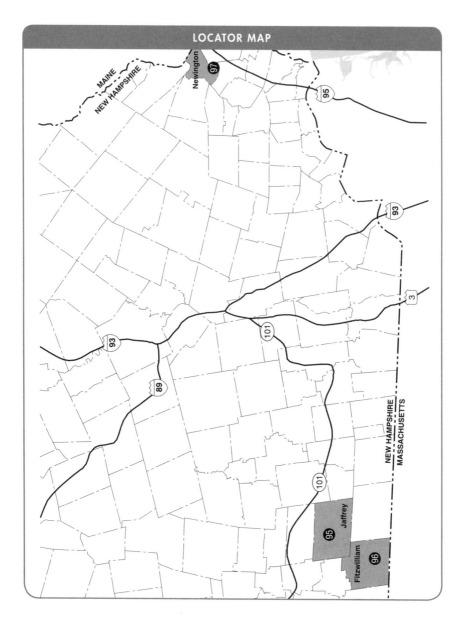

LOCATOR MAP

Trip 95

Ages 9–12

Monadnock State Park

With a steady uphill climb that's not too steep, Mount Monadnock makes a great first summit for older kids.

Address: Mountain Road, Jaffrey, NH
Hours: Dawn to dusk daily
Fee: Adults, $4; children ages 6–11, $2
Contact: nhstateparks.org; 603-532-8862
Bathrooms: At the campground
Water/Snacks: Water fountains in the picnic area and at the campground; snacks and drinks at the park store
Map: USGS Monadnock; nhstateparks.org/uploads/pdf/MonadnockHikingTrailsMap_All_2010.pdf; *AMC's Southern New Hampshire Trail Map*
Directions by Car: From Boston, take I-93 North to Exit 37B onto I-95 South. Take Exit 32A to merge onto US 3 North, then take Exit 33 toward Westford. Merge onto MA 40 West and follow until a slight right onto MA 119. After 10 miles, turn right onto Canal Street, then continue onto Mason Road, then onto NH 124 West. After 21 miles, the parking is on the right. *GPS coordinates: 42° 50.731′ N, 72° 5.321′ W.*

The bare summit of Mount Monadnock offers 100-mile views southeast all the way to Boston and northeast to the White Mountains of New Hampshire. One of the most-climbed mountains in the world, Monadnock is unlikely to be sparsely populated when you visit, but that won't hinder your fun.

Older kids, more so than younger ones, will likely enjoy the challenge of the climb. Many young children often climb the mountain (or attempt to), but only you know what your child can handle at any given age. All hikers on Monadnock should wear proper hiking shoes and carry at least 2 quarts of water.

Forty miles of hiking trails crisscross the park, heading toward the summit from all sides. Speak to the rangers when you arrive; they can offer suggestions and tips. Dublin Trail and White Dot Trail are two of the most popular routes. For a different route, try White Arrow Trail, which offers a rocky scramble in its 4.6-mile round-trip to the summit. From the parking lot, take Old Halfway House Trail, a well-packed trail that is fairly level until it joins Old Toll Road just before the Halfway House site—a hotel once stood in what is now a

Visitors to Mount Monadnock can camp overnight at the park's campground.

meadow. White Arrow Trail starts across the meadow. Follow its rocky, wide path 1.1 miles to the summit—kids will enjoy the adventurous trek over the rocks and will be rewarded with views and a nice rest atop the summit. After enjoying the view and the company, head back the way you came.

Remember: The summit of Mount Monadnock is above treeline, and the weather can be harsh. Plan accordingly; even if the weather seems mild at home, it can change drastically at the summit.

PLAN B: Turn your day trip into an overnight at the park's Gilson Pond Campground. Call 877-nhparks (877-647-2757) to make reservations.

WHERE TO EAT NEARBY: Jaffrey has a number of cafés, restaurants, and markets if you want to purchase picnic supplies.

Trip 96

Rhododendron State Park

At Rhododendron State Park, explore the largest grove of rhododendrons in northern New England.

Address: NH 119 West, Fitzwilliam, NH
Hours: Dawn to dusk daily
Fee: Suggested donation: adults, $4; children ages 6–11, $2 (a self-pay box is at the trailhead)
Contact: nhstateparks.org; 603-532-8862
Bathrooms: Portable toilets to the left of the parking lot (open year-round)
Water/Snacks: None
Map: USGS Monadnock; nhstateparks.org/uploads/pdf/RhododendronMaps.pdf
Directions by Car: From Boston, take I-93 North to I-495 South. After about 20 miles, take Exit 29B to MA 2 West, which turns into MA 140 North. After 10 miles, this road changes names to MA 12 North. Stay on this for another 10 miles, and make a slight left to get onto NH 119 West. The park and its small parking lot are about 1 mile ahead on the right. *GPS coordinates:* 42° 46.901′ N, 72° 11.387′ W.

Rhododendron State Park is named for the 16-acre grove of *Rhododendron maximum* found here, which draws crowds in July when the shrubs' enormous pink-and-white blossoms are in full bloom, but the park offers a fascinating excursion any time of year.

The grove is just a small part of the 2,723-acre park, but it is unique. Rhododendrons grow in acidic soil like that found in the southern Appalachians and in evergreen swamps. Conditions at this site match those found there, allowing this grove to thrive at the northern limit of the species' range. This is the largest grove in northern New England and was designated a National Natural Landmark in 1982.

As you wander through the park, you can easily imagine you are far from New England, since the leaves of the plants look so tropical. Some of the branches of the rhododendron grow so tall that you walk under sections that are almost like tunnels. The shady paths, however, are easy to traverse and the 0.5-mile Rhododendron Trail is universally accessible. Wildflower Trail and Laurel Trail are easy enough to push a stroller over as well. Wandering along all three trails is a lot of fun for kids. Look for the Fitzwilliam Garden Club

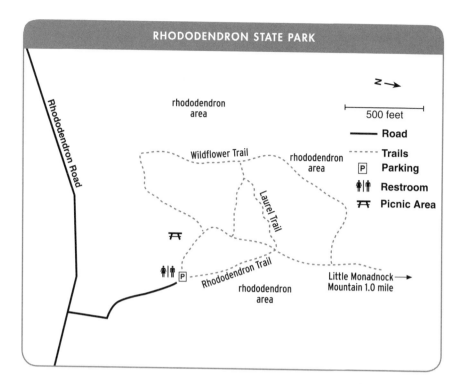

RHODODENDRON STATE PARK

rhododendron area

Wildflower Trail

rhododendron area

Laurel Trail

Rhododendron Trail

rhododendron area

Little Monadnock → Mountain 1.0 mile

500 feet

━━ Road
- - - Trails
P Parking
🚻 Restroom
🏓 Picnic Area

Rhododendron Road

visitor registration station on Wildflower Trail, where you and your kids can sign your names in the notebook found there.

This property was once owned by the Appalachian Mountain Club (AMC), which received the land as a donation in 1903 with the stipulation that the rhododendron grove and pine forest remain a public reservation forever. In 1946, AMC gifted the property to the New Hampshire Division of Parks and Recreation.

Remember: You can spot quite a lot of different mushrooms alongside the trails. Bring a mushroom guide and see how many kinds the kids can identify.

PLAN B: A 1-mile trail here leads to Little Mount Monadnock, which offers views of Mount Mondanock and Mount Sunapee.

WHERE TO EAT NEARBY: A convenience store, a pizza place, and an ice cream shop are located where NH 12 meets NH 119.

Trip 97

Great Bay National Wildlife Refuge

Formerly part of an Air Force base, Great Bay is now an important bird refuge and offers easy walks.

Address: Arboretum Drive, Newington, NH
Hours: Dawn to dusk daily
Fee: Free
Contact: fws.gov/northeast/greatbay; 978-465-5753
Bathrooms: At the comfort station next to the parking lot
Water/Snacks: None
Map: USGS Portsmouth; fws.gov/northeast/greatbay/pdf/Great%20Bay%20 Trail%20Map.pdf
Directions by Car: From Boston, take I-95 North to Exit 4 for NH 16/US 4. Take Exit 1 off NH 16 or Spaulding Turnpike and turn onto Pease Boulevard (toward Pease International Tradeport). Go through one light. At the next stop sign, turn right on Arboretum Drive. Follow signs for 3 miles to the refuge and park in the large lot. *GPS coordinates:* 43° 05.356′ N, 70° 50.610′ W.

Two trails are found at the Great Bay National Wildlife Refuge, both of which are perfect for families. The property is one of more than 550 refuges in the National Wildlife Refuge System, run by the U.S. Fish and Wildlife Service. This refuge was once part of the Pease Air Force Base, which closed in 1989 and in 1992 was turned into a 1,000-plus-acre sanctuary along the eastern shore of New Hampshire's Great Bay.

Today, it is an important migration and wintering habitat for the federally protected bald eagle and a prime migration habitat for the peregrine falcon. Depending on your kids, you can take Ferry Way Trail, a 2-mile round-trip hike that leads to a scenic overlook where you can peer through mounted binoculars at the boats and scenery in Great Bay, or you can choose the 0.5-mile Peverly Pond Trail, which goes along one side of the pond. If you're feeling up to it, walk both trails to see the variety of habitats, which include mud flats, saltwater and freshwater marshes, swamps, ponds, streams, woodlands, and fields.

Ferry Way starts from the asphalt path adjacent to the chain-link fence across the road from the parking lot. After following the fence line, you'll see a

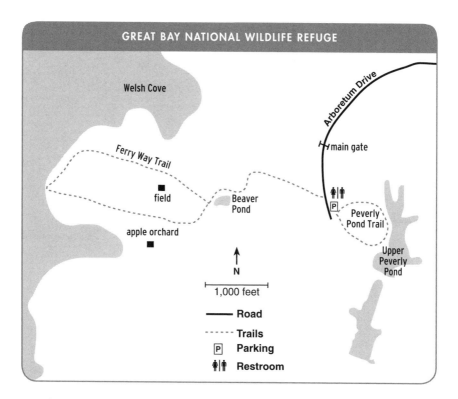

GREAT BAY NATIONAL WILDLIFE REFUGE

Welsh Cove

Arboretum Drive

main gate

Ferry Way Trail

field

Beaver Pond

apple orchard

Peverly Pond Trail

Upper Peverly Pond

N

1,000 feet

———— Road

- - - - - Trails

P   Parking

🛉🛉   Restroom

sign for the trail. Walking is easy on the abandoned dirt road here, which leads to woods. Along the way, interpretive signs tell you about the area. Peverly Pond Trail begins to the left of the parking lot and meanders through a forest to Upper Peverly Pond. In season, you can check out vernal pools.

Remember: While full-service bathrooms are in the comfort station, no drinkable water is available here.

PLAN B: The charming town of Portsmouth, a 15-minute drive from here, is fun to explore on foot.

WHERE TO EAT NEARBY: The Newington Mall has numerous restaurants, and US 1 toward Portsmouth also offers a lot of options.

Section 11

Southern Maine

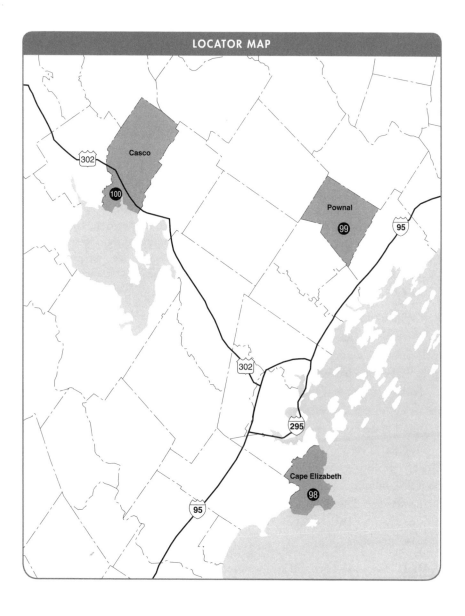

LOCATOR MAP

302 | Casco
100
Pownal
99
95
302
295
Cape Elizabeth
98
95

Trip 98

Fort Williams Park

This oceanside park offers stunning views, the chance to get up close to Maine's oldest lighthouse, and paved paths for strolling near the shore.

Address: 1000 Shore Road, Cape Elizabeth, ME
Hours: Dawn to dusk daily
Fee: Free
Contact: capeelizabeth.com; 207-799-2868.
Bathrooms: Portable toilets in several areas of the park
Water/Snacks: None
Map: USGS Cape Elizabeth
Directions by Car: From Boston, take I-95 North for 85 miles to I-295 North. Take Exit 1 for US 1, then merge onto Maine Turnpike Approach. Turn left onto Main Street, slight right onto Broadway, and turn right to stay on Broadway. Then turn right onto Cottage Road, and continue onto Shore Road and follow signs for the entrance. Once you get to the park, you'll see several parking areas. *GPS coordinates:* 43° 37.360' N, 70° 12.660' W.

Fort Williams Park, home to the oldest lighthouse in Maine, is about as picture-postcard perfect as it gets. Don't forget to bring your camera! Ocean views, historic properties, and plenty of paved paths, swings, picnic tables, and cooking grills make for a perfect outing for families.

Fort Williams was once a military asset during World War II, protecting the shoreline of Cape Elizabeth. It was officially closed and deactivated in 1963. Portland Head Light, the centerpiece of the park, has a museum and gift shop.

The park has views of Ram Island Ledge Light and the islands of Casco Bay as well as playing fields and tennis courts. The paved paths are great for bicylcles. In winter, the park offers great places to cross-country ski or sled.

Remember: The museum—which has a number of lighthouse lenses and interpretive displays—is open seasonally with limited hours. Call or visit its website for details.

PLAN B: Head into Portland and wander around the historic Old Port section of town.

WHERE TO EAT NEARBY: Cottage Road offers a variety of ice cream shops and pizza places.

Trip 99

Bradbury Mountain State Park: West Side

Climb to the summit of Bradbury Mountain on an adventurous hike and enjoy gorgeous views at the top.

Address: 528 Hallowell Road (ME 9), Pownal, ME
Hours: 9 A.M. to sunset
Fee: Adults, $4.50; children ages 5–12, $1
Contact: bradburymountain.com; 207-688-4712
Bathrooms: Portable toilets at the parking lots
Water/Snacks: Water fountains near the parking lots
Map: USGS North Pownal; bradburymountain.com/trail-maps.html
Directions by Car: From Boston, take I-95 North for 93 miles to Exit 53 toward ME 26/ME 100 West. Turn right onto Falmouth Road, then left onto Winn Road. Turn left onto ME 9/Main Street for 3.0 miles, then turn left onto ME 115 West/Walnut Hill Road. Take the second right onto ME 9 East/Memorial Highway, and continue to follow ME 9 East for 3.4 miles. When the road forks, head right and after about 3 miles you'll enter the park. *GPS coordinates:* 43° 54.013′ N, 70° 10.769′ W.

Bradbury Mountain State Park, sculpted by glaciers thousands of years ago, is one of Maine's five original state parks and offers a multitude of activities for lovers of the outdoors year-round. Horseback riders, hikers, mountain bikers, picnickers, and snowmobilers all can enjoy the 800-acre park.

You can reach the 485-foot-high summit of Bradbury Mountain by a short, steep climb—less than 0.5 mile long—or by more circuitous routes. Mountain bikers flock to Bradbury Mountain in summer for its great trails, as do snowmobilers in winter, who use former ski trails to race around. In the 1940s, downhill skiing was available, but it is no longer offered. Snowshoes are available for rent if you're on foot.

The 1.0-mile wooded Northern Loop is a wide, gradual ascent to the top of Bradbury Mountain, but kids who like to climb will prefer the short Summit Trail, which gets you to the top in 0.3 mile. You can gain access to the trail, marked with white blazes, from the parking lot. This is not a trail for short

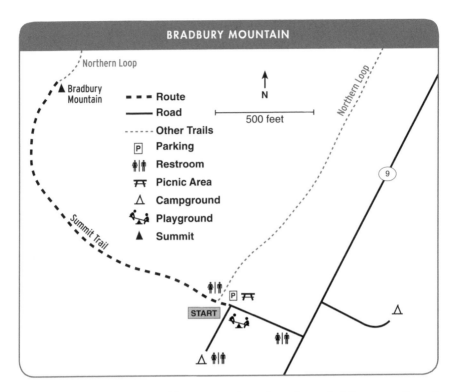

BRADBURY MOUNTAIN

Northern Loop

▲ Bradbury Mountain

- - - Route
— Road
----- Other Trails
P Parking
♦|♦ Restroom
🛆 Picnic Area
△ Campground
👫 Playground
▲ Summit

N

500 feet

Northern Loop

9

Summit Trail

START

little legs or anyone with bad knees! One benefit is that only hikers are allowed on the trail, so you don't have to keep an eye out for bicycles. Once you reach the top, the plateau makes for picture-perfect views. At the bottom of the mountain are picnic tables and a large playground.

Remember: The park has 35 rustic campsites, so you can easily make this a fun weekend adventure. However, plan ahead! Sites fill up quickly. Keep your dog on a leash and clean up after it.

PLAN B: Casco Bay Trail at Wolfe's Neck Woods State Park takes you along Maine's rocky shoreline.

WHERE TO EAT NEARBY: The village of Freeport, south of Pownal, offers plenty of dining options.

Camping is a great family activity, whether you choose close-to-home overnights or weeklong adventures. Here are some tips as you're planning:

- *Practice makes perfect.* Consider a trial run. Pitch a tent in the backyard for your first overnight with kids, and let them help out setting up camp. Experiment with sleeping bags, mattress pads, even sleeping arrangements.

- *Do your homework.* Scout out trails, campsites, and the weather before you head into the woods. Ask your kids where they'd like to go—the answers might surprise and inspire you.

- *Know your children's limitations.* Consider "car camping" at a drive-in campground with amenities such as bathhouses as a start. When you are ready to venture farther, try walk-in campsites, which provide more quiet and a stronger connection with nature. AMC's Cardigan Lodge has wooded sites less than a 10-minute walk from the lodge. Try backpacking or hut-to-hut hiking as your children's abilities and interests expand.

- *Get the right gear.* Wilderness veterans know that having the right gear is crucial. Pack plenty of layers. Buy or borrow a tent sized for at least one more person than the number in your group. Remember the child-safe bug repellent.

- *Engage if feasible.* The great outdoors is an unparalleled educational opportunity, but try to avoid the "classroom" feeling. Fire your child's imagination with lessons about wildlife, the surrounding trees, the change of seasons. Teach them map and compass skills.

- *Distract if necessary.* Have a few favorite props handy—a Frisbee, a ball, coloring books, a harmonica.

- *Remember to play.* Fishing, swimming, tree-climbing, or telling ghost stories might not qualify as high adventure, but they're all fun.

- *Fuel up.* Bring plenty of nutritious food, including kid-friendly snacks for on the trail and before bedtime, and encourage children to drink lots of water to prevent dehydration.

- *Be ready when nature calls.* On the trail, or at a primitive site, show children how to be self-sufficient (always pack toilet paper!) and teach them Leave No Trace guidelines.

- *Build memories.* Take plenty of pictures and have children keep journals. Both help capture memories and generate excitement for the next adventure.

- *Camp often.* The more familiar kids become with the outdoors, the more comfortable they will be. Every outing doesn't have to be an epic, and even most urban areas have state parks nearby that allow overnight camping.

Trip 100

All Ages

Sebago Lake State Park

Sebago Lake State Park, a paradise for water sports lovers, is one of Maine's most popular parks.

Address: 11 Park Access Road, Casco, ME
Hours: Dawn to dusk daily
Fee: Adults, $6.50; children ages 3–11, $1
Contact: maine.gov; 207-693-6613
Bathrooms: At the day use area
Water/Snacks: Water fountains near the bathrooms
Map: USGS Naples (maps available at park entrance)
Directions by Car: From Boston, take the Tobin Bridge to I-95 North and drive for about 100 miles. Take Exit 63 and follow signs for ME 115 West. After about 6.5 miles, turn right onto ME 35 North and follow for 10 miles. Turn left onto State Park Road, and after 1.5 miles make a sharp left on Park Access Road into the parking lot. *GPS coordinates: 43° 55.489′ N, 70° 34.116′ W.*

This 1,400-acre state park, which opened in 1938, is one of Maine's five original state parks. The 45-square-mile Sebago Lake, for which the park is named, is an absolute haven for water sports lovers, who come to sail, kayak, canoe, fish, swim, and sunbathe.

When you're not in the water, enjoy beaches, woods, ponds, bogs, a river, and a variety of plant and animal life, along with miles of trails accessible from the park's day-use area. If you camp overnight at the park, you have access to even more trails.

Trails from the day area are mostly flat and gravel-packed, making them popular with cyclists of all ages. In winter, the trails are groomed for cross-country skiing. For an excursion away from the busy beach area, the 3-mile Woodland Trail takes you through the forest. A shorter option is the 1.5-mile Songo River Trail, which takes you along the river, where kids will enjoy seeing boats passing through the hand-cranked locks. Since the water level on Long Lake (located north of Sebago) is 4 feet higher than that on Sebago, boats have to use the locks to get to Sebago. At the day area, you can enjoy horseshoe pits, a ball field, picnic tables, and a playground.

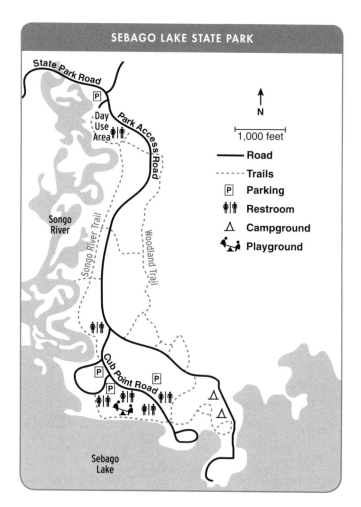

Remember: If you want to turn your visit into an overnight, make a reservation at the 250-site campground.

PLAN B: An unexpected attraction for so far north is the Songo River Queen II, a replica of a Mississippi River stern paddle wheeler. Take a ride to enjoy the state park from another vantage point.

WHERE TO EAT NEARBY: On ME 35, as you head to the park, you'll see cafés and convenience stores where you can pick up snacks or stop for a bite.

RESOURCES AND CONTACT INFORMATION

APPALACHIAN MOUNTAIN CLUB
800-372-1758; outdoors.org

BAY CIRCUIT ALLIANCE
978-470-1982; baycircuit.org

BOSTON HARBOR ISLANDS NATIONAL PARK
617-223-8666; bostonharborislands.org

BOSTON NATURAL AREAS NETWORK
617-542-7696; bostonnatural.org

BROOKLINE PARKS AND OPEN SPACE DIVISION
617-730 2069; brooklinema.gov

CAMBRIDGE OFFICE FOR TOURISM
617-441-2884; cambridge-usa.org

CAPE COD CHAMBER OF COMMERCE
508-362-3225; capecodchamber.org

CONNECTICUT COMMISSION ON CULTURE & TOURISM
888-288-4748; ctvisit.com

GREATER BOSTON CONVENTION & VISITORS BUREAU
617-536-4100; bostonusa.com

MAINE TOURISM
888-624-6345; visitmaine.com

MASS AUDUBON SOCIETY
781-259-9500; massaudubon.org

MASSACHUSETTS DEPARTMENT OF CONSERVATION AND RECREATION
617-626-1250; mass.gov/dcr

MASSACHUSETTS STATE PARKS
617-626-1250; massparks.org

NEW HAMPSHIRE TOURISM
603-271-2665; visitnh.gov

NEWTON RECREATION AREAS AND FACILITIES
617-796-1500; ci.newton.ma.us/parks/areas.htm

RESERVE AMERICA (CAMPSITES)
877-422-6762; reserveamerica.com

THE TRUSTEES OF RESERVATIONS
781-784-0567; thetrustees.org

SPECIAL OUTDOORS EVENTS THROUGHOUT THE YEAR

JANUARY
Neponset First Day Hike, Neponset; bostonnatural.org
Seafarer's Island Holiday, Boston Harbor Islands; bostonislands.org

FEBRUARY
Winterfest, Lowell; lowell.org/Pages/Winterfest.aspx

MARCH
Maple Sugar Days, various locations statewide; mass.gov.dcr

APRIL
Patriots' Day Parade and Reenactments, Lexington and Concord; nps.gov
Sheepshearing Festival, Waltham; goreplace.org
Swan Boats Resume at Public Garden; swanboats.com

MAY
Duckling Day Parade; friendsof thepublicgarden.org
Franklin Park Bike & Kite Festival; franklinparkcoalition.org
Lilac Sunday; aboretum.harvard.edu
Memorial Day Powwow, Spencer; 508-528-6885
Wake Up the Earth Day Festival; spontaneouscelebrations.org

JUNE
Brockton Fair, Brockton; brocktonfair.com
Father's Day Road Race & Walk, Easton; childrensmuseumineaston.org
National Trails Day, various locations; americanhiking.org/national-trails-day

JULY
Boston Harborfest; bostonharborfest.com
Barnstable County Fair, East Falmouth; barnstablecountyfair.org
Houghton's Pond Fish Festival; mass.gov/dcr
Lantern Festival; foresthilltrust.org

AUGUST
Tour de Farms; zerve.com/adventours/tdf
Crane Beach Sandblast; thetrustees.org
Red Fire Farm Tomato Festival, Wareham; redfirefarm.com/news/tomatofestival

SEPTEMBER
Eastern States Exposition (Big E), Springfield, MA; thebige.com
Gloucester Schooner Festival, Gloucester; capeannvacations.com/schooner
Topsfield Fair, Topsfield; topsfieldfair.org

OCTOBER
Zoo Howl, Boston and Stoneham; zoonewengland.com
Cranberry Harvest Festival, Wareham; cranberryharvest.org
Keene Pumpkin Festival, Keene, N.H.; pumpkinfestival2012.org
Head of the Charles Regatta; hocr.org

NOVEMBER
Ice Rink Opens at Frog Pond; bostonfrogpond.com
America's Hometown Thanksgiving Festival, Plymouth; visit-plymouth.com

DECEMBER
Boston Common Tree Lighting; cityofboston.gov
Boston Tea Party Reenactment; oldsouthmeetinghouse.org
First Night Boston; firstnight.org

CAMPING

GENERAL
Reserve America
877-422-6762; reserveamerica.com

MASSACHUSETTS
Blue Hills Reservation: Ponkapoag Pond (Trip 27)
781-961-7007 (AMC); outdoors.org

Wompatuck State Park (Trip 64)
781-749-7160; mass.gov/dcr

Myles Standish State Forest (Trip 68)
508-866-2526; mass.gov/dcr

Scusset Beach State Reservation (Trip 69)
508-888-0859; mass.gov/dcr

Wellfleet Bay Wildlife Sanctuary (Trip 70)
508-349-2615; massaudubon.org

Harold Parker State Forest (Trip 74)
978-686-3391; mass.gov/dcr

Tully Lake (Trip 85)
978-249-4957; thetrustees.org

Noble View Outdoor Center
413-572-4501; nobleviewoutdoorcenter.org

MAINE
Maine State Park Camping
800-332-1501 or 207-624-9950; campwithme.com

Bradbury Mountain State Park (Trip 99)
207-688-4712; bradburymountain.com

Sebago Lake State Park (Trip 100)
207-693-6613; maine.gov

CONNECTICUT
Department of Energy and Environmental Protection
860-424-3000; ct.gov/dep

Mashamoquet Brook State Park (Trip 93)
860-928-6121; ct.gov/dep

NEW HAMPSHIRE
Division of Parks and Recreation
603-271-3556; nhstateparks.org

Monadnock State Park (Trip 95)
603-532-2416; nhstateparks.org

INDEX

ABOUT THE AUTHOR

Kim Foley MacKinnon has been writing about what to do in New England with kids ever since her daughter was born 13 years ago, and learned that the best way to transform a cranky child instantly into a happy one was to go outside. She has written for the *Boston Globe*, *Boston Herald*, *AAA Horizons*, and many other publications. Although she travels the world in pursuit of adventures to write about, she is constantly amazed by what she can find in her own backyard. This is her fifth guidebook.

APPALACHIAN MOUNTAIN CLUB

Founded in 1876, AMC is the nation's oldest outdoor recreation and conservation organization. AMC promotes the protection, enjoyment, and understanding of the mountains, forests, waters, and trails of the Northeast outdoors.

People

We are more than 100,000 members, advocates, and supporters, including 12 local chapters, more than 16,000 volunteers, and over 450 full-time and seasonal staff. Our chapters reach from Maine to Washington, D.C.

Outdoor Adventure and Fun

We offer more than 8,000 trips each year, from local chapter activities to adventure travel worldwide, for every ability level and outdoor interest— from hiking and climbing to paddling, snowshoeing, and skiing.

Great Places to Stay

We host more than 150,000 guests each year at our AMC lodges, huts, camps, shelters, and campgrounds. Each AMC destination is a model for environmental education and stewardship.

Opportunities for Learning

We teach people skills to safely enjoy the outdoors and to care for the natural world around us through programs for children, teens, and adults, as well as outdoor leadership training.

Caring for Trails

We maintain more than 1,500 miles of trails throughout the Northeast, including nearly 350 miles of the Appalachian Trail in five states.

Protecting Wild Places

We advocate for land and riverway conservation, monitor air quality, research climate change, and work to protect alpine and forest ecosystems throughout the Northern Forest and Mid-Atlantic Highlands regions.

Engaging the Public

We seek to educate and inform our own members and an additional 2 million people annually through the media, AMC Books, our website, our White Mountain visitor centers, and AMC destinations.

Join Us!

Members meet other like-minded people and support our mission while enjoying great AMC programs, our award-winning *AMC Outdoors* magazine, and special discounts. Visit outdoors.org or call 800-372-1758 for more information.

APPALACHIAN MOUNTAIN CLUB
Recreation • Education • Conservation
outdoors.org

AMC IN EASTERN MASSACHUSETTS

The AMC Boston Chapter is AMC's largest chapter, with more than 20,000 members. It offers a variety of hiking, backpacking, paddling, bicycling, skiing, and climbing trips each year, as well as social, family, and young member programs and instructional workshops. Members also lead trips, maintain trails, and teach others about outdoor skills.

The AMC Southeastern Massachusetts Chapter offers outdoor activities, conducts trail work, and addresses local conservation issues south of Boston and on Cape Cod and the Islands. Programs range from hiking and cycling to skiing, paddling, and backpacking.

The AMC Worcester Chapter is dedicated to the outdoor resources of Central Massachusetts, and offers activities and trips for all levels. Chapter members partake in a wide range of social events and educational programs.

To view a list of AMC activities in Massachusetts and other parts of the Northeast, visit activities.outdoors.org.

AMC BOOK UPDATES

AMC Books strives to keep our guidebooks as up-to-date as possible to help you plan safe and enjoyable adventures. If after publishing a book we learn that trails have been relocated or route or contact information has changed, we will post the updated information online. Before you hit the trail, check for updates at outdoors.org/bookupdates.

While hiking, biking, or paddling, if you notice discrepancies with the trail description or map, or if you find any other errors in the book, please let us know by submitting them to amcbookupdates@outdoors.org or in writing to Books Editor, c/o AMC, 5 Joy Street, Boston, MA 02108. We will verify all submissions and post key updates each month. AMC Books is dedicated to being a recognized leader in outdoor publishing. Thank you for your participation.

AMC's Best Day Hikes Near Boston
2nd edition
Michael Tougias and John S. Burk

From the barrier beach on Plum Island, the Middlesex Fells and the Blue Hills, to the South Shore and Cape Cod, this guide offers a variety of trails for all ability levels and interests. This fully revised new edition adds ten more hikes for beginner and intermediate hikers.

$18.95 • 978-1-934028-47-6

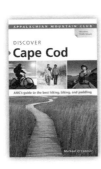

AMC's Best Day Hikes in the White Mountains
2nd edition
Robert N. Buchsbaum

This fully updated four-season guide from the publishers of the best-selling *White Mountain Guide* leads you to 60 of the finest views and best trails of the region. Explore the peaks bordering Franconia, Crawford, and Pinkham notches and visit several of AMC's huts.

$18.95 • 978-1-934028-43-8

Discover Cape Cod
Michael O'Connor

This trusted guidebook details 50 of the best hikes, mountain bike trails, and paddling routes in this beautiful coastal area, including many trips within the Cape Cod National Seashore. For short, one-hour excursions, day-long adventures, or weekend afternoons, this book provides the best outdoor experiences for vacationers and residents alike.

$18.95 • 978-1-934028-17-9

Discover Martha's Vineyard
Lee Sinai

This multi-sport guidebook includes 45 of the best hikes, on- and off-road bike trails, and paddling routes this peaceful destination offers. This trusted resource will lead visitors and residents alike to winding hiking and biking trails and unforgettable paddling routes within the island's most unforgettable spots.

$18.95 • 978-1-934028-24-7